Dogging It

Through Divorce and Beyond

JONATHAN WAGNER

Dogging It

Through Divorce and Beyond

JONATHAN WAGNER

www.mascotbooks.com

Dogging It Through Divorce and Beyond

For more information, please contact:
Mascot Books
620 Herndon Parkway #320
Herndon, VA 20170
info@mascotbooks.com

Library of Congress Control Number: 2017911121

CPSIA Code: PBANG0418A
ISBN: 978-1-68401-462-0

Printed in the United States

To my four wonderful Labrador Retriever-loving children:
Nathaniel, Johanna, Sarah, and Robert.

To Scott Snyder, the owner of Black Hawk Kennels,
for providing me and my family with seven marvelous Labs.

To David Fuller, former President of Minot State University, for
his insightful critique of my manuscript and his enthusiastic
support of it.

To Mary, my beautiful friend, for her positive acceptance of my
Labs and me and for teaching me to recognize the inherent
beauty of spirituality.

INTRODUCTION

Announcement of My 2003 Christmas Visit to My Parents at

My Boyhood Home in Aurora, Ohio.

Sister-in-law Martha: "Hilda (my-98-year-old, 90-percent blind mother), Jon's just arrived."

Hilda: "Which of his wives did he bring this time?"

Martha: "None. He just brought his dogs. He's divorced."

Hilda: "That's queer."

My Three Musketeers

"I think dogs were put in this world to remind humanity that love, loyalty, devotion, courage, patience and good humor are the qualities that, with honesty, are the essence of admirable character and the very definition of a life well lived."

— Dean Koontz, *Seize the Night*, p. 115

Despite what the title might imply, this book is neither a diatribe against ex-wives, nor a jeremiad lamenting the failure of the institution of marriage. Rather, it is a story about the dogs that appeared in my life before I married, during my married years from 1963 to 2003 and afterwards to the present. As the text will show, I'm a devoted dog person, that is, someone who loves canines and who includes them in his life willingly. This love for dogs has been with me since my childhood. Now as a retiree living with more than one dog, I have been asking myself where that love came from and what was, or is, its significance. This book attempts to answer those questions.

From the onset, my canine interests and dog affinities complicated my marriages and divorces. I never understood just how much until I undertook this project of writing specifically about my several dogs and the roles they played during my married life. As I considered the careers of my several canines, beginning with first puppy Satchel and continuing on to my post-married life with its present two Labrador Retrievers, I became increasingly aware of how these dogs fit into the total span of my life, how they affected it, and the legacy they bequeathed.

In brief, this book represents an opportunity for me to understand the importance of dogs in my life and why and how I exhibit such a strong affinity for dogs, especially Labrador Retrievers. As I have come to understand, my view of the world changed as I aged. I discovered how this maturation related to my dogs. I became aware of how my dogs served as both mentors and affirmation sources and trainers. Thus, as I aged, my dogs became increasingly important. In the text that follows, I will attempt to explain how and why that happened.

Beyond me, the dogs have exerted positive influences on my four children, providing buffers and sources of love and sanity amidst the trials and tribulations associated with the divorces affecting our family. It is no accident that at the time of this writing, three of my children have Labrador Retrievers in their homes; one of them has three versions of the breed, a black, a yellow, and a chocolate. My fourth child Robert, who graduated from college last spring, represents the exception. He told me recently, however, that when he moves into a more permanent residence, he plans to acquire a Lab puppy.

In the pages of this book, I have consciously tried to separate the dogs from the wives as much as possible. I have sought to describe how my canine friends have served in lieu of wives for devotion and fidelity. In my account, the dogs have relieved pain but also inspired joy. In essence, this book represents the confessions of a three-time divorced man who loved and loves his furry companions, those wonderful faithful friends who accompanied him during the periods of loneliness, descents into despair and the difficult recuperations afterward.

Through writing this book, I now understand better how my dogs "nourished me," how their love and devotion buffered "the effects of loneliness and social isolation." My Labrador Retrievers, those beautiful creatures I call *My Sweet Spirits,* represented for me a kind of Platonic ideal of love and devotion. To me, they increasingly appeared as God-sent friends, dropped mysteriously into my life from some source beyond choice or reason.

Besides celebrating these gifts and the canine ideal, the book provides a commentary on my own evolution, growth and development. In detailing the lives of my dogs, I have described the several periods of my life: childhood, adolescence, early adulthood, mid-life, and now retirement. As the dogs accompanied me through these several stages, they taught me lessons about my youth, maturity, aging and ultimately about coping with death. Thus, although the dogs were and are real, they also reflected and influenced metaphysical themes in my life.

From caring for puppies, I learned about youth and adolescence;

from training and hunting with my dogs, I learned about confidence, competence and carrying through with a job or task; from having to put my dogs down, I learned about death, a sad but natural thing not to be feared but accepted. On my life's scales, the dog legacy of love has always outweighed the sadness of death. Finally, as a diagnosed neurotic (told that by the several marriage counselors and psychologists during counseling sessions), I have come to accept my dogs as more often than not right rather than wrong in their acts and choices. All of my Sweet Spirits shared the Lab qualities of loyalty, affection, ruggedness, and *joie de vivre* (joy in life) celebrated so often by devoted fans of the breed. Nevertheless, to me my dogs always remained unique, each different in his or her own wonderful fashion.

Throughout the individual Lab stories, hunting plays an important role in the text because for me, each individual dog represented not only a friend and pet at home, but also a hunting companion. Emphasizing hunting seemed justified and logical because, from its origins, the Labrador Retriever often functioned as a working/hunting dog. Long before I acquired my first Lab puppy, the breed established itself in Europe and then in North America both on land and in the water as one of the world's leading hunting breeds. I always purchased my Lab puppies with their hunting potential in mind.

Again let me emphasize, I never intended my book as a way to cast aspersions on marriage or former wives. Rather, it is much more an encomium, a paean like Saint Francis's Ode to the Sun. Its main purpose has always been to celebrate my precious dogs, all of whom have blessed my life, made me more understanding and sympathetic and, I hope, a better person.

They have given me the joy the great German literary figure Friedrich Schiller celebrated in his *Ode to Joy* (*An die Freude*) and which the even more famous Ludwig von Beethoven immortalized in his Ninth Symphony version of that poem. To me, my Labs have appeared as embodiments of the Schiller/Beethoven ideal, as true "Tochter aus Elysium", as "daughters from Elysium."

Viewing my dogs as creatures of Elysium introduced me to the spirituality of my dog experience. For the classical Greeks, Elysium described the residence after death of the blessed. It represents their version of heaven, a place where love and peace prevail. For Schiller, Elysium also constituted a place where "Freude" or joy, that "schoener Goetterfunken" or "beautiful spark of the Gods" existed.

Over the course of several years and the lifetimes of more than one of my Labs, I have come to believe that my canines, the sources of so much joy for me, were in fact creatures embodying the Schiller ideal. The joy they created for me seemed indeed like the "sanfte Fleugel" (gentle wings) Schiller described, that is, the joy and love I experienced embraced me like "gentle wings." This way of thinking introduced me to a new spirituality that has increasingly affected me.

In short, my dogs, those vessels of joy, appeared increasingly as spiritual entities, as creatures reflecting the beauty of God's creation not only physically, but even more so through their love and concern for me. I came to view them as blessings, vehicles conveying the spirit of God to me, as teaching me not only about the grace of divine love, but also the beauty of creation itself. All this was new to me. The spirituality which characterizes my present religious beliefs owes, I believe, its origin to this transformation. Because my Labs opened up for me this new spiritual life, I am profoundly thankful to each and every one of them.

Finally, I want to express my gratitude to my human offspring who knew and loved the animals I celebrate. I talked to my children and grandchildren about my dogs and their Labs and what they remember as most special about each. I sought to get their takes and reminiscences to flesh out my own thoughts. In my interviews and their emails, they provided valuable information, much of which I had forgotten or did not know. I incorporated many of their impressions into the text.

The process of canvassing my offspring and hearing what they recalled about our departed and present dog-family members was both fun and enlightening. I was surprised, impressed and touched to learn just how my dogs and their own Labs influenced them. My thanks go out to daughters, Johanna and Sarah, sons, Nathaniel and Robert, and grandchildren, Samantha, Clare, and Thomas. Love to you all.

Finally, the photographs that appear throughout most of the text were taken by me or my family. The absence of such pictures in chapter one, which describes the period of my childhood and adolescence, was due to my not learning how to use a camera until after I married!

CHAPTER ONE

MY CANINE BAPTISM

"We long for an affection altogether ignorant of our faults. Heaven has accorded this to us in the uncritical canine attachment."

— George Elliot

Although my dog experiences began in grade school, my first pet was a cat. In my family, my mother had the most influence in household matters, including pets. A shy, introverted, intellectual, amber-eyed brunette, she loved art and literature more than politics or other mundane matters, including home-making. At home, the former librarian spent much of her day reading.

I remember one of my youthful New Year's Resolutions that she not scorch any more food. I still have occasional flashbacks of smoke wafting out of the kitchen from incinerated peas or a glowing red hot tea kettle while Mom, engrossed in a book, sat warming her feet over the register in the living room. For pets, she preferred cats. I was seven when the issue of having my own pet arose.

To my question about why she liked cats, she answered: "Because they're easy to take care of. Fix a sand box for them to do their thing in, set out their day's food in the morning, provide water. That's it."

"But, you gotta like how they act too?" I said.

"I do. Love their purring. Like them sitting in my lap while I read. Nice soft creatures and they get mice. I hate mice," she said.

Disappointed, I said, "You don't like dogs?"

"Too uncouth," she said.

"What's that mean?

"Uncivilized."

"What's uncivilized?" I said, frowning.

"Too much noise. Barking and growling. Too much ruckus."

"Not all dogs bark."

"Most do."

"Dogs my friends have don't bark much," I said.

"Dogs're more trouble than they're worth. Always have to take them out to do their business. A kitten playing with a ball of yarn beats a growling puppy chewing up a shoe or gnawing on an antique table leg. Never had a dog. Grandpa couldn't stand barking," she said and returned to her reading.

Of my two siblings, brother Tim, eight years older than I, and sister Polly, three years my senior, only Polly lobbied with me for a pet. Brother Tim had grown beyond such distractions. In his fifteenth year, he favored baseball and football over any animals.

Being realists, my sister and I accepted Mom's and Grandpa's pet preferences and lobbied for a kitten. In 1947, we received our first feline. From the get go, Polly took charge of our little furry gift. Because it was totally black, she named it Inky. Polly fed it and supervised its play times. During the night, it stayed with Polly.

At one point, I asked my dear sister, "Could Inky stay with me some nights?"

"No," Polly replied, "she's my cat. She stays with me."

I thought that ended my cat hopes, but relief was on the way. Never spayed, Inky became a kitten factory. She birthed her multiple litters in odd places, such as beneath our house undergoing remodeling or in the upstairs closet across from my bedroom. Those are the ones I remember. From Inky's first litter, the one from under the house, my mother decreed the first pick for me. Thus, I got the first animal I could call my own, a black male with a white throat. I name my kitten Joe.

Joe quickly matured and became a tom. I don't remember many

details, but Joe apparently couldn't or didn't care a fig about his alleged master, me. He much preferred prowling to sitting on my lap. On one of his nightly escapades, he was run over.

I don't recall exactly when that happened but the day after Joe's demise my father, on his drive home from work in Cleveland, recognized Joe's carcass by the side of the road. He stopped, retrieved the body and brought it home for burial. Again, the details remain sketchy, but I don't think I was particularly upset by the loss. Joe never became my buddy. He seemed then and even more so now an abstraction, an entity doing its own thing. I can't even remember if he purred.

Not long after Joe's death, my dear father, a kind man of few words and fewer overt emotions, came home from work one day and asked, "Jonny, would you be interested in having a dog?"

I said, "Yes, I sure would."

"A work colleague's female Cocker Spaniel had a litter of puppies. They need good homes. She offered one to us. Whadda you think?"

Jumping up and down, I said, "I'd love to have my own puppy. Take good care of it. I promise, I promise."

"I'll check with Mom. She agrees, I'll bring a puppy home."

"Oh, Dad," I said," that'd be great." I went to bed that night with my fingers crossed, hoping my mother would change her opinion of dogs and let my wish come true.

The next morning as my father was leaving for work he said to me, "Talked to Mom about the dog. She's not opposed. So if you're still interested, I'll get a puppy."

"I am; I am. Please do!" I couldn't believe Mom's acquiescence but loved her for it.

That night my father returned home with a little, two-month-old black male puppy in a shoe box. The dog was supposed to be a Cocker Spaniel, but was not entirely. I didn't care. At that time, I had no idea what pedigree meant. I only cared that he was mine. As soon as I saw him, I fell in love. Of course, I had no idea he would turn me into the dog lover I am today. But first, he needed a name.

SATCHEL

As implied, I grew up not far from Cleveland, Ohio. My childhood home town was Aurora, Ohio just 25 short miles from Cleveland's traditional central monument, the Terminal Tower. Originally a farming community first settled in 1799, Aurora had just begun during the 1940s and 1950s its evolution into the commuter center it became for both Cleveland to the north and Akron to the south.

According to the 2010 census, Aurora's population numbered 15,548 residents. The number for my time growing up in the 1940s and 1950s just exceeded 500. The small-town Aurora I knew as a youth was a quiet, laid-back place with little vehicular traffic. No stop lights existed in town and most of the roads beyond the town's center remained unpaved, gravel ones.

Hudson, eight miles southwest, a slightly larger town with the closest movie theater, was accessible to me and my friends via our bicycles. A fifteen minute trip by car to Hudson today required an hour biking for us. I remember those Hudson dirt-road bike rides over and back as great fun. With light provided by flashlights taped to our bikes' handle bars, we would return after the movie singing loudly, swearing and laughing to our heart's content. Meeting a car going or coming was unusual.

For Aurora's rural context, I was and still am most grateful. It allowed me to develop from childhood my lifelong outdoor perspective with its love for woods, fields and streams. In 1950, a five-minute walk from my village home put me in the town's water works, a ten-acre stretch of woods where I first learned how to hunt cottontail rabbits and fox squirrels. In the 1950s, Aurora was a great place for me to have a hunting dog.

At the time of my puppy's arrival in the summer of 1948, Cleveland possessed a professional baseball team that would win the World Series. No Indian team since then, including the 2016 team, has been so successful. In 1948, all the former or present ball players in my household from Grandpa to Dad to big brother and me were devoted

Indian fans. (As non-baseball players, my mother, grandmother, and sister were uninterested.)

In addition, the family had a special attachment to the ball club. Cleveland Indian regular game and season tickets were sold in several Cleveland downtown businesses, one of them being the Burrows Brothers Book Store and Office Supplies where my father worked as merchandise manager. Lucky for my brother Tim and me, Dad often brought home tickets for Indians and Browns games.

In 1948, Cleveland Indians owner Bill Veeck did for the American League what Branch Rickey accomplished for the National Baseball League: hired the first African-American player. In fact, by 1948 Veeck had outdone Rickey by adding two African-American standouts to his roster. While Rickey had signed Jackie Robinson, Veeck added a gifted young outfielder named Larry Doby and the aged, legendary Negro League pitcher Satchel Paige.

In the summer of 1948 when I got my puppy, Satchel Paige had become a Cleveland Indian fan favorite. By that year, Paige's once great skills (none other than Joe Dimaggio described him as the fastest pitcher he'd ever seen) had declined. Nevertheless, the 45-year-old Paige still had enough different pitches and deliveries to get the majority of major league batters out. And Cleveland fans loved him: his skills, his unconventional deliveries, his creative showmanship. I did as well. When I named my new gift Satchel, I intended to celebrate the inspiring pitcher Paige.

Satchel, the two-month-old puppy, became my ward. I fed him, played with him, took him out to go potty, cleaned up after him when he failed to do his duty outside. As I grew, Satchel grew faster. He became my pal and ever-present confidant. I can't imagine my childhood without him.

When I was ten, I had a paper route delivering the *Cleveland News*. Each day, Satchel ran alongside me as I rode my bike from one subscriber household to the next. On a hot day, I'd stop at Hackbart's General Store to share ice cream cones with him: chocolate for me vanilla for him.

Of course, Satchel slept on my bed. Later as a twelve- and thirteen-year-old, I helped my dad deliver the *Cleveland Plain Dealer* in the early morning. Before joining my father, I would pull sleeping Satchel from the foot of the bed up to my pillow, put his head on it and snuggle the covers up around him to make sure he remained warm and comfortable during my absence. I don't think my parents ever knew about that favoritism.

As an adult, Satchel resembled neither a pure-bred Beagle nor a Cocker Spaniel, yet he possessed recognizable elements from both breeds. To begin with, he had the Beagle/Cocker Spaniel size, much smaller than my later Labrador Retrievers. I would guess he weighed about 25 pounds, maybe less.

From what my Dad told me, he resembled his Cocker Spaniel mother in being completely black, with no trace of Beagle brown or white. He had not only a Beagle body, but Beagle legs as well, longer ones than his mother's. Moreover, his ears differed from the Cocker Spaniel's elongated ones. Beagle size, they did not extend below the muzzle. As a whole, his snout and face resembled a Beagle's, except for the color.

At the other end of his body his tail remained in its natural state, not clipped like so many Cockers. Although the tail length was standard Beagle, it had thicker hair. Satchel's coat followed his tail in being denser than the usual Beagle one, but not as curly as the typical Cocker's either. My first dog's hairy coat resembled more closely what would be characteristic for my future Labrador Retrievers. Satchel shed like one too.

During my Satchel time, which corresponded to my elementary/middle school years from the third to eighth grades, I developed a fascination with nature. To start with, I became a serious bird watcher. In pursuing my bird interest, I made long walks to Aurora's Bird Sanctuary, a wooded preserve two miles east of town owned by the Cleveland Audubon Society.

On those trips, I always took along my copy of Roger Tory Peterson's *Birds of America*, the first of many bird books I would own. At the time, I had no idea who Roger Tory Peterson was. Only later did I learn about the role he played not only in the history of bird watching in the United States, but also in the conservation movement that took off in the 1950s. Much to my delight, my discovery of and fascination with birds mirrored Peterson's own experience for, as tradition has it, he was eleven when the bird enthusiasm "took over his life."

The source most responsible for my childhood bird interest was a kindly neighbor named Carl Haman. I came to know Mr. Haman from mowing his lawn each week. A tall, thin, soft-spoken, partly-bald retiree who kept in shape by making long walks pursuing his interest in Ohio's birds, Carl knew all the local birds by sight and song. Several times he took me on early morning excursions to Aurora's Bird Sanctuary, which he knew intimately. There and in his yard, he coached me on how to act as an authentic birder.

I remember his basic bird advice: "Jonny, when birding, you must move slowly, stop often to look up as well and down and always listen carefully. If you don't use your ears, you'll miss many neat birds. Hearing birds is often easier than seeing them."

His best teaching example, I remember, was the Warbling Vireo. One day when I was in his yard mowing his grass, he came over and signaled for me to shut off the mower. I did.

He said, "Follow me, got something to show you."

I followed him over to one of the big elm trees in the yard. He pointed to the top of the tree and said "Listen to that bird. Can you see the bird making that call?"

I looked up to where he pointed but could see nothing. I shook my head. However, I could hear the bird's call clearly, a subtle, lilting, series of soft, rising notes.

"Jonny," he said, "that's a Warbling Vireo singing. Isn't it beautiful?"

"Sure is," I said.

On another occasion when he took me to the Bird Sanctuary, he explained one of his favorite bird watching procedures. "Jonny, there's a trick you should know. It's a way to get birds to come in close. When you do it, you've got to be absolutely still. Then you make this sound: 'pisst, pisst, pisst, pisst, pisst.' Birds hear this. They become curious, come in close. Neat way to get a bird's eye view!" He smiled at his pun.

Over the years, I've had success with this method, especially with one of my favorite birds, the black capped chickadee. For example, I used the Haman "pisst. pisst etc." to cope with boredom while sitting in the woods deer hunting. If I "pisst" enough, I could get the occasional chickadee to perch on a branch four or five feet from me and look me in the eyes, trying to figure out what "pisst, pisst, pisst..." meant.

Carl tendered advice not only on how to watch and listen, but also on bird behavior and habitat. I remember on another Bird Sanctuary trip when we were walking in the woods, he said "Jonny come here. Got something to show you." He pointed at a small tree, moved up to it and parted the branches.

"Look at this. You know what that is?" he asked.

I peered at the object he was pointing out and said, "No, what is it?"

"That's a Ruby-throated Humming Bird's nest," he said smiling.

The nest was the size of an old fifty cent piece, a beautifully crafted tiny grey bowl. I was impressed.

On the same trip walking through the woods, he stopped and motioned toward the canopy of leaves above us and said, "Hear that call?"

I nodded and he said, "That's the call of the Red-eyed Vireo, a cousin of our Warbling Vireo on Maple Lane."

The song was more forceful, less subtle, more confident sounding than the sweet sounds of its Warbling cousin.

Mr. Haman continued, "You know, Jonny, Red-eyed Vireos are almost as common around here as our Robins."

Again, I was impressed. I still am. From the deck of my summer place in Wisconsin, I hear the Red-eyed Vireos sing nearly every day. When I do, I often think of that gentle, kindly neighbor who took a ten-year-old boy under his wing and taught him to love bird songs. My fondness for beautiful sounds today stretches back to Mr. Haman. A direct connection exists between my present fondness for Mozart, Beethoven or Puccini and the Warbling Vireo, I believe.

While on that same Red-eyed Vireo outing, we walked along the shore of the Bird Sanctuary's pond where Carl introduced me to the lake's fly catchers: the Alder, Acadian, and Crested ones, all of which I had never seen before. They contrasted with the Vireos in being close to the ground and easier to see. I don't remember their calls but I do the adroit, air-born maneuverings they used to catch flying insects.

During my middle-school birding years, my interest in nature expanded beyond winged creatures to the frontier and the wilderness of an earlier age. At that time, I discovered James Fennimore Cooper's *Leather Stocking Tales*. To this day, I love Cooper, even after having read Mark Twain's satire of him! My two favorite Leather Stocking volumes were and remain *The Deerslayer* and *Last of the Mohicans*. There's a reason why my elder son's name is Nathaniel. I often call him Natty (after Cooper's hero Natty Bumpo) when to everyone else in the family he's simply Nat.

Moreover, during this time my fascination with Canada developed. The reason for this derives from several sources. To begin with, my sympathy for Canada came naturally because my father was born and raised in Kitchener, Ontario. He moved to the United States as a young man in the late 1920s. But even more so, a book I first read and took to heart in the seventh grade, a volume borrowed from the Cleveland Public Library, influenced me.

Entitled *Trap Lines North, a True Story of the Canadian Woods*, the book's narrative was set in Canada during the early 1930s. It describes the experiences of a 17-year-old Canadian youth who, because of his father's illness, had to take over the business of running the family's many-mile-long trap line in the Canadian Pre-Cambrian Shield north of Thunder Bay in Northwestern Ontario. The author Stephen A. Meader based his account on the diaries kept by the young man he described. More specifically, the book details the daily life experienced by the intrepid youth travelling by canoe or snow shoes to check his traps, sleeping in primitive cabins and lean-tos in temperatures often well below zero.

Hooked on the first go round, I reread the book several times. It inspired in me the desire to imitate the young Canadian, to have my own trap line in the far North. I remember spending happy hours sitting at the desk in my Aurora bedroom with a Sears Roebuck catalogue in front of me, making lists of what supplies and gear I would need to duplicate the young Canadian's adventure.

At the time, I planned to go to Canada and trap during the winter after graduating from high school. Aware of my imaginings, neither parent made light of my thoughts nor tried to discourage me. In fact, they humored me. Evidence of such humoring appeared one Christmas in the form of a coonskin hat a la Daniel Boone.

Today, I'm amused by my preadolescent attachments and my parents' dilemma. Looking back, I realize now that neither parent could identify with my nature, my wilderness fixation, because they weren't Romantic. Of course, my Canadian trapping dream never materialized. In the end, time, age and other ambitions prevented the realization of that boyhood fantasy. However, the fascination with nature, the wild world of birds, fish and animals would extend well beyond my childhood to become a life-long interest and commitment.

Satchel, who was with me as I conjured up such dreams, did his best to support and expand my nature affinity. In my middle school years, he served both as my household pal and my fishing and hunting companion. I don't remember when I started fishing but it was early, not long after Satchel's puppyhood.

In the small town of Aurora, everything seemed to be within walking or biking distance, including fishing opportunities. As a budding child angler, I considered myself fortunate to have the Chagrin River flowing through our town. In the summer, Satchel would follow me on my bike to the river and we would spend the day fishing for Blue Gills and Cat Fish—all easy prey for earth worms dug out of our garden.

In the beginning, I fished only with such bait under a bobber. The dog would stay with me and watch me fish, sometimes going in the water but usually lying down next to me waiting for the next fish. When finished, I would tie the stringer with the day's keepers on my bike's handle bar, rouse the dog and peddle home.

In 1953, when I was 13, the fishing routine became more challenging. I started fly fishing. Another wonderful neighbor named Everette Petoe, who resided across the street from my home and three houses down from Carl Haman's, gave me my first fly rod and taught me how to use it. Married to my Sunday school teacher, Everette, a tall bespectacled, sixty-year old fellow with a ready smile and an authoritative voice, had been a life-long fly fishing enthusiast. He told me how when he was growing up, his father, who owned a shoe store in Cleveland, would turn the store over to subordinates so the family could spend the summer camping in the Maine woods.

Their son Everette became both an accomplished hunter and fisherman. On one occasion, he showed me a picture of his adolescent, grinning self displaying a hefty brook trout caught on a fly in the Maine woods. On other occasions, he displayed photos of pheasant hunting in South Dakota and goose hunting in North Carolina. What I saw both captivated and inspired me. I wanted to be like him.

Everette's fly fishing instructions were simple. He followed the KISS routine (Keep It Simple Stupid). My basic instructions from him began the day I took a new fly rod that I had just bought over to show him. To try it out, we went into his back yard. He made a few casts and shook his head.

He said, "Jonny, this won't do. The rod's not stiff enough. The line doesn't fit either. You need something better, something that'll give you more control. Hold on. I'll be right back."

He went into the house and came back with one of his own rods, a seven-footer obviously used but in good condition. It had a smoothly functioning reel on it with the correct weight line. Telling me to stand aside, he then demonstrated the proper way to cast. With the line moving back and forth, he announced, "There are two basics to fly casting. The first is you must work your rod between ten o'clock and two o'clock. You got a watch, Jonny?"

I shook my head.

"Okay, but you know what the clock in your school room looks like, right?"

He looked at me. This time I said, "Yes."

"Here, watch me. Watch how when I cast forward my rod doesn't go beyond two o'clock on our invisible clock. Back cast comes back only as far as ten o'clock. You see? If you cast this way, the line'll straighten out properly. You need to get it to do that."

I nodded.

"Second thing you must remember is to keep your wrist straight. Don't bend it when you move your arm from ten to two."

"You right handed, like me?" he asked.

"Yeah," I said.

He cast some more, his left hand feeding out more line with each movement of his right arm forward. Then he stopped. "Come here," he said. "Take the rod and see if you can do what I just did."

I tried and when I went beyond ten on the back cast or two on the forward cast, he told me so. To drive the lesson home, he picked up a garden stake and took a position behind me, holding the stake at nine o'clock. Every time I hit it with the rod, he said, "Too far, too far."

He would also tell me, "No, no, you're bending your wrist. Keep it straight, keep it straight."

When I began to get the routine right, he was very encouraging. We did this for fifteen minutes and stopped.

He said, "Take my rod home and practice with it. If you get good enough with it, I'll give it to you. Come back in a couple of weeks. See you then."

I did what he said. I practiced and practiced. Two weeks later at the second try out, he watched without saying anything as I cast. I worked the rod for about five minutes. Finally, I stopped and turned to him.

Smiling, he said, "Jonny, you got yourself a new rod. You're getting the hang of it. You still need more practice but you know what to do. So, go do it."

I followed his advice as closely as I could. I worked at practicing my casting at home in the back yard, but also at the river. When I first started, I would watch both my forward and my back casts, moving my head back and forth awkwardly.

As I improved, I no longer needed to trace the backward motion. With my ability and confidence augmented, I applied my new skill in the rivers and lakes around Aurora. In doing so, my passion for fly fishing grew. I became not only a fan, but an advocate as well.

Later, when I had children I would attempt to pass on to them what Mr. Petoe had bequeathed to me. I came to love fly fishing for several reasons. I loved the physical part, the skills it took to deliver the fly effectively to a specific place. I loved the intellectual part, the ability to figure out which fly to present where, on the water's surface or below it at the right depth. Finally, I loved the aesthetic part of fly fishing as an art. It is beautiful to watch and to perform. To me, it represents artistic motion in air over water with the rod, the line, the fisherman's body all moving in sync, not unlike a miniature ballet.

Fly fishing has historically been involved in catching the most beautiful of our fish, especially North America's brown, rainbow and brook trout. Even today, more than sixty years after my youthful introduction, watching a skilled fly fisherman perform thrills me. For teaching me how to fish with a fly rod, I am eternally grateful to my neighbor Everette Petoe. I consider his teaching a gesture of shared love, the greatest of gifts. Today, three of my children are accomplished fly fishers. Sadly, none of my wives had any interest in fly fishing. I tried my best sales pitch but it never worked.

Once I learned how to cast a fly, I could fish Aurora's Chagrin River more successfully. As a fly fisherman, one does not remain sedentary, but wades and moves. Doing so, I covered much more water and now caught fish on flies that had been uninspired by worms. For example, I used artificial bugs and flies to catch the stream's Crappies that had previously spurned my worms. Some of my flies I purchased, but I also began to tie my own flies that summer. Most of my home creations looked pretty primitive, but they worked. I found it great fun to watch a big blue gill with its roseate throat patch rise up slowly from the stream's bottom and then suddenly snatch my floating fly off the surface. When I fly fished, Satchel, of course, accompanied me. In fact, I think he liked the fly routine better than sedentary bait fishing. Moving along the river and smelling new smells apparently beat simply lying and watching his master's bobbers.

Everette Petoe was also the person most responsible for beginning my career as a hunter. Somehow my parents, who knew virtually nothing about hunting or guns and cared even less, came to accept that their eighth-grade son was old enough to own and operate a shotgun. The reason for this: they talked to Petoe.

My fly-fishing mentor, whom my parents knew as a friend and respected, convinced them to grant my wish. Fortuitously, it turned out Everette had a friend in Cleveland who ran a respectable gun shop. From there and with my caddying money, Everette purchased a used 16 gauge, double barreled Ithica shotgun for me. (That particular gun, now an impressive antique, presently adorns a wall in my northern Wisconsin summer home.)

With my Ithica, Satchel and I hunted cottontail rabbits in the fields and woods around Aurora. Hunting came naturally to my little black dog. The Beagle in him emerged with a vengeance. He knew instinctively how to run rabbits. He wasn't fast enough to chase them to ground, so the bunnies would do their circling thing. While in pursuit, Satchel didn't bellow like a real Beagle. He yipped. Nevertheless, he did it loudly enough so I knew from which direction the rabbit would reappear. In 1953, we got lots of rabbits and the reason was my star companion Satchel.

My hunting career with Satchel lasted two seasons. In the fall of my 14th year, I went away to boarding school in Hudson, Ohio and my close relationship with my faithful dog-friend all but ended. I hunted some during vacations in 1954 and 1955, but high school sports and my prep school friends soon took Satchel's place. Away from home I missed him, but not as much as I thought I would. I was too busy with academics.

In the fall of 1956, my parents had Satchel put to sleep. I learned about it several months after the fact. Although heart-broken, I tried to understand as best I could by putting myself in their place. I recognized that neither parent had ever been much interested in the dog. They were not "dog people." For them, Satchel represented an intrusion into their lives. In our family, Satchel never became anyone else's special pal except mine.

Today, I don't talk very often about Satchel. That was not the case when my three children from my wife Shannon were growing up. I'm referring to the 1970s. To entertain them, I often told stories from my childhood. The ones they liked the best, more often than not, were my Satchel accounts—those stories about my pal and the crazy things we did together.

I had a bevy of such yarns, some embellished for effect, but for most I didn't need to exaggerate to get a laugh or a smile. I can still hear my elder daughter Johanna as a seven or eight-year old pleading, "Dad, Dad tell us another Satchel story." When I talked to her recently about this manuscript, I asked if she could remember any of her favorites. Here are two, the Paper Route Saga and the Piano Fiasco.

As noted above, I helped my Dad with the *Cleveland Plain Dealer* deliveries. The route included about a hundred subscribers. We delivered the papers by automobile at daybreak. My Dad drove. Riding shotgun, my job was to fill the customer mailboxes or Plain Dealer tubes on the right side of the road.

On the story day, Satchel managed to get out of the house just as we drove off to start delivery. Imagining himself a Greyhound rather than a Beagle, he set out after us. The first part of the route went north two miles. In that stretch we stopped at four mail boxes.

The dog didn't cease chasing after the first hundred yards, or even the first mile. As we slowed down for a mailbox, he would gain. When we drove away, he would lose ground. This happened with all four of the first deliveries. I noted Satchel shortly after we started out but didn't say anything to Dad. I assumed the dog would get tired and quit. He didn't.

After the first two miles, we turned west to cover a stretch where the subscribers lived more closely together. The dog had lost ground in the race's first leg, but not heart. With more frequent stops, Satchel gained ground. When he was less than fifty yards behind, Dad finally noticed our pursuer. Begrudgingly, he gave in to Satchel's persistence. We stopped and waited for the dog to catch up.

When he did, I opened my door and got out to make room for him. Satchel was heaving and panting and had dropped to the ground. But his tail still wagged. I didn't think he had enough energy to jump into the car, so I picked him up and helped him into the back seat. I got back into the car. We started up again.

After we delivered a couple more newspapers, I heard "haauuk, haauuk, haauuk" from the back seat. Satchel vomited his entire breakfast and more. Not on the floor, but on the seat. My Dad didn't say "Oh Shit" or "God Damn that dog," but I knew he wasn't happy. The dog had upchucked in the new Ford my Dad had bought the month before.

My father always devoted special care to his cars and this Ford was no exception. It seemed almost as if he washed and vacuumed it nearly every week. My wise-ass sister once remarked with regard to Dad's automobiles: "There aren't three children in this family but four, and Dad's favorite lives in the garage." There was some truth to that. Satchel won no accolades the day of his vomiting. I felt sorry for both father and dog.

Johanna's second favorite Satchel story went like this. I was home alone with Satchel late one winter afternoon. Don't remember the year. My family and I lived in a large late nineteenth century Victorian home which my mother, father, aunt and uncle purchased together in 1938. It would serve as a kind of old fashioned duplex. My mother told me that at the time they bought it, the bank considered it a "White Elephant" because in 1938 few could afford such an extravagance.

When my parents, aunt and uncle and maternal grandparents moved in, the three-storied house possessed four bathrooms, seven bedrooms (two with fire places), three living rooms, also with accompanying fire places, and two kitchens. The ceilings on the first-floor rooms extended to eleven feet. On the second floor, they were the conventional eight. On our side of the house the upstairs was accessible via an elegant staircase with a walnut banister, which for years I enjoyed sliding down.

The third floor served as an attic used exclusively for storage. This attic also provided living space for a variety of wild life, including red squirrels, mice, spiders and especially bats. Of these various varmints, the bats appeared to visit downstairs most frequently. They would somehow manage to crawl under the door at the bottom of the attic stairs and then invade the lower levels. My mother had a thing about bats and would become hysterical whenever one escaped the attic to fly about on the second or first floors.

On this particular Satchel-story day, a bat appeared before Satchel and me in the main living room. Making itself "to home," as the locals might say, it flew in from the parlor to visit us. What Satchel and I were doing at the time I don't recall. But the bat appeared suddenly, startling both of us. It was flying about in circles five to ten feet off the floor. I hustled to the kitchen entry way to get a broom to knock it down.

When I returned with my weapon, the beast was still doing its thing. As it flew by me, I swung at it and missed. I swung again and again. No luck. The dog entered the fray as well. Every time the bat swooped down to five feet or less the dog leaped up snapping at it. He jumped more times than I swung. I encouraged him with repeated "Get it Satch, get it Satch." The contest went on for several minutes until the bat finally gave up flying (it probably realized the yahoos swinging and jumping at it were no threat) and attached itself at the top of one of the eight-foot-long curtains hanging in one of the room's two main windows.

Satchel noted where the bat landed. The nearest piece of furniture to the window and subsequently, the bat, was the room's baby grand piano. Using his hunter savvy, Satchel jumped up on the piano bench and then onto the top of the piano.

The piano was only a few inches from the curtain. Believing himself within catching distance, Satchel jumped at the bat on the curtain. His initial jump fell short. Undeterred, he tried again and again. More often than not when he came down from a jump, he slid across the piano's top. Several times his toenails scratched the piano's elegant finish. Realizing what was happening, I got Satchel down off the piano. With my broom, I knocked the bat off the curtain and took it out of the house.

But the damage was done. What should I do? If Mom found out, Satch and I were in serious trouble. To deal with the crisis, I got furniture polish and mixed it with some dust from the fire place to cover up the scratches. The effort worked, at least for the time being. When my parents arrived home that evening, neither one noticed the scratches.

The damage was discovered later. I'm not sure when. The dog's role in the scratches remained a secret. Much to my relief, my pal had survived another day. Although fearful and guilt-ridden, I never confessed Satchel's act. Several years later when my father began refinishing the piano, the scratches became apparent and the truth came out. No big deal. By then, my beautiful friend resided in doggie heaven.

Looking back from the vantage point of 2017, I think I understand Satchel's position in my childhood much better now than I ever did before attempting this manuscript. My understanding of Satchel has become clearer because I have had the experience of eight dog companions after him. I asked myself: why did you have so many dogs after Satchel? The answer was and is Satchel's unique legacy for me. Just exactly what do I mean by that? I think an accurate answer to that question lies in the non-affirmation context of my human family life.

No one among my human family shared my interests in nature, fishing or hunting. Even my non-outdoor school activities generated little interest for the family. For example, neither parent attended any of my varsity baseball games at my boarding school, Western Reserve Academy, where I started as the varsity baseball team catcher for three years. Coming to a game now and then wouldn't have been a problem, since they lived only ten miles away. Other team member parents were a regular feature at our home games.

In such a non-affirmation family context, Satchel stood out as the polar opposite. He functioned as both my affirmation source and my affirmation trainer. Satchel became the family member who participated in my life most fully, the one who became in my outdoor engagements and everyday activities the partner who enthusiastically shared with me the most.

He gave me love, attention and an escape from solitude. He became for me not an intrusion into my life as he was for the other members of my human family, but a vital part of my existence. By his example, Satchel also taught me how to affirm others. As I have come to recognize while working on this memoir, Satchel's legacy of love and sharing not only shaped and influenced my future dog commitments, but, as we shall see, it also affected my children.

INTERREGNUM

Between 1955 and 1968, I possessed no canines. The reason was simple: too much schooling and no time for dogs. The 1954 move to Western Reserve Academy in Hudson, Ohio in effect ended my youthful Romantic period with its attachment to and involvement with nature.

Most of my hunting and fishing ceased at that time. I entered a markedly different social and intellectual milieu. The boarding school years ushered in a more serious age for me, a time of rationalism and intellectual endeavors. The student body had been carefully screened for academic aptitude and skill. Hence the academic challenges were significantly greater than those of the Aurora school system. I loved Western Reserve Academy but beyond sports and academic work, little time existed for engaging nature.

Of the many English, social studies or history papers I produced during my four years in Hudson, only one dealt with nature. In 1955, for the freshman essay contest I submitted a short piece which described my discovering at the Aurora Bird Sanctuary the nest of a Blue Grey Gnat Catcher, a very small, uncommon but beautiful Ohio song bird. The essay didn't win, but it did receive an honorable mention. That made me happy.

After graduating from Western Reserve Academy in 1958, I went off to Bowdoin College in Maine. During that period, I had the same problem as at Reserve: an absence of time for non-school related activities. Although a frat brat, I was wise enough for all four years to live in the dorms rather than the fraternity house.

I had three other fraternity brothers in my class who shared my aversion to residing in the Animal House and stayed in the dorms. We ate our meals at the fraternity and partied there after football games or other social events, but that was it. A Boxer who lived in the fraternity house represented my only dog contact during that stretch of years. I can't remember who owned him or even whether he had been adopted by the group. He seemed to be most attached to a member from Pittsburg whose scholarship job involved helping in the house's kitchen.

I can't recall either the dog's name or the brother presumed to be his master. I do remember the dog as friendly, but his most memorable characteristic lay not in his social skills but rather in his drooling. He had mastered the art. At breakfast, he would sit next to you and stare hard as you ate, the object and expectation being a part of what you were chewing. All the while he concentrated, he'd drool. Occasionally he'd lick his chops. The drools would sometimes extend from his jowls to the floor, 15 to 18 inches below.

Though disconcerting, the Kappa Sigma Boxer's drooling never reached the disgusting level of James Herriot's farting Boxer Cedric. The drooling never prevented me from consuming my usual breakfast of three dropped eggs. I have no idea what happened to him. He did leave a legacy for me however: his drooling turned me off Boxers.

I graduated from Bowdoin in 1962 and moved on to do a master's degree in early modern-medieval history at the University of Pennsylvania in Philadelphia. During my time at Penn (1962-1963), I came to realize that my three years of Latin language study at Reserve were not sufficient enough for me to maintain momentum in medieval studies.

Finished with Penn's M. A. program, I changed direction, choosing instead to concentrate on modern European history and, more specifically, the history of Germany. Having minored in German at Bowdoin, I felt more comfortable with that language choice. To pursue a history Ph.D. program, I changed universities, opting this time for the University of Wisconsin in Madison.

In August 1963, I married first wife Shannon, an attractive, intelligent, five-foot six inch, brown-eyed brunette whom I dated during the last two years of my college stint in Maine. A year younger than I, Shannon had majored in French at Colby College. More devoted to music than her avowed major, she spent most of her enthusiasm and effort during her undergraduate years honing her considerable singing talent. With a beautiful contralto voice, she starred in a variety of her college's vocal groups.

During those years, Shannon studied with several voice instructors. She would follow her singing passion throughout our time in Madison and well beyond. The musical thing represented a major difference between the two of us, for I had then and have now no musical ability. Although unmusical, I attended her various performances faithfully throughout our married years and I very much enjoyed doing so.

Unfortunately, in the end I think my musical non-aptitude would be a crucial factor in our ultimate separation.

Shannon's and my Madison period lasted from the fall of 1963 until the end of the spring term in 1968. The only interruption during that period was a nine month stretch in Germany (1966-67) which enabled me to finish my doctoral dissertation research. We returned to Madison in late 1967.

In the spring of 1968, the University of Winnipeg in Winnipeg, Manitoba hired me to teach German and European History. I began my teaching career there in September 1968. In May 1969, the family had a new arrival, our son Nathaniel. The next year at about the same time, our second child, Johanna, arrived. A final daughter, Sarah, was born in early 1972.

CHAPTER TWO

Jason of the Golden Fleece
Water Dog Incarnate

Jason launching himself into the Saint Lawrence River

"If you have a dog, you will most likely outlive it; to get a dog is to open yourself to profound joy and prospectively, to equally profound sadness."

— Marjorie Garber

I was sitting in the University of Winnipeg's student union one afternoon in April 1970, having coffee with several history colleagues when the subject of dogs arose. Included among the group was the department's Canadian historian, Ross McCormack. I knew dapper, dark haired Ross, a handsome, preppy-looking, 26-year-old and favorite son of the department's chair, owned a dog. I met his canine, an elegant (non-drooling) boxer, at a Christmas party he and his wife held during the preceding holiday season. Of the history faculty, Ross was the only Winnipeg native and alumnus of the college that employed us. As a result, I assumed he knew more about the city than anybody else on staff and he did.

"Ross," I said, "you're a dog guy. Maybe you can help. Been thinking about getting a dog for hunting ducks and geese. Know any good sporting dog breeders in town?"

"Lots of different sporting dogs. Any special breed in mind?" he said.

"Yeah, Labrador Retrievers. Been doing some research. They seem to be the most popular dog," I said.

Ross said, "Lucky you asked. I've got a friend whose female black Lab had a litter of puppies a couple of months ago. He's in the process of selling them as we speak. Wife and I saw the litter last weekend. Took our daughter over to play with the puppies. When we arrived, there were eight puppies left, half black, half yellow. All beautiful. Mother impressive as well."

"Are they purebred?" I asked.

"Yeah. As far as I know. Friend's asking a couple of hundred dollars for each so must be the real thing," he said.

"What's your buddy's name?"

Ross gave it to me and I called his friend that day after I got home. The owner told me he had six puppies left from the original nine. I realized we needed to move quickly if we were serious about getting a dog. After supper that evening, Shannon and I went over to take a look.

The puppies were in a fenced off area of the owner's basement, their mother suckling them. A large black Lab, the mother impressed me as a gentle, calm, sweet tempered, even regal canine. When the owner called her, she got up and left the puppies to us.

Choosing one from the litter was both fun and difficult. It took half an hour of scrutinizing, holding them upside down, making strange sounds at them and embracing the several puppies before we decided to take one of the yellow males. We came away happy. The dog we fetched that day would be with us for the next ten memorable years. It would convert me to the breed from virtually his first day as a member of the family. We named our new yellow dog Jason after the Greek myth featuring the adventures of Jason and his Argonaut cohorts in their quest for the golden-fleeced lamb.

The motivation behind the choice to go with a Labrador Retriever grew out of a series of events unrelated to dogs. As noted, Shannon and I moved out of Madison in August, 1968 so I could join the history faculty at the University of Winnipeg. From the start, we liked "Winterpeg," as some of the locals dubbed it.

Settling in came easy. Shannon had wonderful musical opportunities with the city's symphony chorus and other smaller operatic and choral groups. I had fishing. My initial Canadian angling efforts involved lake fishing from a boat for Walleyed Pike. Although these first angling efforts employed live bait and a sedentary approach, I hadn't lost interest in fly fishing.

In fact, in Madison I restarted my fly fishing career in Black Earth Creek, a small stream with rainbow and brown trout. The creek, located about half an hour's drive from Madison, or the time it took for me to smoke a cigar, provided considerable relief from my graduate studies. In Winnipeg, my renewed fly fishing interest and activities led to a friendship which ultimately prompted me to purchase and train a Labrador Retriever.

The impetus was accidental. Sometime in early 1969, while in a sporting goods store in North Winnipeg inquiring about fly fishing equipment, I was overheard by a tall, blond young man with a crew-cut dressed in jeans and a red University of Manitoba sweatshirt also shopping for fly fishing materials. Curious about my interest in fly fishing he said, "Excuse me for interrupting but are you a fly fisherman?"

Surprised, I said, "Yeah, have been since my teenage years. You fly fish?"

"For sure," he said.

"I'm new to Winnipeg so maybe you can help me. Don't know anything about fly fishing opportunities here. Do they exist?"

"Yeah, good ones too," he said.

"But I'm interested in trout fishing. Any trout opportunities?"

"Yeah, good ones too."

"Great, how do I find out about em? Somebody at the Manitoba Department of Natural Resources I can contact?"

"Don't have to do that. There's a better source, our fly fishing club, the Manitoba Fly Fishers," he said.

"Can anybody join?"

"Yep, we're open to all who love to fly fish," he said.

"Who do I contact about joining?" I asked.

My new friend then filled me in on the details. According to him, the club met once a month to tie flies, watch films, hear lecturers and share trout experiences. He invited me to attend the next month's meeting and gave me the name of Don McMaster, the club's president and editor of its monthly newsletter.

A couple of days later, I called Don to introduce myself and have him tell me more about the club. A gracious fellow, he sounded pleased I had called and encouraged me to join the group. I did. Thus began a friendship that would include not only fly fishing outings but also hunting adventures as well.

A good half a dozen years older than I, Don was a native Winnipegger and an active, creative outdoors man. A tall fellow with close-cut, light brown hair that covered only part of his balding head, Don worked as a school administer in one of the city's high schools. The former biology teacher possessed impressive artistic and taxidermist skills. His bird and fish mounts, particularly his big game heads, equaled most museum pieces.

Over the next few years, we became good friends and outdoor companions. His family and mine meshed as well. Don's wife taught music in the city schools; his two children were the same ages as my Nathaniel and Johanna. All four children attended the same grade school in Winnipeg's River Heights. The children and wives developed their own friendships and as families, we enjoyed activities including camping and ice fishing together.

Don's influence on my dog preference stemmed from his interest in waterfowl hunting. An avid hunter, he made duck hunting into an art. He traditionally hunted waterfowl on Lake Winnipeg just north of Riverton, Manitoba.

His duck hunting routine involved a canoe and considerable paddling. He took me along for the first time in the fall of 1969, on a Saturday morning in October. He picked me up in his red IH Travalall with an aluminum canoe on its top at four-thirty a.m. We drove north, ending up at the lake an hour and a half later. He parked the vehicle off the road on the edge of what looked like a large marsh.

As we got out of the truck, Don said, "We'll put the canoe in here in this ditch. You'll see as it gets lighter the ditch runs into a canal that'll take us out through the marsh to the lake's edge. Once there, we'll put out the decoys, hide the canoe in the cattails and wait for the action to begin."

"How long's the paddle?" I asked

"Not too long, maybe half an hour or so. Advantage of the long paddle is we avoid other hunters. Too much work for the average Joe. Don't have a problem with that, do you?"

"Not at all. Like to canoe. Do a lot of it at my in-law's summer place in Ontario," I said.

"Good, I'll hold you to that," he said.

We pulled on our marsh camo-clothes and chest waders, placed the decoys, ammo, guns and lunches in the canoe, climbed in and pushed off. We paddled for about a hundred yards down the ditch/canal and then cut through the marsh out to the lake. The trip took about the half hour Don had described, most of it carried out in the dark. Once at the edge of open water, we set out the decoys in the shape of a U, pulled the canoe into the adjacent cattails and waited for the ducks to arrive.

We didn't wait long. As soon as it became light, we had ducks:

Mallards, Blue-bills (scaup), Teal, and Gadwalls flying about, some coming into the decoys. They swooped in as singles, doubles, triples and even small flocks. The shooting was fantastic. When it let up, we'd pull the canoe out of its cover and paddle out to pick up the downed ducks. By ten o'clock a.m. we had our limit of eight ducks a piece and headed back to the truck. I'd never enjoyed hunting as much as on that day.

Don took me out several more times that fall and my conversion to waterfowl hunting became complete. Although it took considerable work to reach the place to hunt and setup, the effort was well worth it. We had the lake to ourselves. The only thing lacking for me was a dog—a hound to fetch the ducks we downed.

Don didn't see the need for a dog. He had hunted without one since high school. With my Satchel experiences, I knew what a dog could do for a hunt. In a wonderful exercise like this, a good duck dog could only magnify the overall pleasure of the hunt. The kind of duck-dog to get now became the question.

To find out about an appropriate duck-dog, I did some reading, specifically looking at a number of *Field and Stream* and *Sports Afield* articles describing duck hunting with dogs. In 1970, the most common duck dog in America, I discovered, was the Labrador Retriever. On the belief that Labs would fill my need, I responded to my colleague's information about the litter of available puppies.

Looking back, I realize I really didn't know what I was doing but fortuitously the decision to buy Jason turned out to be positive. Once I had my puppy, I began to think about the training he'd need. Cocky enough to believe I could do the training myself if I had a good book to follow, I bought a copy of *Water Dog* by Richard Wolters. That represented one of the best book purchases I ever made.

When I bought the book, I knew nothing about the author, or of his interests beyond dog training. As it turned out, he and I had a host of things in common besides Labrador Retrievers. These included duck hunting, fly fishing and even college teaching.

During his lifetime, Wolters, a man of many talents, produced a spate of books on dogs and dog training besides *Water Dog*. These included *Gun Dog*, *Game Dog*, and *Home Dog*. Recently I acquired his major work *The Labrador Retriever The History... The People... Revisited*. As a historian, I'm impressed with the time and effort he dedicated to this work and with the scope and scale of his research into the subject. The short Labrador Retriever historical sketch which follows summarizes Wolters' definitive conclusions about my Jason's breed and its origin in Europe and America.

The antecedents of the modern Labrador Retriever are not known with any degree of certainty. According to Wolters, who did extensive research into the origin topic, much bad ink has been spilled trying to describe the breed's beginnings. For example, extensive claims have been made about the dog's relationship to the indigenous Newfoundland dogs. Almost all such assertions, Wolters insists, have suffered from faulty or inadequate evidence.

The reasons for this are clear. In the 17th and 18th centuries, Newfoundland was a distant, primitive, sparsely populated place. Before 1800 adequate records simply did not exist to allow for certainty as to the dog's beginnings. More recent explanations have complicated the issue by describing influences not only from Newfoundland (St. John's Dog) but also from Britain or even France (St. Hubert's Dog). Not until the 19th century did significant records appear to allow for more certainty as to the dog's origin and development.

According to Wolters, the modern prototype of what we know as the Labrador Retriever did not evolve until the nineteenth century and it occurred most obviously in Great Britain. Even from that time, however, the records depicting the animal's development are sketchy because the dog was almost exclusively in the hands of a small, aloof English aristocracy, whose world more often than not was limited to their own ilk.

Nevertheless, in 1903 the English Kennel Club recognized the Labrador as a separate breed. Five years later in 1908 Labs were exhibiting superiority in that country's field trials. Throughout the 19th and into the 20th century it should be noted that in Britain hunting remained an exclusive aristocratic activity.

As the years passed, the Lab's popularity as a hunting dog increased. By 1930, it had developed among the British aristocracy into one of their most popular shooting dogs. This trend continued. The present Queen Elizabeth still maintains royal kennels with Labrador Retrievers. Fondness for and commitment to Labs would eventually make its way across the pond to North America.

American imitation of the British aristocracy's adoption of the Labrador Retriever didn't begin until well into the twentieth century though. As Wolters points out, it commenced in the interwar period of the 1920s and 1930s as part of a faddish imitation of Britain's aristocrats by east coast American rich folk. Having a Lab or better yet, a kennel full of Labs, became a symbol of social status.

Such pretentions were particularly evident among New York's Long Island patricians. For several decades, this exclusive eastern tradition continued having little influence beyond the rich and well-born. Only after World War II and the Depression's end did interest in Labs expand among the not-privileged.

A couple of reasons exist for this: the first and most important being the increasing wealth and leisure time activities of a growing American middle class and second the spread among this expanding middle-class hunter group of an awareness of the Lab's great hunting and retrieving potential.

As news of the dog's hunting skills spread, so too did a consciousness of the breed's other positive features such as affection, tractability, and versatility in a social sense. Increasing numbers of American non-hunters adopted the dog for its role as companion and family member. Writing in the 1980s, Wolters summed up the process with these words:

> "The change in ownership of the Labrador was similar to that of the automobile; everyone could now afford to have

one.... In America from a mere handful of Labs in the thirties there were now hundreds of thousands. The Labrador became just as much at home in the family station wagon as he was in the kennel" (*The Labrador Retriever,* p. 108).

One of today's most popular and prolific dog authors, namely Jonathan Katz, who has published on a variety of different dog breeds, claims that the "best all round breed pound for pound is...a Lab, one of the best working dogs, one of the best family dogs, one of the best dogs period."

Katz describes Lab water skills in this fashion: "Labs exhibit an amazing amphibian construction—head above water, tail acting as a rudder, strong lungs powering the strokes, sleek oily hair sliding through water." Most often, Katz concentrates his discussion on the breed's positive personality and character traits.

To begin with, he describes Labs as non-belligerent, being "uninterested in expending the kind of energy it takes to get into a fight." Non-aggressive Labs, he claims, tend to "think no ill, do no harm, spread love and happiness." In his words, they are "relentlessly affectionate, tolerant, genial and easy to please."

In manifesting such socializing characteristics, they become "utterly dependable." For Katz, the effects of such dependable behavior make Labs "portable happiness generators, with their peacefulness and eagerness to please having a calming effect not only on their masters but on other humans as well" (Katz, *Izzy & Lenore*, 77).

I bought the Wolters *Water Dog* when Jason was six months old. His training began shortly thereafter. By Wolters' standards, I delayed unnecessarily long and should have begun the day I brought the dog home. Nevertheless, I tried to follow the master's guidelines.

I quickly discovered that Wolters was a perfectionist and dog training was not some minor exercise one engaged in at infrequent leisure times. His program required repetition, precision and commitment by both dog and master. I didn't have the time or necessary sense of purpose to duplicate his model.

Although impressed, I read his advice and followed it selectively, picking and choosing in an effort to end up with a dog that would obey enough basic commands to be a suitable pet at home and a respectable hunting companion as well. I had no desire to own a field trial candidate. My intentions remained much less ambitious.

The Wolters program I followed included the basics: sitting on command, heeling, lying down, staying and coming when called. How to teach these procedures the Wolters book described in detail. When Jason had learned the basic obedience requirements, I started on the retrieving.

As Wolters advised, I used dummies. I had the dog practice short retrieves, then longer ones and eventually multiple retrieves. I owned three dummies for the more complex exercises. (In one exercise, Wolters used sixteen different ones!) I never used live birds in any of Jason's practice sessions. I did try to teach the baseball procedure Wolters described in his manual. That was fun for both Jason and me.

Playing baseball with Jason went like this. I rigged up a make-believe baseball diamond in the back yard. I commanded Jason to sit and stay at the designated pitcher's mound while I stood at home plate. A dummy had been place at first base, second and third. I began by yelling "Jason, fetch" and then would signal with my right arm which base for the dog to fetch from. If I wanted him to retrieve the dummy on first, I would wave my right arm in the direction of first, indicating for him to bring the dummy on first to me. For second base the signal would be my arm straight forward toward him accompanied by the command "Back."

The whole baseball routine was designed to teach the dog to take a direction for his retrieve. We practiced this little fun game enough so he got the basic idea: look to me for a line and then take it. Later when hunting ducks, Jason's mastery of this skill turned out to be a boon for both of us. It prevented many a lost duck.

After the obedience sessions, I worked on training him to ignore the sound of shooting, to accept it as part of the game. For this, I borrowed a colleague from the University of Winnipeg's history department as a helper.

The introduction of gun shots required two sessions, the first with the gun at fifty yards' distance and the second with the shot at a tenth of that. On both occasions, Jason was distracted by being fed while the guns discharged. I repeated the routine a couple of times after without a partner. By opening of the hunting season, Jason had adapted to gun retorts nicely. This didn't surprise me because he was neither a nervous nor an easily intimidated canine. His self-confidence facilitated adaption.

The only complication in Winnipeg for my training routine occurred when I moved to introduce feathers; that is, have him fetch a real bird. I started with a dead pigeon. I let Jason smell the bird then tossed it ten yards away. Jason was excited for sure but he held his position. When I commanded "fetch," he galloped to the bird, grabbed it and began to eat it. I arrived just before he started to swallow. I grabbed his head, reached into his mouth, and shouted "Give, give!" He resisted, tried to turn his head away so I couldn't interfere with his culinary prize. I persisted and extracted the pigeon.

When both of us had calmed down and Jason was back in the sitting position beside my left knee, I tossed the mangled bird again and ordered him to fetch. Apparently afraid of what he would get if he grabbed it a second time, he refused. I gave the fetch command again but in a gentler, more coaxing tone. After a couple of minutes, this worked. He went to the bird, picked it up, brought it back to me and rendered it up. We repeated the lesson several times and I figured he had the routine down. The duck season was about to begin that next weekend in September. I was pleased with Jason and his progress.

Besides dog training, preparations for the season included my securing a canoe (a la Don McMaster), a dozen Mallard decoys with strings and weights, and a 12 gauge pump shotgun. I still owned my childhood 16 gauge side by side but had decided Lake Winnipeg waterfowl hunting required more gun. I painted the canoe a light orange/

brown color to match the fall's cattails and phragmites common to the Lake Winnipeg shoreline. Finally, I secured a car-top carrier rig for the canoe and a kennel to house Jason in the back of my station wagon.

On opening day, I hunted by myself with Jason in the general area north of Riverton that Don had introduced me to. I told Don I wanted to hunt Jason for the first time by myself so I could concentrate on seeing if he would do what I wanted him to do without other distractions.

Physically, the puppy who became the mature hunter developed steadily into an impressive figure. Throughout his growth, his color remained a solid yellow, the average hue for the breed's yellow version; that is, it was darker than the whites but lighter than the reds which have become popular of late.

As an adult, Jason weighed about 90 pounds, meaning that he was a bit bigger than average but certainly not a brute. As a mature dog, his most distinguishing feature was his longer than average pointed snout. The lady who ran the Winnipeg Labrador Club in the 1970s referred to him as "an ugly Lab" because of his snout. That comment offended me, but she did such a wonderful job looking after Jason the nine months of 1975-1976 when the family and I were in Germany on sabbatical leave, I made a point of ignoring the insult.

I hunted waterfowl with Jason for nearly a decade in Manitoba before returning to Wisconsin to attend law school in 1980. Most of that hunting involved trips to Lake Winnipeg. It took Jason only a couple of times out in his first season to learn what was expected of him in the canoe and the makeshift blind we would construct once on the lake.

In paddling out to the big water, Jason had to learn to lie quietly in the canoe. If he were to move about or try to jump out, he might have upended the boat. When I paddled, I wore my chest waders and had I fallen overboard, it might have been difficult to avoid drowning. Knowing this, I kept a tight rein on Jason. In the canoe, he had to lie at my feet with his head in my lap. If he tried to get up, I would smack him with a piece of rubber hose. He learned quickly to stay put.

My bright, serious, athletic son Nathaniel, born the year before we got Jason, accompanied me on numerous duck hunting trips during his grade school years. During that period, he became a devoted hunting companion for both me and Jason. Recently, he commented on Jason's excited anticipation for the hunt.

"I remember one evening before the opening of duck season, you lifted your shotgun off the gun rack and pumped it once, then replaced it. Jason heard the noise and it set him trembling and whining most of the night because he thought there would be hunting the next morning." In the canoe, Nat continued, "I remember him shaking with anticipation in the floor of our aluminum canoe, making the whole craft rattle." Because of this excitement, I always talked to Jason in a calm voice as I paddled, praising him for being such a good doggie and not trying to move from his position at my feet.

Son Nathaniel and Jason with the results of
a successful Lake Winnipeg hunt

Over the years, my magnificent yellow dog became an exceptional Retriever. He could retrieve from the thickest vegetation or in the roughest waters, even waves of a foot or so. Any duck or goose I shot, he eagerly fetched. The dead ones were easy work for him. Retrieving cripples presented more of a challenge, but Jason became expert at that task as well.

41

He developed an impressive routine for cripples, one he learned without any help from me. Being a strong and fast swimmer, Jason could catch any wounded foul that tried to swim away. More often than not, the crippled bird would seek to avoid the approaching dog by diving. Lake Winnipeg Bluebills, for example, were particularly adept at this. Jason learned how to cope with divers by swimming in circles around the spot where the wounded duck had disappeared. Normally the bird would stay submerged for less than a minute. When it resurfaced, Jason would go for it. The bird would repeat the dive and Jason would swim another circle until the duck reappeared.

This procedure might be repeated three or four times before the bird resurfaced close enough so Jason could grab it before another submergence. It was a fascinating routine to watch and one that impressed even my buddy Don McMaster. I can't recall Jason ever being bested at this little game. A few cripples did manage to avoid him by flying, but that happened infrequently.

Jason retrieving a Lake Winnipeg Bluebill

On my duck hunting trips, I occasionally took my second oldest child, daughter Johanna, with me as well. Presently a Presbyterian minister in Missouri, Johanna loves to tell the story about the time her father shot her while hunting ducks. Johanna, my blonde, smiling jokester was eight at the time of the hunt.

We left Winnipeg at four o'clock a.m. and drove to the lake, arriving according to plan about a half hour before sunrise. After I got the canoe off the station wagon and into the water, I loaded it with decoys, shells, lunches, dog and daughter. Johanna sat in the front. We paddled through the marsh out to the lake, found a suitable spot to conceal the canoe, and set out the decoys. We finished the set just as dawn was breaking and began our wait for the ducks.

Before any ducks appeared, a small flock of Canadian geese came off the lake several hundred yards to our left and turned in our direction flying along the shore line. They looked as if they might fly over us.

I told Johanna, "Hunker down and don't move. They might fly right over us and give us a good opportunity."

She complied.

The geese did as I hoped. The six-member flock stayed on the shoreline flying about 30 feet above it. As the geese flew over us, I emptied my gun and knocked down two birds. With my third shot I missed.

After I fired the third time, Johanna yelled "I'm shot. I'm shot." And she started to cry. I was mortified. I knew I hadn't shot her, but had no idea why she was being so hysterical.

Here's what happened. After my third shot, the ejected shell casing hit Johanna on the cheek. She had indeed been hit, but not by any BB's. I examined her cheek. No bruise, but her face was red from crying (or embarrassment). I've told this story more than once and it always amuses me to do so. Johanna's version, embellished I'm sure as only my lovely daughter can do, also amuses her listeners. Unmoved by Johanna's histrionics, Jason dutifully retrieved both downed geese. By noon we had our limit of ducks and the two geese. We headed off. Johanna slept peacefully most of the trip home.

The only exception to my Lake Winnipeg waterfowl routine was Snow Goose hunting north of Winnipeg on Hutterite Colony land. For several seasons, I went out in late August or early September to the colony and rented a quarter section of one of their fields for half a dozen dates in early November. The colony's land lay close to

Lake Winnipeg's Netley Marsh which received in the course of the fall migration thousands of these geese stopping off on their trip south.

Sometimes there were no geese in the marsh and none to come into my decoys. However, in the course of the month, geese would eventually show up in vast numbers on more than one of my dates. A student of mine named Clifford Klump, who had grown up hunting geese, kindly donated two dozen Snow Goose silhouettes to me. I used these on my goose hunts. When the birds were in the marsh, the decoys worked wonders.

Of course, Jason accompanied me on these hunts. We'd arrive before daylight at the field. I'd dig a shallow trough for us to lie in, collect straw for cover, put out the decoys, and wait for the morning rush. Jason would lie beside me, covered with a straw-colored camo cloth. I whispered encouragements to try to get him to relax. It never worked. He would whine and shake in anticipation of the action to come but never move enough to queer the geese.

If the birds had arrived at Netley Marsh, the shooting on the adjacent Hutterite lands would be frenetic. As one flock was driven off by the gun's retorts, another one would be settling in. There seemed to be no let up. It reminded me of the 4th of July parades from my youth: first the marching band, then VFW men, boy scouts, girl scouts, school cheer leaders, etc.

Jason would do his Retriever thing as well on Hutterite land as at the lake. Oftentimes before noon we'd have our limit, pack up and leave. As I recall, the daily limit in the 1970s was seven geese, much less than the several dozen or more characteristic of today's totals. The seven geese we brought home after such a hunt, however, constituted more than enough table fair for me, my family and faithful dog.

When I think of those Snow Goose outings, one less serious trip always comes to mind. On that hunt, I included the same daughter I'd allegedly shot while hunting ducks. I don't recall much of the details of that specific Snow Goose outing except the difficulty Johanna had in adjusting to the requirement of lying down flat on the ground in the makeshift trough blind I'd dug and remaining quiet while the geese overhead considered our decoys and the possibility of their landing to join them. On that day when the first flocks started to come over the decoys, all of us including me, Jason and Jo-Jo were lying flat according to plan.

As the geese approached, I whispered to Jo-Jo, who was right next to me, "Remember be still. Don't move. Freeze."

As the geese got closer, I said, "Be absolutely still."

When they were just about over us, she wiggled her arms and legs. The first flock flared off. The next approached shortly thereafter.

"Honk, honk, honk" from the geese.

From me, "Quiet, shush, freeze."

From Jo-Jo wiggle, wiggle, wiggle. Another flock flared. She couldn't, or wouldn't, not wiggle!

After the third flock fiasco, I took my little girl back to the station wagon and said, "You stay here, Sweetheart. Jason and I'll be back shortly."

As I shut the door, I added, "You can now wiggle a much as you want."

Years later my dear daughter explained her wiggling. "Dad, I couldn't stay still because the sound of your gun was so loud. Hurt my ears. I tried to cover them with my hands when you got ready to shoot. Didn't work. That's why I moved so much. Also, I remember when you and Jason came back, you had six geese."

During his life, Jason spent only a small percentage of his time hunting. The vast majority of his hours he lived out with his family in our house. Jason wasn't a trouble-free puppy, but nearly so. He had his place in the basement for the times we were busy or away.

For the first year, he was restrained to his basement area by a chain attached to a drain pipe. He could maneuver about to get comfortable on his rug or go potty on the newspapers spread for that situation. The chain and papers routine I learned from the Wolters book. The formal house breaking came along slowly, but eventually he knew when and where to go. From the basement abode, he had little opportunity to engage in the destructive chewing and door-busting activities John Grogan described for his Marley.

The only troubling incident from his puppyhood arose from his chewing his bedding rug. He ate a portion of the rug and it impacted in his intestines. After he threw up several times and refused to eat, I took him to the nearest veterinarian I could find in west Winnipeg.

The vet I chose, a man of Ukrainian descent named Balko, turned out to be God-sent. A heavily accented, tall, balding, brusque man, who seemed always in a hurry, Dr. Balko had a unique way of dealing with his "duggies." He'd approach big dogs like Jason by confronting them with his buttocks: that is, by putting his ass in their face. His idea, I guessed, was a buttock was less likely to be bitten than a hand or finger. The buttock-in-face immediately intimidated my Jason and allowed the gruff doctor to do his will.

After introductions, I followed the doctor into the examination room and he said, "What's wrong with beautiful duggie?"

I said, "Not eating. Hasn't for the past 3-4 days. Everything I've fed him he's thrown up. I'm worried. Think he may have eaten part of his sleeping rug and it's stuck in his stomach."

Dr. Balko and I lifted Jason up onto the examination table. He looked into Jason's eyes, felt his stomach and underside, and listened to his heart. He turned to me and said, "Your duggie don't look too good. Tell you what I do. I attack problem from both ends. Medicine in mouth, medicine in butt. See what happens. Okay?"

"What happens if he doesn't pass anything"? I said.

"Then must operate. Don't like to. Is dangerous. Costs much more. Want to try other first. That okay?"

"Yeah, doctor, whatever you think is best. I love this dog, want him healthy."

"Okay, you leave him. We look after him. We call when we have something to report. Okay?"

"Yeah, that'll be fine. Thanks, Doctor." And I left.

Four days later, Dr. Balko's office called to tell me Jason could be picked up. The oral/anal treatment had succeeded. The rug piece passed. I was much relieved.

When I brought Jason home, he looked like walking death—his eyes appeared sunken; his ribs were showing; he seemed listless. Nevertheless, he began to eat almost immediately. In a week, his appearance changed dramatically. His eyes sparkled again; his ribs no longer protruded, his old *joi de vivre* reappeared. I was much indebted to the good doctor for saving my "beautiful duggie."

The adult Jason who matured in our home evolved into much more than a Retriever of game. Indeed, he became a solid member of his human family, embodying the Wolters ideal of good citizenship. He was calm, confident and caring. He barked infrequently, never at persons who came to our door or at other dogs viewed while travelling with us in the family station wagon. The most serious barking situation I can remember occurred on one of our trips east from Winnipeg.

It took place at a campground near Wawa, Ontario. For supper that evening we had campfire-cooked pork chops purchased in Wawa. One of those chops, the one I ate, was spoiled. At two o'clock a.m., I left the tent in a rush to puke. The regurgitation was loud and dramatic.

Before the obnoxious noise began, Jason had been asleep on his bed beneath our boat. My strident throwing up apparently terrorized or befuddled him. He began to bellow, to make long, drawn out, desperate sounds that called for an equally serious remedy. Apparently, he felt obliged to broadcast to us and the entire campground the danger implied by the God-awful sound I made. The whole affair embarrassed me, but I couldn't fault Jason. He was only doing his good citizen thing and notifying us and the other campers of the source of the dangerous noise.

In sharing his puppy years and adulthood not only with me, his hunting companion, but also with my wife Shannon and our three children Nathaniel, Johanna, and Sarah, Jason left many positive memories of his acts of love, concern, and enjoyment with his human family. Our first Labrador Retriever fit so well into the family group as a puppy and later when mature because of his positive character traits.

Throughout his time with us, Jason exhibited intelligence, liveliness, and a fondness for fun. He loved attention and responded with appropriate affection. The children liked to play with him, tease him, or try to get him to do something naughty. Jason responded to the tail pullers and ear twisters by licking the perpetrator's face. It always worked; hands to human face and off his tail or ears. When they tried to ride him, he moved out from under Nat or Jo-Jo with his tail wagging.

My three children came to identify with Jason as one of them. I witnessed an example of this one day while stopping for groceries. I left the children in the station wagon because I had only a quick stop to make. When I returned to the vehicle five minutes later, the three of them had climbed over the station wagon's back seat and somehow managed to squeeze into Jason's kennel. They'd even pulled the gate closed.

A bit shocked and amused at seeing them in the kennel, I opened the back gate and said "What are you Moroons doing?" I liked to quote Bugs Bunny, whose wisdom and language I'd picked up watching Looney Toons on Saturday mornings in Winnipeg with the children during those wicked winter days when it was more than "meat locker" cold to do anything outside.

The smiling Maroons responded "Woof, woof, woof!"

Laughing, I repeated, "What are you doing?"

Nat said, "We're being Jason."

His sisters agreed: "Woof, woof, woof!"

The woofers came out of the kennel without a battle. I felt fortunate I managed to get them out of the cage before some other adult called the police on me!

In 1975, Shannon's parents donated to us the smaller of their two island holdings on the Canadian side of the Saint Lawrence River's Thousand Island group. A year later we had a summer cottage built on that island. A small property 225 feet long and 60 feet wide, it was essentially a rock with sparse soil extending out of the river.

Nevertheless, its plant life included several White Pines and a surprising abundance of blueberry bushes.

For the first several years, conditions remained primitive. We had no running water, no electricity, and no flush toilet. In 1978, we had electricity brought over from an adjacent island. That provided light, heat to cook with and the power to run a Swedish electric toilet, a great improvement over the chemical one we had been relying upon.

Each summer from 1975 to 1980 we spent two months on the island. Both Shannon and I loved the beauty of the place, its peace and serenity. So did our three children and our grand golden-fleeced water dog Jason.

The children each have favorite Jason stories. Here are a couple examples from our time in Winnipeg. Nathaniel likes to tell about his Christmas present fiasco. According to him, his mother and I only let the children open one Christmas present before seven o'clock a.m. Christmas morning. They had been instructed not to awaken their parents before that hour, they were told, because both Shannon and I had been up very late Christmas Eve wrapping their presents and needed extra sleep. On the Christmas morning in the story, Nat recalled, Sarah and Johanna each had opened a present and were happily playing with their new toys.

Nat's efforts were not so successful. Well before Christmas morning, he developed an enthusiasm for Canada's national game, hockey. He had a team to play on at Winnipeg's River Heights Community Center and a net to shoot pucks at in our basement. His presents that year included a new hockey stick and a hard rubber ball to go with it.

The morning's problem arose from Jason being naughty. When Nat unwrapped the stick and ball and started stick- handling in the living room, Jason joined the game by grabbing the ball. Once in possession, Jason refused to give up his prize. Frustrated, Nat came up to the parent's bedroom to get help.

"Dad, Dad, wake up, wake up. I need your help," he said.

No response.

He tried again, "Dad, get up, get up."

According to him, I rolled over, looked at the clock and mumbled, "It's only six-thirty. Go back to bed."

"I know," he said, "but I need your help now."

I responded, "What'd we tell you last night? No bothering before seven o'clock. Now go away."

"Did what you told me last night. Only opened one present. Jason took it. Need your help to get it back."

"Let me sleep," I said.

"Dad, I need your help."

"Alright, damn it." I got up.

As I shuffled down the stairs, I said, "What present are you talking about?"

"Jason's got my new hockey ball."

I shook my head in disbelief. "Where's the dog?" I muttered.

"In the kitchen with the ball," my remorseless son said.

I entered the kitchen, saw the dog standing in front of the refrigerator with his tail wagging and yelled, "Jason, what are you doing? Bad dog."

At my harsh words, his demeanor changed. Guilt replaced joy: his tail stopped moving back and forth, his ears drooped, the sparkle disappeared from his eyes.

When I commanded again, "No. Bad Dog, drop it," he looked at me as if to say, "Dad, don't get all upset. We're just playing, having fun. He's got his stick; I got the ball. We're even."

To no avail. I yelled again, only more loudly. "Jason, drop it. Drop it."

My tone and anger worked. Jason complied. As Nat tells the story, Jason nodded his head and the ball dropped from his mouth, going "bonk" on the floor. Bonk, that's the word my son used in remembering the sound. It still reverberated for him 35 years later!

End of story: I returned to bed, couldn't get back to sleep, came back downstairs and told the children to go ahead and open the rest of their presents. Shortly after they started, Shannon joined us.

Nat's sisters had favorite Jason stories as well. Johanna, for example, enjoys hearing me tell about the time Jason starred at Winnipeg's Queenston Elementary School's "pet showing day."

On that day I took Jason over to her school room and had him do the usual obedience routine: heel, sit, stay, and come. I also brought a retrieving dummy to conclude the act. For that I stood at the front of the classroom next to the teacher's desk and had Jason sit beside me on my left. I tossed the dummy down the middle isle between the rows of desks. Jason held steady until I said "fetch." At the command, he launched himself after the prize.

His enthusiasm, magnified by the school room's waxed floor, carried him skidding past the dummy. He quickly recovered, grabbed it, and returned it to me. His great yellow tail wagged throughout the act. When he delivered the fetched object, the children clapped their approval. That evening at home Johanna said "Dad, everybody loved the dog show and so did I." That my little girl was pleased made me happy.

As strong as Jason's fondness for the family was, his attachment to me, his hunting pal, appeared even greater. At home he followed me about from room to room. He would lie next to me when I worked at my desk in the study or when I watched television. At the island, the same routine prevailed.

At the summer place he would watch my daily jogs on our home turf. I ran for about 45 minutes in the afternoon an hour or so before supper. That exercise represented an attempt to maintain a regular jogging routine I'd started in the early 1970s.

On our small island I ran over a 90-foot-long path through the blueberry bushes up to the house and then back down to the water's edge. It was hard on the knees and one had to concentrate on not tripping because of the uneven, rough, root-strewn, rocky path. Nevertheless, I always felt good when I'd finished. Weather permitting, I ran nearly every day. While I ran, Jason would lie on a rock next to the house and patiently watch me throughout the workout. He did so because he knew the routine always included a wonderful finale for him. After a jog, I'd go for a dip in the river and include him.

In the post-jog swim, the children and Shannon usually joined us. It became a family swimming affair in which Jason was intimately involved. He loved to swim alone or with company. He took advantage of any opportunity to enter the water. For example, he liked to chase Mallard ducks from our shoreline. Those that he thought had come too close, he would swim out after, forcing them to fly.

Jason watching me run at the island

He always returned from such outings, I thought, with a smile on his face. But being the social animal he was, he enjoyed even more swimming with us. He could swim for three quarters of an hour non-stop, his body moving gracefully through the water, his great otter-like tail guiding his turns and moves.

In a recent sermon on fear, Minister Johanna included these words to describe her childhood swimming experiences with our yellow dog. "When I was a child, my family would vacation in the Thousand Island Region of the St. Lawrence River with our older cousins who, not to put too fine a point on it, loved to terrorize my siblings and me. My grandparents had an old outboard motor.

Our cousins would tell us stories about the kind of things that could happen to people run over by boats like theirs... Fishing trips would become litanies of stories about all the different ways a hook would find its way into someone's eyelid...

But maybe the worst thing was the stories our cousins liked to tell us, usually at night, when we would be at their mercy, alone with them at the kid's table, about all the different kinds of toe-eating fish there were infesting the waters near our grandparent's swimming rock. There were man-eating northern pike. The finger-devouring large-mouth bass. The king or the river, the fearsome muskellunge—that could basically tear off a small child's leg. It got so we could barely wade in the river.

But then one day it occurred to us, the logic of childhood—that this must be why our family's faithful Labrador Retriever, Jason, would always swim around us when we were in the water. He was protecting us from all those fish!

It suddenly made sense why Jason had that habit of batting the water with his big yellow paws—and then snapping at the splash. This was how he let all those toe-eating fish know that he meant business: better not come around his family!

We were terrified. There were creatures lurking in the dark river water beneath us. Sometimes one of us would think that they had caught a glimpse of something dark and oily and scaly and serpentine and we would freeze and stare and try not to breathe. And then we noticed Jason, his golden fleece bright in the sunlight, patiently paddling around the three of us, keeping the bad fish away, and the three of us were so happy, feeling so safe and secure."

Johanna's sister Sarah had comparable memories of Jason. Here's what she wrote me several summers ago in response to my email request on her Jason thoughts. She was at the island still owned by Shannon when she answered.

> "Being up here at the island, I think of Jason, such a regal, loyal dog. Also he had the patience of Job. When we lived in Winnipeg, when I was probably five or six, I went through a stage where I would play with his ears. They were so velvety

soft, irresistible, especially as I would try out new 'hairdos' on him. I'd fold his ears, curl up his ears, smooth down his ears. And he would bear it all. I remember hearing you tell us that the summer when we went to stay for a few weeks with Grandmommy and Grandpappy at the island how Jason would be on constant vigil for us... Then there is that beautiful photo of him up at the island lying on the rock in the sunshine. He will always be the prince of this place."

Jason fishing with Johanna at the island

As all the Labs I've owned over the years, Jason possessed remarkable skill at discerning the intentions of his master and family. At his beloved island, Jason knew when we were preparing to depart for good and not just intending to run into town for groceries.

When the boat was loaded up for the last trip to shore and he was obliged to enter it with us, he would go to the boat's front and stand with his paws on the bow and bark. As we moved away, he barked not in the panicked, warning way he had at the Wawa campground. Rather, he howled doleful lamentations. He wailed his departing good-byes with his head pointed skyward. He continued his canine requiem all the way to the dock. It was indeed a sad sight and sound. I think I understood what he sought to convey. I shared his sadness.

Jason spent his last days at the island in the summer of 1981. His time there lasted several weeks and I was not present during his visit. He had Shannon, Nat, Johanna and Sarah as companions. I had to remain in Madison because the University of Wisconsin Law School offered the opportunity to earn a J. D. in two rather than three years. One could do this by attending two semester summer sessions.

The family returned from the St. Lawrence at the end of August during a particularly hot day. The drive through Chicago rush-hour traffic had exacerbated the heat. Our station wagon had no air conditioning. Jason rode in the vehicle's back, in his kennel the entire trip. As I recall, he acted strangely that evening. He appeared unable to find a comfortable place to lie down. At the time, I attributed his discomfort to fatigue and stress. At eleven o'clock p.m. after we had all gone to bed, I heard a loud noise coming from the basement, like something tumbling down the stairs. I arose and went to find out what had happened.

I found Jason collapsed half way down the stairs, gasping his last breaths. I held his head in my hands and repeated, "Don't die, don't die Sweet Dog, don't die." He didn't obey.

At the time, Jason's death represented the most devastating blow I'd ever received. During my childhood, I experienced the deaths of both of my mother's parents who were living with us. Their departures were sad, but they appeared natural at the time because both were old persons in their eighties.

Jason's death was different. It seemed odd, shocking and inexplicable. When he left with the family to go on vacation, he had appeared healthy and happy, his normal fun self. Although in his tenth year, Jason didn't appear old. It seemed neither right, nor fair that he should die when he did.

In a state of shock, I wrapped Jason in a blanket and took him out to the garage. I didn't want the children to see him in his deceased state. Then I returned to bed to tell Shannon what had happened. I was numb and sobbing when I did.

"What's the matter? Why'd you jump out of bed and leave?" she said.

"Jason collapsed, fell down the basement stairs. He died." I nearly gagged as I spoke.

"What time is it?" she said.

"Did you hear what I said? Jason died."

"I heard. What'd you do with the body?"

"Jason died; he's dead. Our beautiful dog is gone," I sobbed.

"I'm sorry," she said.

I climbed back into bed and wept alone.

The next morning after telling the children what happened, I called a local veterinary clinic to arrange for the Jason's disposal. When I delivered the corpse that afternoon, the young woman at the office asked me how he died. I mumbled the words "old age." I held back the tears until I reached the car and then let loose the suppress sobs.

Depressed and feeling desolate, I drove home, entered the house and picked up the want ads section of Madison's *Capital Times* to see if there were any Labrador puppies available for purchase in the area. As luck would have it, there were.

I noted the puppy-vender's address and took nine-year-old Sarah, who was the first child home from school, to accompany me to see what was available. The backyard breeder we visited had two puppies left from a litter of eight. The two available were both chocolate males. In five minutes, I decided to go with the bigger puppy. I paid the 100 dollar price and we left with our new dog.

On the drive home, Sarah said, "Dad, I got a name for our new puppy."

"What is it?" I said.

"Boomerang, because he's a Retriever and boomerangs always come back to the thrower. So that's a good name for a Retriever, don't you think?" she said.

"Yeah, I do," I said. The name stuck. We had our Boomer, our second Lab.

Today, looking back and considering the spontaneous, almost hysterical purchase of my second Lab, the act seems foolish and irrational. To me, Jason's death happened so suddenly, so unexpectedly, so unfairly. I had no time to face the totally unexpected heartbreak and despair of his death, no time to get ready for his nonexistence, no time to prepare to cope. In a sense, I panicked.

Shannon offered me no solace, no sharing of my grief. I was alone in my sorrow. To cope with the loss, to ward off the enveloping despair, my response was to replace Jason with another Lab and hope the new dog would fill some of the gaping hole in my life that Jason's sudden, unanticipated death caused. As it turned out, Boomer managed to fill some of the chasm.

New puppies normally require more attention than grownups. My preoccupation with the new dog did defuse some of my sadness. For that I was grateful. The memory of my loss persisted but as time passed the despair faded and the memories of Jason's legacy, his special contributions to me and my family grew and became almost enshrined. He would become the measuring stick for all the Labs that followed.

I will argue in the following chapters that each of my Labs was or is unique, that is, distinct in his or her own special way. Jason certainly was unique not only in being my first Lab but also my most skilled water dog and hunting enthusiast.

To me, he remains the superb professional, the ideal hunting companion. He set the pace for the others to follow in both spheres. My children recognized his unique qualities early on. Johanna with her story of Jason swimming around them fending off water threats illustrates both her appreciation of him as a defender of the family but also her recognition of his special water skills.

Jason also was a model of patience and gentleness. Sarah's hairdo story describes both his extraordinary patience and gentleness. Finally, Nat, who is presently a college athletic coach, summed up Jason's unique hunting legacy and its impact on me with these words:

"Jason was born to water and loved hunting as much as I have witnessed any creature love any activity. It was truly a *raison d'etre* for him—instinct and passion in potent combination, and that shared love of hunting forged an incredible bond between my Dad and the dog. Indirectly

Jason and my Dad taught me how close two individuals could grow through a shared love of an activity. Maybe that seeped into my love of coaching too—faith in shared endeavors to forge such bonds."

Jason's uniqueness extended well beyond his capacities for swimming, hunting and gentleness. A model of civility, sociability, calmness, patience, and obedience, Jason knew how to love, experience joy and create relationships with other dogs and humans. He was never an outsider or an intrusion into his human family but always an appropriate, appreciative member.

Of all my dogs, he represented the one who did the best job of reuniting me with what Satchel had done, that is, binding me to nature. Moreover, as his pose in the photo of him lying on the rock next to our island cottage and his patient observation of my many jogging sessions illustrate, Jason possessed a capacity for serenity. He accepted life's peaceful times as easily as he did the ones filled with action.

In his loyalty and devotion to me and the family, Jason set not only a precedent but the standard for what I wanted from the Labs to follow. He won me over to the breed; he was the one who inspired in me the dual expectation of work but also love that I would seek and receive from the Labs that followed. As his fleece illustrated and name proclaimed, he was my golden dog ideal. I could not have been blessed with a better model.

Nearly thirty years after Jason's demise, daughter Sarah sent me an email expressing her sadness at hearing of the death of my second beautiful yellow Lab Clio (more on her to come). In her condolence note, Sarah incorporated the following celebrated Rainbow Bridge Poem.

"Just this side of heaven is a place called the Rainbow Bridge.

When an animal dies that has been especially close to someone that pet goes to the Rainbow Bridge. There are meadows and hills for all of our special friends so they can run and play together. There is plenty of food, water and sunshine, and our friends are warm and comfortable. All the animals who had been ill and old are restored to heath and vigor. Those who were hurt or maimed are made whole and strong again, just as we remember them in our dreams of days and time gone by. The animals are happy and content, except for one small thing; they miss someone very special to them, who had to be left behind.

They all run and play together, but the day comes when one suddenly stops and looks into the distance. His bright eyes are intent. His eager body quivers. Suddenly he begins to run from the group, flying over the green grass, his legs carrying him faster and faster.

You have been spotted, and when you and your special friend finally meet, you cling together in joyous reunion, never to be parted again. The happy kisses rain upon your face; your hands again caress the beloved head, and you look once more into the trusting eyes of your pet, so long gone from your life but never absent from your heart.

You cross the Rainbow Bridge together."

Today, as I finish this celebration of the first of my Sweet Spirits, I still feel much sadness for Jason. I continue to rue that he did not have two or three or even one more year to live. I grieve over Jason's death because it did not allow me to witness and relate to his decline physically and mentally. The absence of this deprived me of a lesson in the overall mortality issue in life. I would learn those lessons from his successors.

I am saddened also that at the time of Jason's death I did not have a partner with whom I could share my grief. In the days, months or years after Jason departed, Shannon and I never engaged in nor shared the kind of positive reminiscing about Jason that John Grogan and his wife did after their Marly left them.

In writing this chapter's conclusion, I have tried to fill in some of those absent recollections by reference to the Jason thoughts of my adult children as the dog related to them. That has been both rewarding and enjoyable, but it has not replaced what might have been with Shannon.

One last Jason thought before moving on to Boomer. If there's any truth to the Rainbow Bridge poem, I know Jason will be the first of my Sweet Spirits to welcome me and my later Labs into that happy place on the other side of the bridge.

CHAPTER THREE

BOOMERANG (AKA BOOMER OR BOOM-BOOM)
"HE'S MY TEEN AGER'S DOG," NAT WAGNER

Nat with his buddy Boomer

"Pets complement and augment human relationships. They add a new and unique dimension to human social life and thereby help to buffer the effects of loneliness and social isolation."

— James Serfell

If Jason embodied the ideal of good citizenship, Boomer did not. During his ten-year lifetime Boomer, my first Chocolate Lab but not my last, would qualify as one of John Grogan's (*Marley & Me*) endearing "bad dogs." Moreover, he seemed to justify the belief that bad dogs, rather than respectable canines, had more fun.

From puppyhood, Boomer knew how to enjoy doing his own thing—whatever that might be. No matter how naughty he seemed, no matter what his flaws, I couldn't help loving him to the end. He was expert at making me laugh and for me, inspiring laughter has always been a saving grace.

As noted in the last chapter, Boomer entered the family while I was hard at it trying to finish law school. Feeling guilty because Shannon had to return to work to help support the family, I applied for and acquired a clerking job with a Madison law firm in the first semester of my first year. I worked fifteen to twenty hours a week doing gopher work or whatever else my lawyer employers needed. If the clerking had monetary/psychological advantages, it also had a downside. This applied particularly to my activities at home with the children.

In Winnipeg I coached son Nat's soccer team for the five years prior to leaving for law school. That memorable period provided a host of wonderful experiences. When my former Winnipeg soccer boys called me after they won the 11-year-old Provincial soccer championship in the fall of 1980, I nearly cried for not having been present at their victory. Such comparable involvement with my children during my law school and law practice times was simply not possible given my schedule.

What applied to the family also held true for my hunting and fishing activities. Moreover, the time constraints in Madison affected my relations with our new dog. I never had the time to spend with Boomer that I had for Jason. This included not only hunting and daily companionship but, more importantly, obedience training. By comparison with his yellow predecessor, Boomer suffered neglect. The undisciplined puppy became a wild and crazy grown up, albeit a sweet one.

Physically, puppy Boomer was Labrador cute. His attractive puppy features included his well-proportioned head, body, and tail, and an especially rich, dark chocolate coat. Nevertheless, when first with us, his puppy personality seemed odd.

Not active, nor curious, he appeared almost sullen and lackadaisical. I never had a puppy so reticent and passive as little Boomer. That stolid condition lasted for about a week until I took him to see a veterinarian. The diagnosis had the dog suffering from an ear infection, the cause of his lethargy.

After a week of antibiotics, our new family member began to reveal his true self. He had energy in abundance manifested in chewing on things indiscriminately, carefree romping about the house, tail chasing and playing with whatever thing or human he could get to respond to his enthusiasm. As the months and years passed, Boomer developed into a beautiful, albeit a crazy adult. During maturation, he grew to a good size, not as large as Jason but just as muscular and nicely filled out.

His head and face appeared as classic Labrador. He had a large, broad head, his muzzle more square and less pointed than Jason's. His one untypical Labrador feature, a white star on his chest, became his hallmark.

Looking back, I think Boomer's craziness reflected the many abrupt and significant changes and uncertainties that affected me and the family as a whole during the 1980s. That decade began with me in the midst of a midlife crisis which precipitated the decision to go to law school.

The law school stint lasted until August 1982 when I graduated with my J. D. That month we moved out of our rented Madison property and purchased a house in nearby McFarland, Wisconsin. Residence there allowed Shannon to continue her legal secretary job in the Capital city.

In September 1982, I secured attorney work with two different law firms in two locations. The mornings I spent in Madison, the afternoons in Jefferson, Wisconsin, 30 miles to the East. Neither position paid well, and the work (mostly bad divorces, collections, and drunken driving cases) depressed me. After a year doing this double duty, I hooked up with a friend from my law school class who had started his own law business. It involved servicing three offices in three different towns: Platteville for the main one and branch offices in Highland and Muscoda, all in western Wisconsin near the Iowa border.

To me, the daily routine seemed something like what riding the legal circuit must have been in Abraham Lincoln's day. Because of distance, I spent the week in Platteville, returning to McFarland only on weekends and holidays. Pay wise, this routine differed little from my first year of legal services. The two of us were struggling to make the law business work. I had neither the patience nor the will to pursue.

In the winter of 1983, I decided to turn the clock back and return to my previous career teaching history. This did not turn out to be as easy as I thought it would be. A number of problems existed, the worst being a spate of recently graduated or previously employed history teachers now unemployed and a corresponding dearth of available positions.

The competition proved to be fierce. I applied at over three dozen schools in different parts of the country and Canada and managed to make the final interview list at only three institutions, one in upstate New York, one in Tennessee and the last in North Dakota. From the three interviews only one job offer resulted, that came from Minot State College in Minot, North Dakota. With the support of the family, I accepted the offer. We sold the place in McFarland and headed west in late July 1984.

Shortly after I started teaching at Minot, I learned from a younger history colleague there had been over 200 applications for the position. Initially, I couldn't comprehend how or why I'd been so lucky. After a few weeks on the job however, I learned the reason. Bless his soul, Henry Dugarm, the head of the history contingent and American history instructor, fancied himself something of a legal scholar. He liked to talk about seminal legal decisions and legal history. For this reason, he admitted to me he found my candidacy with its legal element not obnoxious, but attractive.

Henry became an outspoken advocate for me. Dale Elhardt, the head of the Social Science Division, supported Henry's choice and offered me the job. How lucky had I been? Very lucky indeed! Then as now, I think most historians would oppose hiring a lawyer, even an apostate one. Too many, if not all, the line from Shakespeare's Henry IV that "The first thing we do, let's kill all the lawyers," would seem more fitting than bringing one on board.

For the next four years, I taught history at Minot State. By 1988, I developed a new fantasy: an ambition to be an academic dean. To pursue this dream, I applied for and secured an assistant dean's position back east at Washington and Jefferson College in Washington, Pennsylvania, not far from my boyhood home in Aurora, Ohio.

For Shannon, I think the move to Washington and Jefferson was the last straw. Shortly after Christmas, the marriage collapsed. She informed me the marriage had ended. Her exact words were, "I want out of the marriage." I tried to convince her to go with me for marriage counseling. She agreed briefly. We went twice to a counselor.

After the second meeting, I asked the psychologist, "Is there any possibility that we might recoup, might save the marriage?"

He responded, "I don't think so. There's nothing there for her. She feels the marriage is, in her words, 'hollow' and no reason to prolong it."

Before or after leaving, she never attempted to explain her actions. I was never told that my fondness for beer was tedious, my enjoyment in killing fish and animals disgusted her, my falling asleep during Wagnerian operas illustrated my philistinism or even that history was a bore.

In my efforts to figure out her leaving, I think all of the above probably applied, but I also believe my non-musical self played a role. I tried to appreciate her skills, but I don't think that succeeded. As I look back, I think she always needed a husband with whom she could share her gifts. As it turns out, she found such a man and married him.

The initial impetus for Shannon's remarriage exhibits, I believe, considerable irony. Shortly after we arrived in Washington, Pennsylvania and before she left me, I made a phone call to neighboring Pittsburg to the director of that city's illustrious Mendelsohn Choir. In my call, unbeknownst to Shannon, I arranged a date for her audition with that world-renowned choral group. Although never acknowledging that favor, Shannon happily tried out and succeeded.

For the next twenty-plus years, she would be a prominent and devoted member of the choir, even serving a stint as one of the choir's executives. Her happiness with the group was augmented by one of its members, the man she would take as her second husband. That marriage between the two musical people has lasted to the present. Today, I am happy she finally found someone with whom she could share the musical passion and skill I never possessed.

Depressed by Shannon's departure, I called my friend Dale Elhardt, now chair of the Social Science Division in Minot, to see if there might be a way I could return to Minot's history department. The fates smiled on me. My original supporter Henry Dugarm had decided to retire, leaving his spot in history open. My understanding, compassionate friend Dale pushed my candidacy and I was rehired.

In my first week back at Minot State, the college's president Gordon Olson, a six-foot, six-inch-tall, heavy set, authoritative fellow who intimidated nearly everyone on campus including me, summoned me to his office. When I arrived at his office at nine o'clock a.m. my first day back, his secretary sent me right in. President Olson was sitting as his desk. He glanced at me and said, "Jonathan, good to see you. Have a seat." I did as told. The president finished what he was doing, looked up, slid his chair back and started in.

"Jonathan," he said, "I wanted to talk to you and get a couple of things straight right from the beginning. First, let me say, I've never done this before, never rehired a faculty member who'd abandoned us and then tried to come back on board. Against my best inclinations.

You had a chance here and then rejected us. What's to keep me from thinking you'll not do it again?" He waited for my answer while staring intensely at me.

"Dr. Olson," I said, "I'm sorry for the mistake I made in leaving Minot State. I'm very conscious of the forbearance and kindness of this institution in being willing to rehire me. I'll not repeat my mistake. I'm more grateful to this school than you'll ever know. You offer me a great break. I'll not let you down, not disappoint you. I promise."

"Okay, I'll take you at your word. But I'll be keeping an eye on you. Don't disappoint me again. You understand?" he said.

"I won't, Sir. Thanks again for what you've done for me. I won't forget."

He motioned that our meeting was over; I got up and walked out breathing a great sigh of relief. In the end, I did not disappoint him. I remained at Minot State for the next 22 years, until retiring in 2010.

The move back to Minot State and North Dakota involved a new twist residence wise. With the support and urging of Nat, I bought a house out in the country, 17 miles from Minot and seven from Surry, the closest small town on the way into Minot. A large, roomy two-story dwelling, the house included on its several floors four bedrooms, two baths, an upstairs living room and kitchen, plus a large finished family room in the basement.

Initially, the new country location seemed to have several advantages, one of the most positive being its authentic North Dakota prairie landscape. Not entirely flat but slightly rolling, its site reflected the agricultural side of the state beautifully. Fields of wheat, soybeans, sunflowers and corn stretched out in all four directions. Pasteur land for livestock broke up the planted sections now and again but didn't upset the wide-open, cultivated-spaces aspect. Initially, the view from my new home had an exhilarating, freeing effect. It allowed my eyes to roam from my residence as never before.

Although my years in Canada had been spent in an essentially agricultural province, my urban Winnipeg home had been much removed from the prairie. Likewise, my earlier Minot residence and the place in Washington, Pennsylvania had both been in city contexts. Now in my second North Dakota residence, I experienced for the first time actually living on the prairie.

Previous camping trips or hunting and fishing adventures beyond Winnipeg or Minot into a prairie context had been limited ventures into open space. Living north of Surry constituted for me a genuine back-to nature move. On the prairie, I could imagine what it had been like living on the original Romantic frontier.

The more immediate, less distant, external elements of my north-of-Surry home included a large lawn of several acres, plus a vegetable garden plot of nearly an acre. The residence proper sat a hundred yards removed from the gravel road leading into the town of Surry.

Like the road into town, the driveway was gravel. Beyond our yard and buildings, the property included eight acres of fenced, closely cropped pasture land which the previous owner had rented out to a local farmer for his half dozen or so beef cattle. The pasture possessed not only grazing space but a pothole for the cattle's water.

All in all, the new homestead left the impression of being very much North Dakota: surrounded by enough space to engender a sense of freedom but isolated enough to ensure privacy. Indeed, the closest neighbor, whose house was barely visible to the south, lived three quarters of a mile away.

The move to Surry impacted the children less than some of my other moves. Nat, who had spent his freshman year at Washington and Jefferson College, successfully transferred for the 1989-1990 academic year to Carleton College in Northfield, Minnesota. He was happy there from day one.

His sisters Johanna and Sarah had been enrolled at my prep school, Western Reserve Academy, in Hudson, Ohio for the two preceding years so they did not have to change schools with the move. Thus, for them as for their brother, the move to rural North Dakota represented no major problem. All three could return for vacation breaks to Surry and at the same time resume their earlier Minot friendships.

For Boomer, the move to the country seemed like a dream come true. At last, it seemed, he could do his own thing or things unencumbered. During his Madison, McFarland and Washington, PA years, Boomer's trips out of doors were always escorted ones on a leash. If not tethered, he would have run off.

Despite our best intentions, he did occasionally escape the house and dash for freedom. That a car or truck in Minot or Washington did not run him over seemed like a miracle to me. He had no fear of motor vehicles. Even heavy traffic never deterred him. He ran where the spirit urged.

Boomer playing fetch at the island

Before the period in the house on the prairie, the only unfettered time Boomer ever experienced was at our island in the St. Lawrence River. During my law school and law practicing days, Boomer's and my trips to the summer cottage were much shorter than the ones Jason experienced. Certainly Boomer enjoyed his free times at the island, but these did not compare to the life he would lead once we moved to the North Dakota prairie.

During our first full summer north of Surry in 1990, all three children came home. They found work at various jobs: waitressing for Johanna, employment at MacDonald's for Sarah and bartending for

Nat. In an effort to augment their earnings and provide some extra money for their school times, I followed the advice of a very clever, Jack-of-all-trades student of mine named Kyle Frame who suggested I rent a field from a neighboring farmer and raise sweet corn which, at ripening time, we could sell out of our truck in Minot.

We followed his advice and rented five acres three miles north of our house. Another student's father agreed to "blow in;" that is, plant our corn while doing his sunflowers in an adjacent field. The costs for seed and assistance in planting were minimal. By mid-June, our substantial crop had sprouted. We were all excited. Naturally that summer, I taught summer school (with three children in private schools, I could not afford not to).

On my way back from Minot or from the Air Force Base 19 miles north of the city where I also taught twice a week, I would stop off to check the crop's condition. I found that a great way to end the work day. By late July, the corn had ripened enough for marketing. We drove into Minot and set up stands in several places about town where permitted.

All of us, myself included, had fun with this project. The only problem arose when Nat fell asleep driving the pickup truck back for another load of corn and crashed into an oncoming car. Fortunately no injuries occurred, but the cost of repairs to the truck pretty much wiped out the profits from our corn venture.

When the children returned to their respective schools, I remained alone in the new home with its multiple rooms and rural location. Initially, I had a hard time dealing with being alone. Depression, sadness, a sense of personal failure all began to burden me. The world that had been so good to me for so long now seemed empty. How, I asked myself, did you manage to screw things up so profoundly? Why did you get this place in the middle of nowhere? In short, I felt lost, biter, angry and resentful.

For me, the fall season had traditionally been a fascinating period of transition, of both cessation and recovery. Now at my home there was no one to share in the season's beauty, no one to sit with on my deck drinking coffee after diner and marvel at the golden fields, no one to listen to the sound of forlorn coyotes calling from nearby, no one to watch the passing of beautifully symmetrical flocks of migrating Sandhill Cranes or the larger more disjointed ones of Snow Geese, no one to share the pungent fragrance of North Dakota's harvest season.

Boomer, on the other hand, had no such regrets. He suffered from no resentments, no disappointments, and no what-might-have–been thoughts at the new residence. No longer penned up in the back yard or always restricted by a leash as on his walks in Pennsylvania, Boomer now enjoyed free reign both inside and outside the North Dakota ranch house. Boomer developed his own routine on being let out in the mornings.

He ran about the property and engaged his particular interests: check out the grounds about the house to see if any new foreign scents (rabbits, foxes, ground hogs, etc.) had impinged on his turf, hunt an eatable mouse, or bother the cows in the adjacent pasture. The dog's new freedom meant he could perfect some of his traditional fun things and devise new ones as well. Boomer's enthusiasm for our new home ultimately would be the balm that would raise my spirits and enable me to accept our new circumstances.

In his early years, Boomer developed several unique entertainments, one of these being his obsession with human hats. Begun during his puppy days, this hat passion would continue throughout his life. How or why it developed remains a mystery. I think it began in Madison during his first winter with us.

Initially it involved the children, the dog's house mates. As I recall, Sarah fell victim most frequently to Boomer's bad hat jokes. When it was cold and snowy, she usually wore a woolen stocking hat. If Boomer saw Sarah with her hat on, he would run after her and try to grab it off her head.

Sarah, a small person, had trouble thwarting the big brute. More often than not, he would knock her down in the snow and then snatch her hat while she lay on the ground. With his prize, he'd then run off a ways and wait with his tail wagging for her to come after him to get the hat back. Sarah would usually end up crying because Boomer's grab caused pain. Inevitably, he pulled her hair as he pilfered her head piece.

How many times I had to go after the dog, take the hat back, and reprimand him, I don't recall. But my disapproval and reprimands had no effect on the trickster. Boomer pursued hats his entire life. Some of his hat snatches came at the expense of innocent, unsuspecting non-family members as well.

The most dramatic one occurred at the prairie home in the fall of 1989. After we moved into the new place, the furnishings we brought began to seem skimpy to me given the available square feet. The main living room on the second level in particular appeared to lack comfortable furniture.

To remedy this, I bought a large, dark brown sofa at a Minot furniture store and had it delivered. The piece, seven feet in length, three feet wide with T shaped cushions and a wooden base, weighed a great deal. In size and weight, it was a real brute. Two days after purchase, the furniture store's truck with two delivery persons showed up in the morning.

The sofa's bulk wouldn't fit through the garage door, so I told the delivery men, "Take the piece around to the back of the house, up the porch steps and into the living room from the door off the deck." They nodded agreement.

The men took the sofa out of the truck and carried it around to the back of the house to the deck stairway without a problem. Because of the piece's weight and size and the guys totting not being particularly big, the task of getting it up onto the deck was another story.

After more than a few grunts, some swear words and a good deal of straining, the first guy backing up the stairs reached the deck. The second man who carried most of the weight had advanced as well but was having trouble navigating the last three steps. As his head came up parallel with the deck's floor, Boomer, who had fixated on the whole process from the deck, leaned out over the stairs and snatched the hat off the second delivery man. With his prize, he then jumped back and ran into the living room.

The heist stunned and confused the delivery man. He staggered, moved back a step and yelled, "What the hell!" In my teenage years we had an appropriate phrase for his condition—"He didn't know whether to shit or go blind."

As he staggered, I thought he'd fall. But he recovered, held on and managed to get the sofa up the last three steps onto the deck from where the two men easily moved it into the living room. His partner was laughing; I was trying to keep a straight face. I cursed Boomer and apologized profusely to the dog's victim. My efforts had little effect. The hatless fellow was not happy even when I returned his hat. Scowling at me, he mumbled something about keeping your "God-damn dog" away. I couldn't blame him for his words or sentiment. I was too embarrassed.

Just recently I was obliged to move that same piece of furniture out of storage. On that day, I discovered firsthand the sofa's great weight and cumbersomeness. I also recognized how strong the mover dude had been who anchored the sofa's journey up those deck stairs. Likewise, I understood that if the hatless fellow had stumbled and fallen and the brute come crashing down upon him, he would, no doubt, have been seriously injured.

As a short-time lawyer whose favorite class in law school had been torts, I let my imagination go with the worst possible accident scenario. Here's what I envisioned would have been reported in the legal section of the *Minot Daily News*: "Severely injured delivery man sues successfully; grossly negligent Labrador Retriever owner permits his antisocial dog to attack a defenseless delivery man, causing multiple injuries including a fractured back, broken ribs and multiple head lacerations. The plaintiff reputedly received an award settlement of six figures." Thank God that was only fantasy!

After the men left, Boomer got a good scolding. But as usual it had no effect. He'd had his fun. I remember his larcenous posture when I went into the living room to take back the hat—he stood there, hat in mouth, tail wagging, and a happy gloat on his face. He expressed in his look and body language both delight and joy. He seemed to be saying, "Dad, wasn't that the coolest grab you've ever seen? Ain't I too much, the grooviest dog ever?"

After the sofa delivery snatch, I watched Boomer more closely when we had guests in the house. If someone had a hat on in the house or outside the home for that matter, that person continued to be fair game for my big brown jokester. I recall another much less serious snatching instance not long after the couch affair.

In October of that same year, Boomer and I, who had been hunting with a friend named Carl Pelto, returned to the house after a morning duck outing. Carl and I were sitting at the dining room table drinking coffee. Before sitting down, Carl had taken off his hunting coat but not his hat. As we chatted, Boomer ambled over and plopped down next to Carl.

Boomer was never one of those dogs reluctant to stare straight at you, eyes matching eyes. When you fixed your gaze upon him, he fixed right back. More often than not, he stared not aggressively but mischievously, as if he knew something fun were possible. His look seemed to be saying "Life is really a game. You shouldn't take it or yourself too seriously."

As we chatted, Carl noticed the dog's rapt attention. "Why's Boomer staring at me like that?" he said. "What's he want? A piece of my muffin?"

Thinking he was about to bend down and give Boomer a tidbit, I snapped "Don't give him anything. If you do, you'll regret it."

"Why not? He's a wonderful beggar. Deserves a reward for fetching this morning."

Before I could repeat my warning, Carl leaned over to oblige the dog. In a flash, Boomer ignored the hand with the muffin parcel, grabbed the hat and yanked it off Carl's head. Boomer pranced off into the living room with it and turned to face us. Wagging his tail, he had the same devilish smile on his face that always accompanied a successful snatch. "Come get if you can" his posture said. Of all my dogs, Boomer mastered the post-naughty-act gloat better than any of my other Labs.

Among my children, Boomer's most famous/infamous snatch occurred in August 1990 while future wife Ann and I were travelling in Maine. Upon our return, Ann dropped me off at the north-of-Surry home in the early evening. I entered and greeted my children Johanna and Nat, who were watching television.

"How'd you guys get along in my absence?" I said as I put down my suitcase.

Nat said, "Okay. Managed to keep occupied."

Johanna said, "Threw a party out here while you were away."

"Good. Have fun? Who'd you have out?" I said.

Johanna said, "Friends from Minot. Pot luck supper. Cook out. Everything went well except for the dog!"

"What'd he do?" I said.

"He was a real asshole," Johanna said.

"Not my big brown clown," I said, beginning to laugh.

"Asshole's the right word, Dad. He was a real jerk," she said, shaking her head.

"What'd he do?"

"He ruined the party for two of my friends."

"How so?"

"I told you it was a potluck. Well, he ate one of the dishes my friends brought."

"He enjoy it?" I said, trying not to laugh.

"Not funny, Dad. Jan and Ron brought a deep dish apple pie. Beautiful piece. Dog was out in the drive way playing the welcome wagon when they arrived."

"Hey," I said, "nothing wrong with greeting people?"

Johanna interrupted. "I'm not finished. When they got out of their car and opened the back to get their stuff and the pie. Boomer jumped into the car before they could grab the pie box and dove into it."

"Why didn't they stop him?"

"They couldn't. They tried. He was determined to eat the pie. I was on the deck cooking. Saw the dog jump into the car and heard Jan scream, 'No, no, don't, get away.' He wouldn't budge. I ran down off the porch to the car. Got my arms around his middle and pulled him out of the car. God, I was pissed."

"What about the pie?" I said.

"He'd eaten about half. Total loss. My friends were furious. Jan kept saying 'It was beautiful; it was beautiful. I wanted a piece.'"

"So what'd you do to the dog?"

"Let him finish it. What else could I do?" she snapped.

When Johanna stopped, Nat said, "Dad, you should have seen his gut afterwards. Bloated beyond belief." He laughed.

"Let me guess," I said. "He barfed up what he'd eaten. In the house or outside?"

"Yeah, he barfed but not right away," Nat said. "Had to get a drink first.

Went to the pothole and filled up. Came back and then barfed. Yuk. Unbelievable mess. But he upchucked outside, not in the house, thank God."

Johanna hugging Boomer long before the pie snatch

Johanna spoke again, "I second that Yuk. Boomer was disgusting. During the whole charade the guys were laughing, thought his act hilarious. Stupid jerks."

If Johanna thought Boomer an asshole, Nat had an entirely different view of our naughty Boom-Boom. When I asked him recently to reflect on the dog and give me his thoughts, he happily responded. Nat's email version to me of the brown devil follows. Although I knew he liked the dog, I was unaware of the scope or depth of his attachment.

"Boomer, our big chocolate," he wrote, "was a source of pride and something of a role model for me. He loved to play, making a game of anything—particularly stealing hats and trying to get you to chase him. I would come home and wrestle with him, using the wrestling moves I picked up at middle school wrestling practice and he would growl and grab me, never hurting but sharing in the joy of roughhousing.

I also admired his rebel's spirit. He would regularly strike against authority. He would look at a peanut butter sandwich on the counter, look at you, look back at the sandwich, look at you—knowing he would get smacked and he would say "screw it, it's worth it," and steal the sandwich. That's a form of heroism to a middle school boy. Sometimes sinning for a moment of fun is a hellava lot more fun than behaving.

With all of his flaws, appetites and excesses, he was himself. For a middle school kid, surrounded by young adults trying on various personae and struggling to find and forge an identity, you might say Boomer was the most honest presence in my life. I loved that about him. When Boomer ate, he ate. When he chased a cat, he chased a cat. I would walk him three times a day and I never controlled him. He was irrepressible in his desires and appetites."

Boomer walking Nat

"Boomer," Nat continued, "was fun-loving, proud, athletic, disobedient, tough, independent and beautiful—qualities any teen-age kid would want to emulate. My friends loved the dog too. He was cool—wild, hard to control, a nut but always Boomer. When he ate dead fish, dead beavers, dead rabbits, dead deer and other unrecognizable carcasses in the gravel road ditches of Surry, N. D., he was Boomer. He never took 'no' for an answer, and he always said yes to his impulses, both good and bad."

Nat had a favorite Boomer screw up story as well. It wasn't partying or eating, but hunting where he exhibited his special skills. I had forgotten what follows, maybe on purpose, but Nat's recollections brought back memories and a laugh. These are Nat's words to one of my recent requests for Boomer memorabilia.

"I will never forget," he wrote me, "the time we went duck hunting with Boomer. We were hunkered down in a makeshift blind in some cattails along a pot hole prairie pond, decoys scattered out in front of us. A lone goose flew over us and you rose up and shot it. As the bird fell, it angled not over the water but off to our right over a rise on the shore line behind us. You turned and said sharply, 'Hang on to the dog. I'll be right back.' You climbed out of the blind and ran after the wounded goose. Boomer went ballistic. He lunged after you in an effort to follow. I tackled him, wrapping one arm over his back and one under his chest, snaking my hand inside his collar. He dragged me about fifteen yards down an alkaline beach, bawling and braying like he was being slaughtered. When I finally slowed his momentum, I snapped a leash on him and horsed him back to the blind, tugging and bucking the whole way.

Moments later you returned with the goose and plopped it down about six feet from the dog. Boomer hurled himself at the dead goose, digging into the bird's abdomen, feathers and down flying, jaws working madly. Throughout the show, you beat on the dog's back, screaming 'No, no, stop!'

When we finally pried the dog off the bird, I turned and said, 'Dad, you should have let him get the goose.'

You nodded and muttered, 'Yea, you're right.'"

If secretive or theft eating for Boomer exhibited eccentricity, so too did his normal, every-day consumption routine. For his run-of-the-mill meals, he had his own style and gift. It had to do with speed. All my Labs have been fast eaters; that is, not picky and not hesitant. None of them took much time to smell their offerings (maybe a couple of seconds but that was it) before proceeding to eat. Boomer, however, possessed Olympic style speed in launching into his fodder. He gobbled with a vengeance—no thought, no dainty smell testing, and no tip-of-tongue tasting. No, no, he gulped his food so fast he ingested a good deal of air with each gulp. In the process, he often became so bloated he had to regurgitate what he had just consumed.

What he gobbled and then puked, he ate a second time. In short, he developed a three-stage eating procedure: gobble down, throw up, and eat again. Sometimes he employed a one-stage-dining process, but not very often.

According to Nat, a variation to the one step process did exist, but Boomer only exhibited it on special occasions. He described it this way:

"I'd get Boomer to sit, then take a small pancake and flip it at him, Frisbee-style, with a backhand fling. The dog would sit motionless until I launched the pancake. Then he's snatch it out of the air and swallow it in one smooth motion."

"He didn't chew?" I said.

"No. Open mouth, grab, swallow. All very graceful. As he did it, his eyes sparkled," Nat said.

"When did you do this? I've never seen Boomer perform like that," I said.

"It was an act I reserved for my friends. Did it a couple of times when you weren't here. Cracked em up."

"I'll bet it did. What else did you guys do while I wasn't here?" I said.

"That's a secret. You'll never know,'" he said, smiling.

"Guess, I can live with that," I said.

With regard to what he ate, Boomer didn't differ much from my other Labs. Like the others, he always ate his regular food without hesitation. He would, on occasion, supplement his regular home diet, as Nat indicated, with other things found in his travels abroad—dead animals, maybe a live animal he caught, but no dog or other forms of poop (that I knew of).

His worst food supplement that I can remember occurred on a pheasant hunting trip in his later years. We were hunting south of Hazen, North Dakota in early fall on land owned by a rancher one of my Minot State students recommended. (Boomer's pheasant hunting abilities will be addressed later.) On this particular hunt I don't remember our pheasant harvest, but I do recall vividly the trip home.

On that day, we'd hunted the edges of a small creek that flowed through the proprietor's land. The creek had become a problem for the owner when beavers damned it, causing flooding and difficulties for his cattle to move about. In response, the owner shot several beavers and knocked holes in their damns. Boomer found the corpse of one those beaver villains. And what a treat it was!

He was fifty yards ahead of me when he came upon his treasure. When I reached him, I recognized what he was chomping on and yelled, "No, no, drop it, drop it." He didn't listen of course. But I managed to force him to stop, hoping he'd not consumed too much of the dead animal. There didn't seem to be much left except a dried moldy skin when I examined the animal's remains. We continued hunting. Boomer didn't seem to be any the worse for his snack.

On the way home, however, I learned differently. Boomer always rode in the back of my station wagon where he could lie down. Shortly after we started home, I heard that nasty dog sound, the one that will wake me faster out of a dead sleep than any other sound I know—the ungodly "aauch, aauch, aauch" of a dog retching.

I stopped the vehicle, got out and opened the back door. My brown wonder had eaten more than I thought. He barfed up several pieces of stinking, disgusting, mostly rotten beaver remains. He deposited his upchucking at several places in his sleeping area. With the windows down, I continued our drive homeward, finally reaching a gas station in Hazen. There I stopped and got paper towels to try to clean up the mess. I managed to wipe up most of the vomit but could do nothing about the abiding smell in my station wagon. That lasted for several weeks after the hunt.

My second Boomer eating/barfing story is more serious, more dramatic and more irritating, at least to me at the time. It involved the semi-butchered carcass of a white-tailed deer I'd shot on a Saturday in mid-November 1990 in south west North Dakota. I'd eviscerated the animal in the field and brought the carcass home that same day. Because of the late arrival home, I left the deer carcass on the garage floor, planning to finish my work on it the next morning.

For years, I butchered my own deer. The process was not complicated, just time consuming. In any case, Boomer somehow discovered the dead deer's presence and managed to enter the garage, where he proceeded to feast on the animal.

What he ate, I admitted, displayed considerable carnivore sophistication, for he didn't chew off a shoulder nor munch on a ham from one of the back legs. He passed over these options for one less complicated and, I imagine, tastier. He stuck his head into the cavity where the stomach, intestines, lungs and heart had been and ate the two straps of flesh (the filet mignon) which cushioned the deer's vertebra.

That delicacy apparently satisfied his appetite, for he left the rest of the carcass untouched. When I began the butchering the following day, I noticed right away what the dog had done. Not pleased, I nevertheless blamed myself more than the dog for his escapade. I should have hung the animal from the rafters and not left the carcass on the floor. I finished the butchering and put the venison packages in the freezer.

That Sunday afternoon while shoveling snow off the driveway, I noticed a frozen glob of what looked like bloody meat on the edge of the driveway about fifty feet from the garage. On closer inspection, I recognized it as the pilfered venison filet mignon. Apparently it had been too rich for my ravenous Boomer. For the moment, I left it alone.

The next morning, Monday, as I headed to take my morning shower in preparation for going to work, I called the dog and let him out from the living room door on the deck so that he could do his morning duty. When I finished showering, I went to the deck door to call the dog back to the house. I was nude, not being an exhibitionist but trying to save some time between dressing and getting the dog.

As I opened the glass door and stepped out on the deck, I saw Boomer on the edge of the driveway bent over, apparently eating something. In a flash, it dawned on me that the damn dog was repeating his filet mignon meal! I yelled at him to stop, to come, to get back in the house. No effect. I turned and went back inside to get something to throw at him.

The first missile thing I saw was one of my hunting boots. I grabbed it, rushed back out onto the deck and threw the boot as hard as I could at my disobedient canine.

My missile flew wide of the target. But that didn't the end the crisis. A problem existed on the deck—it was covered with ice. When I launched my bomb with such gusto, my feet slipped out from under me, my naked body flew up into the air maybe three feet off the deck's floor.

I fell back onto the deck landing with a loud bang. The fall's force knocked the wind out of me. Terrified, I thought I might have broken something, maybe my back. I tried to move. I could, thank God, and without much pain. I slowly got to my knees and crawled back into the living room, apparently no worse for wear. At that point, I stopped worrying about the dog, walked slowly back to the bath room, took another hot shower, dried off, went to the bedroom and dressed. Only then did I return to the dog problem.

This time when I called, Boomer responded. Without a word, I put him and his doggie bed in the garage, locked them there together and drove off to work. When I returned that afternoon, Boomer seemed overjoyed to see me. No awareness of sin or wrong doing showed. He may not have learned a lesson, but I had—I needed to learn how to relax. Despite the morning's peccadillo, I found no new mess to clean up in the garage. Boomer had rewarded me after all.

Boomer could find new things to eat and other ways to torment me outside the north-of-Surry home because, as I noted above, he had free reign of the out of doors whenever I was home. In his freedom, he roamed our property but often beyond it as well. Nearly every non-winter day he would visit the pasture's pothole.

There he would chase off any resident duck or tarrying gull, cool off with a dip in its turbid water, or wattle in its slate-colored mud. He would run around me when I cut the grass on the riding mower and when I worked in the vegetable garden.

One afternoon when I was out weeding my tomato and pepper plants, I noticed him a hundred yards off to the south in the pasture scrapping his snout back and forth on the ground. I stopped what I was doing to look more closely. Then it hit me—the smell of skunk. "Oh shit," I muttered, "Boomer got sprayed."

I called him in and for once he responded quickly, no doubt thinking I could help him with his dilemma or at least share in it. He arrived as a stinking mess, the smell nearly overwhelming. He obviously received a full blast at close quarters. I got a rope and tied him to a tree in the back yard and went into the house to see if I could find something to clean him off and eliminate the smell. I didn't know then what I do now about treating skunk smell.

Today, I'm told all you have to do is mix hydrogen peroxide, baking soda and dish detergent in water to produce an effective antidote. At that time from what I'd heard, I thought tomato juice would do the trick. I didn't have that, but I did find half a large can of V-8 juice in the refrigerator. I took that and a pail of warm water mixed with dish detergent out to try and rid the dog of his special aroma.

For the next half an hour I worked on my brown wonder. Despite the effort, I couldn't eliminate the stink. I left him tethered for a while to see if drying out might do the trick. It didn't.

As the sun began to set, I decided Boomer couldn't spend the night in the house or the garage. The stench was just too strong. At his time to retire, I put him in the shed, the out building where I stored my fishing boat. After feeding him, I led him to the shed and left him there. He disapproved.

He started barking at me when I closed the door and he continued barking. He barked loud enough so that I could hear him in the house. And the barking did not cease. When it was time for me to go to bed, I closed both bedroom windows to shut out the exasperating noise. In vain, I could still hear him. As a last hope, I got some toilet paper and made ear plugs. That and a sleeping pill worked.

The next morning, I arose and went out on the deck, listening for barking. I heard nothing. Good start to the day. I fixed the dog's breakfast and went out to the shed to let him out. When I got to the shed, I heard a strange noise coming from it. It sounded like a human suffering from an acute case of laryngitis. I'd never heard anything like it.

When I opened the door, I saw and heard my beautiful Boomer, the source of the noise. He sat with his back to me in front of the shed's only window peering out. He looked forlorn and exhausted. Every three seconds or so, his head would move up and down as he emitted the barely audible sound, "haaaaa, haaaa, haaaa." Then it dawned on me—he was still barking!

I called "Boom, Boom I'm here."

He turned from the window and looked at me. His look seemed to say, "Oh, it's you. Thanks a lot, Dad. I had a memorable night here with the boat and the cement floor. When can I do it again?"

On my second, "Boom, Boom come here, I've got your breakfast. I'm sorry about last night," he stopped the wheezing noise and ran over to me, wagging his tail double time. I felt some guilt for making him suffer isolation and privation. But an upside existed—he no longer smelled like a skunk.

Compared to Jason, Boomer left much to be desired as a hunter. The difference lay not in interest, his nose or any other physical qualities. It related to inadequate training. The fault for that lay with me. As noted, I simply did not have the free time I had had with Jason, plus the fact Boomer had far fewer opportunities in the field. Moreover, in Madison we did not have the numbers of ducks and geese available as in Manitoba.

When the family moved to North Dakota, the conditions for hunting improved significantly. Unfortunately for Boomer, by then my fascination for waterfowl hunting had declined significantly. In North Dakota, I concentrated on hunting pheasants instead of ducks and geese. Nevertheless, I did pursue ducks several times with my chocolate Lab.

The Boomer duck hunt I remember best occurred with my friend Carl at Buffalo Lodge Lake, about 25 miles east of my prairie place. For that outing we took my canoe, some duck decoys and the dog. It represented my effort to duplicate what Jason and I'd done so often on Lake Winnipeg. The situation really didn't compare—less cover, smaller body of water, and far fewer water fowl.

The part of the hunt that stands out involved Carl shooting a Green Winged Teal off the canoe's bow (We were sitting in the canoe as we hunted). When Carl knocked the bird down, Boomer watched it fall near Carl's end of the canoe. To get to the bird, Boomer scrambled toward Carl and tried to climb onto him. Carl ducked and turned away. Undeterred, Boomer then launched himself off Carl's back. As the dog jumped, Carl had the same expression on his face as the poor sofa delivery man. It was a scene right out of a circus act. I couldn't help laughing. Boomer fetched the duck successfully.

Boomer fared better with pheasants. He came to know what we hunted and he flushed birds with skill. The problem lay in distance; Boomer hunted too far ahead of me. In those days, I had no shock collars to restrain the dog and thus no way to force him to hunt close. For example, if we hunted a creek bed, he would chase a bird 50 or 75 yards out in front before it flushed. That might have worked if I'd had a partner to post 100 yards down the creek, but I didn't.

Since I usually hunted by myself, Boomer functioned better in small, finite cattail sloughs where he and the birds couldn't run full out. In the more limited context of the smaller sloughs, we managed to get a few birds. When I did shoot a pheasant amongst the cattails, Boomer would find and fetch it. He retrieved both dead birds and cripples effectively.

If Boomer's exterior activities created considerable anxiety for his owner, his interior antics were less drama filled and problematic. As out of doors, he acted the clown inside. His efforts at drawing attention to himself more often than not brought smiles and laughs, but occasionally some pique as well.

Of all my dogs, his early morning routine amused me the most. Boomer had a very precise morning regimen. He had to eat no later than seven o'clock a.m. If I had not risen or fed him by that time, he would move into crisis mode. In brief, that involved going into Dad's room and posing next to his bed.

Once in position, he would stretch out his front legs and lower his head to the rug. His rump would be almost two feet higher than his head. His tail would be curved up and over his back, not wagging but absolutely still. Once in full position, he would commence his "get your lazy ass out of bed and fetch me my food" noise. His special sound started as a low howl (wooooo) and would grow in intensity as his head rose. This crescendo would end with a sharp "woop." All together is sounded like a continuous "wooooooopp."

He would repeat this noisy show until he drove me out of bed. It amuses me today to write about it, but back then when it was being acted out I found it excruciatingly irritating. For the dog, it worked without fail. He knew that and utilized his advantage as often as needed.

Besides being skillful at getting me out of bed, Boomer knew how to roust his pal Nathaniel out of the covers as well. Nat lived with me at home for his last two and a half college years (1988-1991) when not at Carleton College.

As a late-staged teenager, he liked to sleep well beyond Boomer's and my rising time. On frequent occasions, I would start cooking breakfast and go in to wake him up. More often than not, he would ignore my first summons. If I tried and failed a second time, I'd send in the dog.

"Boomer, go get Natty! Go see Natty!" With his tail wagging, Boomer would happily amble into his room. If Nat's head were close to the bed's edge on say the left side, Boomer would try to lick his face from that angle. If the dog got too close, my boy would roll over to the other side of the bed. Boomer would attempt to fulfill his charge by running around to the bed's right side. This game could go on and on. If the dog failed to roust him, I would move on to plan B.

I'd go to the stereo in the living room (the room next to Nat's bedroom) and play Richard Wagner's "Ride of the Valkyrie" full blast. That's the same music Francis Ford Coppola used in his film *Apocalypse Now* in the scene where the helicopters with their loud speakers blaring Wagnerian cacophony chased Viet Cong down a jungle river. It's the music the film's crazy American commander described as turning the "little bastards (the Viet Cong) into stumps."

It didn't do that to my Nat, but it did get him to stagger out of his room, a big scowl on his face, and sit down to eat his fried eggs. When he appeared, he appreciated neither my laughing nor the dog's nudging him to be petted. For me and my clown Boomer, it was all good fun.

A very different and disturbing event involving Boomer happened at four o'clock a.m. one Saturday night at our north-of-Surry home when the children were away at school. A loud banging on the door to the deck awakened me from a sound sleep. I knew I was miles away from neighbors and minutes away from any police help.

As the banging continued, I got up, put on my bathrobe, and told Boomer, who was sleeping on his doggie bed next to mine, to come with me. I had the dog by the collar as I turned on the deck light to see the source of the noise. My visitor was a tall, dark-haired, heavy-set, rough-looking young man dressed in worn Carhardt coveralls, dusty work boots and a tattered black jacket. I didn't recognize him.

Holding on to my curious dog, I opened the door a crack and said, "What's the matter?"

The fellow looked at the dog and then at me and said, "Me and my friend're stuck in your ditch. Need help to get out?" His head and body swayed back and forth as he spoke.

I said "Where you from? How'd you end up out here?"

He said, "Me and my buddy left Tioga at twelve thirty. Trying to get to Minot but got lost. Don't know where we're at. Now we're stuck in your ditch."

His speech indicated he'd been drinking and I thought to myself "Tioga? That's 90 miles to the west. So it took these yahoos three and a half hours after they closed the bar to get stuck in my driveway! I got a couple of winners here."

"Where's your buddy?" I asked.

"He's in the car. Ain't feelin too good," he said.

I said, "Go back to your car. I'll be out to help in a couple of minutes."

I got dressed, took the dog with me and walked out to view the problem. Their car sat in the ditch with its front end pointing up at about a 45-degree angle. The car's headlights were still on and doing a fine job illuminating the sky.

Apparently, the boys had tried to turn around in my driveway and then backed over the road into the ditch. I went back to the house and got my pickup and a towing chain, came back, hooked the chain to the front bumper and pulled the car back onto the road. The young man, who'd come to the house, thanked me and then asked for directions to Minot. As I told him, his buddy urinated in the ditch. Both fellows then got back in their car and left.

Thinking about the incident later, I thanked my lucky stars that I had my big brown Lab at my side. Boomer, I concluded, may have been an expert at playing the clown but he also posed an impressive physical presence. He looked like a dog that wouldn't tolerate an attack on his boss. I liked that.

Boomer lived with me in my prairie home for another year and a few months after the stuck-in- the-ditch affair. During this time, I met Ann, the woman whom I would marry as my second wife. A colleague at Minot State introduced her to me in early 1990.

An attractive, petite, brown-eyed brunette several inches shorter than I, Ann had grown up in Minot and attended Minot State before heading off to medical school to get her M.D. She had recently returned home to accept a position in Minot as a pediatrician. A calm, soft-spoken, reserved but confident person, I found her intelligence, wry sense of humor and easing-going nature very attractive.

From the beginning, she and I found a number of fun physical activities to share. These included jogging, biking, cross country skiing and even racquet ball, the latter a favorite activity of mine in Winnipeg. The physical thing appealed to me because during my time in Winnipeg I became serious about staying in shape. Ann liked that.

My relationship with her lasted for three years. In that time, we travelled quite a bit. Our first extensive outing involved a ten-day canoe trip in the Boundary Waters of Northern Minnesota in the summer of 1990. The next year we travelled to Maine for a week's vacation. Then in July 1992, we flew to Germany, rented a car, and toured south Germany and Austria. In the fall of that year, we married.

Ann may have liked my fondness for exercise and travel, but she didn't favor Boomerang. Shannon had tolerated Boomer. I don't remember Shannon ever being particularly affectionate or expressing displeasure with the dog. As with Jason, Shannon left the dog to me. She had her music.

Ann, on the other hand, didn't bother to disguise her disdain. Never having had a dog as a child, she did not know much about canines and had, I believe, no reason or reasons to identify with them. For Ann, Boomer always appeared as too big and too hairy. She had a real thing about dog hair in general and Boomer's profuse shedding in particular.

Boomer represented for Ann an unnecessary irritant. Normally soft-spoken, she could become quite different when expressing her non-flattering thoughts on my big brown dog. Her overt dislike disappointed me.

During my second year going with Ann, Boomer began to decline physically. He became incapable of controlling both his bowel movements and bladder functions. That presented a big problem for me, since I was gone for so much of the day at Minot State. I knew what I had to do, but couldn't bring myself to do it.

During my trip to Germany with Ann in the summer of 1992, Nathaniel took matters into his own hands and had the dog put down. He didn't tell me beforehand, but informed me when he picked me up at the airport in Minot.

The news surprised and saddened me, but I felt grateful. My son had done what was necessary and I loved him for it. The issue of Boomer's demise clearly pleased Ann. For a while afterwards our relationship seemed to improve. The improvement was short-lived, however, because in fall of 1992 I acquired another Labrador Retriever, a black puppy named Reginald.

Boomer with a query: When's my next prank?

Before moving on to Reggie, a few final words for Boomerang seem appropriate. My big, chocolate clown dog had most, if not all, the Labrador virtues I admired in the breed; he was loyal, sweet-tempered, affectionate, and enthusiastic. His uniqueness among my several Labs lay in his special view of the world. Of all my dogs before or after, he represented the one who took life the least seriously.

From his early days, he became a creature of humor and laughter. He ranked as my most disobedient dog, the least serious, the one that seemed to have "no innate sense of appropriateness," to prevent him from overreacting or playing the clown.

More cocky than the others, more sure of himself in his independence, his acute sense of humor seemed to imply a high level of intelligence. He could and did deliberately play the fool or bad guy. In doing so, he experienced a level of joy that none of the others knew. That amazed me in his lifetime and amuses and impresses me today.

In the end, his joyfulness brought joy to me as well. He remains my special dog of light and laughter, the one who made me smile and laugh the most. And I think he knew and enjoyed that.

After my sad divorce from Shannon, Boomer helped restore in me my sense of humor, as well as my wonder and delight in the mystery of life. He knew life was a game that shouldn't be taken too seriously. He tried to teach me how to relax. That was a precious lesson I needed to learn to survive my fits of depression and sense of failure from Shannon's leaving me.

Johanna's sister Sarah hugging naughty Boomer

In short, Boomer's *joie de vivre* made him a wonderful companion in my home. Less serious than Jason, less effective as a worker and hunter, Boomer loved his family as much as Jason had. Of all my Labs, Boomer lived through the most tumultuous, uncertain, and difficult decade of my entire life. Divorce, job changing, professional failure, numerous physical moves, and other readjustments to new circumstances complicated not only my life, but the lives of my children, wives, and dog. I am truly sorry there wasn't more stability for my family and my dog.

Despite the tumult, Boomer remained a fun-loving and devoted companion/friend. He may have had his own devious definition of what constituted a Sweet Spirit, but he was one nonetheless. His humor served both as a saving grace and a blessing. When my children remember him, they think of his tricks and they smile. In his delightful picture book (*Life is Good*) celebrating his golden Retriever Trixie, editor Koontz quotes his doggie author as admonishing the readers to "Never miss a chance to share laughs with those you love." That I think nicely sums up my Boom-Boom.

When I appear at the bridge to join my beautiful Jason and the others, Boomer will surely be present. However, he might be a bit disappointed when he first recognizes me, for I suspect he'll be hoping that when I do appear I'll be wearing a hat!

Finally, in the same vein, I'd like to respond to a Garth Stein-prompted thought. If author Stein can have his dog Enzo (*Racing in the Rain*) reincarnated as a formula-one race car driver, I might argue that my Boomerang is among us today generating laughs as a late-night club comedian.

CHAPTER FOUR

REGINALD (REGGIE)

No man nor beast didn't love Reggie

"I think dogs are the most amazing creatures; they give unconditional love. For me they are the role model for being alive."

— Gilda Radner

In August 1991, I sold my prairie house and moved back to Minot. The 17-mile, dirt road drive every day to the university and the inconvenience of being so far from basic conveniences such as a gas station or grocery store had taken its toll.

Living like a misanthropic hermit had grown old. The new home was five minutes from my office and ideally located from whatever conveniences Minot had to offer. Among other things, my new residence had a fenced back yard, roomy enough to accommodate one or more large dogs. Only one major problem—for the first time in over 20 years, I was poochless.

In October 1991, six weeks after I occupied the Minot house and several months after Boomer had been put to sleep, Nathanial phoned from his dormitory at Carlton College in Northfield, Minnesota.

"Dad," he said, "would it be okay if I come home for the weekend?"

"Yeah, of course. Something wrong?"

"No," he said, "just wanted to come home for a couple of days. Bringing a couple of friends with, that okay too?"

"Absolutely. When do you expect to arrive?"

"Oh, mid-afternoon, Saturday. We'll get an early start," he added.

"Okay, I'll look for you then. Drive carefully."

"Will do. Thanks Dad." He hung up.

I didn't know what to think. The call worried me. Nat had been away at school for the past several years and never come home for a surprise visit. I hoped nothing was wrong.

The next day, Saturday, I spent the morning in my office at Minot State doing some grading. At noon, I stopped and went grocery shopping. I enjoy cooking, especially for guests who like to eat. I figured three 20-year-old college boys would eat my fare with gusto. The thought made me smile.

Finished with the grocery shopping at about one o'clock p.m., I headed home. When I arrived, I noted a "puke" (Nat's term) green Chevy sedan with Minnesota plates parked in my drive. Had to be the boys, I thought.

I grabbed the grocery bags and went into the house. Nat and his two friends were sitting on the sofa watching a college football game. Nat introduced his blond companion as Mark and the brunette one as Tom. While he spoke, I noticed something in his hands that looked like a small black Labrador Retriever puppy.

"Hi boys," I said. "Which one of you guys belongs to the dog? Tom? Mark?

Mark said, "Ah, neither of us, Mr. Wagner. It's Nat's."

I smiled and said, "Well son, tell me how you came by the little brut."

"Missed Boomer, Dad. Thought we, and you particularly, needed another dog. Got him last week. Had problems keeping him in the dorm."

*Reggie with Nat in his dorm room at
Carleton College*

"I can imagine," I said.

"Actually, the Dean called me in, said the dog had to go. Didn't like hearing that, but what could I do? Couldn't take him back. Thought maybe you'd take him. He's beautiful. Cutest one in the litter."

"Where'd you get him?" I said.

"In Northfield, answered an ad in the local paper."

"Purebred?"

"That's what I was told."

Nat, stood up and handed me the puppy. The warm little critter didn't object. He licked my fingers and whimpered softly. As I raised him to face level to take a closer look, I knew I was hooked.

"Got a name for him?" I asked.

"Yeah."

"What is it?"

"He's Reggie, named him after Reggie Jackson, the baseball star."

"I know about Mr. October," I said.

"Cool name, don't you think?"

"Yeah," I said nodding.

That's how I got my first black Lab. The baseball name reminded me of Satchel. I liked it. On Sunday, the boys returned to Northfield without the puppy.

Honestly, I didn't have difficulty accepting Nat's gift. I missed having a dog companion and had been seriously contemplating buying a Lab puppy. So in the end, the surprise puppy neither inconvenienced nor upset, but rather pleased me. Looking back, I have to admit Reggie (Reginald) turned out to be one of the nicest presents anyone ever gave me. He would be a joy, a light in my life for the next twelve years.

Nat's gift puppy grew into a beautiful adult, both physically and personality wise. In size, he was relatively small by Lab standards. I would estimate that he never exceeded 60 pounds at his heftiest. He had well balanced features—a nicely proportioned Lab head considerably smaller than Boomer's, a muzzle less pointed than Jason's, an impressive black coat, and substantial "communication device" tail. I never saw his mother or the other members of his litter, so I can't comment on him relative to his canine siblings. Reggie exhibited one physical idiosyncrasy that distinguished him from all the rest of my Labs, with the exception of my present yellow female Toula (more on her to come). That special feature Nat tagged as Reggie's "Butt Run."

The Butt Run involved running at top speed in an uneven way. When Reggie did it, he dropped his rear end down about eight inches below his front. It looked almost as if he wanted to rub his rear on the ground. Not possible. He was scooting too fast. In doing his special act, Reggie manifested a kind of euphoria. Normally, he exhibited the Butt Run out in the back yard after supper. He'd scoot around next to the fence, running rectangles. When "Butt Running," Reggie appeared to be in a kind of trance, having fun, letting off energy—his version of a special *joie de vivre*.

Although the Butt Run was distinctive, the elements that stood out most throughout Reggie's life were not his physical features nor idiosyncrasies, but his character traits. Mild tempered—not exactly insecure, but timid at times—Reggie never barked in the house. I don't remember him ever whining. I may be wrong in this, but I don't think so.

Reggie took scolding more seriously than Boomer or any of my other dogs. In fact, Reggie was easier to discipline than any dog I ever owned. In short, he was a pleasure to have. Reggie didn't beg. If he tried, I would stare at him and say in a disapproving tone, "You're not begging, are you? That's bad, very bad."

At the word "bad" he would snap his head away to look in another direction. Compared to some of my later Labs who had perfected and succeeded in employing the "Please Dad, give me a cookie" stare, Reggie remained a saint. Moreover, he did not climb on the furniture nor engage in any destructive chewing. Reggie seemed only intent on pleasing his master and his family. With a few exceptions, he succeeded. In short, Reggie was a great companion to have around, particularly for a divorced man and his human progeny. My four children loved Reggie almost as much as I did.

Let me start with my favorite scolding story. As a Minot State history professor, one of the distinct advantages of living in Minot and not out on the prairie north of Surry involved the chance to go home for lunch. I did that Monday through Friday, unless a meeting or some other compelling distraction obliged me to remain on campus.

On the day in question, I drove home, arriving at the house around noon. I entered from the front door and walked into the living room as usual. Reggie lay on the floor next to the sofa on the sofa's afghan, which he obviously pulled off the sofa to form his augmented bed. That was a serious no-no.

I deliberately prohibited him from climbing on the furniture, but also from using human bedding as support. When he rose from his makeshift bed to greet me, I said "Bad dog, bad dog. You know you're not to lie on that afghan. Bad dog, bad dog."

Reggie's ears dropped to guilt level and he ran into Nat's bedroom with his tail between his legs. His penitential response made me smile. I didn't have much time so I left the dog to his guilt, fixed my lunch, and ate it. Reggie was still in the bedroom when I returned to the university.

That afternoon I left my office for home about four-thirty. When I walked in the front door, no dog met me. That appeared strange, for he had the acute dog "inner clock" and usually greeted me at the door. He wasn't on the couch and he wasn't lying on the afghan, which remained folded on the sofa just as I had left it.

Pleased that he'd apparently learned a lesson, I said in a voice he could hear wherever he might be, "Where's my good doggie? Reggie, Reggie, where are you?" He heard me and recognized the positive tone, very different from what he'd heard at lunch time. I couldn't see him because he was in the dining room hiding behind the table. When he heard another round of, "Reggie, Reggie, my good doggie, where are you?" he bounded out from behind his hiding place and ran to meet me, his tail wagging double-time. I smiled, reached down to pet him, and said, "Good doggie, good doggie. I love you."

From puppyhood until he was about a year old, I kept him in the basement when not home with the same kind of Wolters' arrangement I used for Jason in his puppyhood. Thus, young Reggie had a basement bed, was restrained there to his bedding area by a chain and had papers on which to do his business. The soiled papers I changed several times every day. Eventually after the house breaking, Reggie would be promoted to the upstairs as described in the afghan story just cited.

I remember a few times when son Robbie, my child from the marriage with Ann, would visit and Reggie would be in the basement. So he could greet and play with the dog, I'd carry him down the basement stairs. Robbie loved to see Reggie, and vice-versa. One memorable time as I toted Rob for his dog visit, I sang a little ditty in German (auf Deutsch) I'd made up for my own amusement.

In my silly act, I pretended to be a Metropolitan opera tenor. For Rob's enlightenment and pleasure, I sang in mock serious tone and like the Herman's Hermits' version of *Henry the Eight I Am I Am*, my second and third verses were the same as the first. The lyrics I sang went like this: "Mein Hunt ist im Keller weil er hat schmuetzige Fuesse." Translation: "My dog's in the basement because he's got dirty feet." I liked singing this for little Rob because it amused me.

Not long after my singing, I visited Ann at her parent's home and learned Rob sang my ditty for his grandparents. What made that particularly amusing for me was this situation: the child sang auf Deutsch (of course, he didn't know what the words he sang meant). But even better, Robbie sang my song on an evening when his grandparents had guests visiting, and these visitors just happened to be German.

As Robbie sang, "Mein Hund ist im Keller…." the lady guest said, "Waaas!" and started laughing. Her husband joined in.

Ann's mother looked quizzically at her visitors and said, "What's so funny?"

The German lady said, "You know what your grandson just sang?"

Ann's mother shook her head and said, "No clue."

"It means, 'my dog's in the basement because he's got dirty feet.'" The lady said smiling. Both Ann's parents joined in the laughter.

As Reggie grew and matured, my relationship with second wife Ann declined. Initially after Robbie's birth in May 1993, I tried to live with Ann in her house. That lasted only a short period. Robbie's birth had not improved our relationship. Both of us found cohabitation troublesome and difficult. Our incompatibility had to do with much more than my dog affinity and her antipathy toward dogs. We had serious differences on many issues.

I moved back into my own house in July 1993. That exacerbated our differences. The incompatibility continued for the next two years and ended in a divorce, finalized in May 1995. After this, my visitation rights became an ongoing battle. Over the next several years I had to go to court a half-dozen times to ensure that Ann would let me see my son.

The legal battles were worth the time and cost. The court orders enabled me to have Rob not only on every other weekend in Minot, but also for extended visits during his summer vacations. These visits allowed me to do with Rob some of the same things I'd done with Nat, such as teach him how to use a fly rod and shoot a shotgun. As a result, my younger son would become, like his elder brother, a great companion for both my hunting and fishing activities.

In the period of the marriage's decline and its visitation battles, I expanded my geographic and residential possibilities by purchasing a piece of undeveloped waterfront property in northern Wisconsin near the town of Florence. The impetus for this came from a trout fishing trip I made with Nat in the summer of 1995. Years before, I taught teenager Nat how to use a fly rod. He became not only a fellow enthusiast, but also a more skilled caster than I. Since my divorce from Shannon terminated my involvement in the St. Lawrence River island property and my use of the summer home there, I had been thinking about finding a new summer place on and off for several years.

I chose Florence, Wisconsin for our 1995 fishing trip because I knew something about the town and area from a visit twenty-five years before. The town of Florence, also the county seat for Florence County, was then and still is a small, semi-isolated village located on US Highway 2 in the state's extreme northeast, on the border with Michigan's Upper Peninsula. According to a recent census, the town of Florence boasts a population today of just over 2500, about five times as large as my youthful Aurora.

Although first surveyed in 1840, the area around Florence remained essentially a hunting and trapping wilderness peopled by several American Indian tribes, most notably the Chippewas, until the 1870s. At the beginning of that decade, iron ore was discovered and the first mine opened in 1873. The town of Florence, named after a mine owner's wife, would be incorporated in that year.

For the next half-century, mining constituted the area's most important economic activity. During that five-decade span, mines would be opened in several county locations. For example, the settlement of Commonwealth adjacent to Florence would support five separate mines until 1925. By the First World War, however, the mining boom had begun to decline. The last mine in Florence County closed in 1931 with the onset of the Great Depression.

During the mining period, another industry which would turn out to be more permanent and sustainable made its appearance in Florence County as well. That industry involved harvesting the vast virginal forests so pervasive to the county. In its initial stage the new logging industry concentrated almost exclusively on harvesting white pine. This benefitted Florence because, according to the local history, "Florence was right in the heart of the pine area when 'Pine was King.'"

Pine logs were not only more valuable than hardwood logs (those from the abundant maple, basswood and oak trees) but they floated better and thus could be transported out of the woods to the saw mills via the area's rivers more easily. In the early days before the railroad appeared, future trout streams including the Pine, Popple, and Brule Rivers served as the means of transporting Florence's harvested logs to the nearby mills located in neighboring Michigan's Upper Peninsula. By the end of the 19th century the scale of log production from Florence County had reached hundreds of million feet. That continued well into the next century.

The mining and logging operations in Florence County at the end of the nineteenth and beginning of the twentieth century created work opportunities for thousands of laborers. Most of the loggers and miners who congregated in and around Florence hailed from beyond Wisconsin. Many of these, mostly young men, arrived without families. To provide for the new laborers, camps sprang up in numerous places within the county. Camps for the loggers were located near the rivers; for the miners, camps appeared adjacent to the mines.

The existence of so many unattached laborers with ready money to spend created not only new social and economic opportunities, but problems as well. According to the local history, Florence had become "one of the worst centers of vice in the state's history" with gambling, prostitution and other forms of crime prominent daily problems by the end of the 19th century.

During this period with Florence "at the height of its brief but lurid hey-day," the town boasted "thirty-one saloons to its discredit, all of them doing a good business." A backlash eventually occurred and the city cleaned up its act.

By the First World War, the town had assumed the more sedate and modern characteristics of its profile today. The logging camps, mines and multiple saloons may no longer exist but the colorful past remains a subject of interest to locals.

Although contemporary Wisconsin is famous for its farms and dairy industry, the Florence area is not now, nor ever really was, a part of that. A few dairy farms do exist today, but they are rare and modest among the predominant forest, which presently covers no less than 80 percent of Florence County.

Today, logging remains an important industry but a far less pervasive one than a century ago. Tourism has become increasingly important of late. Present natives not involved in logging or tourism usually find employment in neighboring Iron Mountain, Michigan, ten miles to the east.

Because of the pervasive forest, wild life in the form of white-tailed deer, black bears, wolves, coyotes and turkeys are common. The main highway through Florence County, US #2, reflects the problem of numerous wild animals in its widely expanded shoulders.

Unlike many areas in the state and the nation, such road clearings in Florence County are deemed necessary to afford drivers the opportunity to see and respond in timely fashion to wildlife crossing before them. Even so, many deer and occasionally bears are killed every year attempting to cross Florence County roads.

Besides abundant game animals, Florence country and its surrounding area also possesses numerous lakes, rivers and streams. The latter attracted me for my first visit in 1970. Specifically, I had read about two first-rate trout streams, namely the Pine and the Popple, being easily accessible from Florence. During the week I spent in Florence, I became familiar with both. Fishing those streams opened my eyes and inspired me. I never had such beautiful, wild country to fish in, nor as much success with trout. When I left, I vowed to return. Unfortunately, it took a quarter of a century to make good on that vow.

Both Nat and I greatly enjoyed our week of fly fishing in the Florence area in July 1995. During that visit, we successfully fished both the Popple and the Pine and duplicated the joy I experienced years before. To me, our time in the woods and on the water together seemed priceless. It had the same effect on my son. On the evening of the fourth day, a day spent on the Popple, we were at the local restaurant eating supper when Nat said, "Dad, this is a great fishing area. Be a good place for a cabin like the one we had on the St. Lawrence."

"Yeah," I said, "been thinking that too. Maybe we should see if there's any waterfront available."

"We got time. Let's do it," he said.

The next morning, we went to the Florence bait and tackle shop out at Keyes Lake to pick up some flies for the day's outing. Shortly after entering, the store's owner, Carl Loppnow, a jowly, heavy-set, nearly bald, bespectacled man in his mid-seventies dressed in blue jeans and a red flannel shirt with the sleeves rolled up to his elbows, greeted us with a smile and a hearty, "Welcome boys. What can I do for you gents?"

I said, "We need trout flies. Got any?"

"Sure do. Let me show you," he said, his glasses magnifying the sparkle of his brown eyes.

Limping noticeably, Carl led us to a counter in the back of the store and said, "Here's what I got."

As we began to consider his selection, he continued, "Where you guys from? Not local, are you?"

"From North Dakota," I said.

"Wow! What brings you down here?" he said.

"My son and I spent a number of years in Madison. We like Wisconsin, particularly the fishing. How long you been running this shop?"

"About 20 years," he said.

"Then you must know something about local real estate, right?"

"You betcha. Interested in land, maybe buying a piece?"

"Could be. Thought crossed my mind," I said.

"What kind of land?" Carl asked.

"Waterfront, but the water's gotta have fish," I said.

"Maybe I can help you," he said.

"How so?"

"Just so happens I've got some waterfront land I'd like to sell."

"Where?" I asked.

"Just north of town. Wanna go take a look?"

"Yeah," I said and looked at Nat, who was nodding.

Carl said, "Okay, let's go look."

He called out to his wife in the next room, told her he'd be gone for a few minutes and led us out the door to his pickup truck. He drove us the two miles into town and then three miles north to what looked like a logging road just wide enough to accommodate the pickup. As we turned onto this, Carl assured us it "paralleled the water."

The road passed through dense woods, which included a variety of mature trees—stately ash, both white and yellow birch trees, a few scattered spruce and pine trees. Nevertheless, impressive sugar maples constituted the overwhelming majority on both sides of the road. For a child of northern Ohio who had gone to college in New England, this maple-dominated arboretum fascinated me. How splendiferous the falls must be in this area, I thought. The reds, yellows, oranges would have been spectacular. Although trees dominated, the forest floor with its extensive crop of lush, vibrant green ferns likewise impressed my boy and me.

We drove down this primitive road/path for about a quarter of a mile. Carl stopped the truck, turned off the ignition and pointed to his left.

"The water's down below a ways. You boys go take a look. I'll wait here. Knees ain't what they used to be," he said.

We climbed out of the truck and started in the direction he'd indicated. For the next few minutes, we walked through the dense woods until we came to the edge of a drop off from where we could just make out the water. The property had clearly captivated us, but we didn't have time to do a proper viewing. We needed to fish, so we returned to Carl.

Back at the truck, a surprised Carl said, "That was fast. You guys not interested?"

"We are, but we gotta get fishing. First things first," I said.

Carl laughed and said, "Okay, fisher boys, no rush. Take your time. I got lots of that."

On the way into town I asked Carl, "What's the name of the river that fronts the property?"

"The Brule," he said.

"Any trout in it?" I asked.

"Yeah, but not in this stretch. For trout, you gotta go about ten to fifteen miles west. This stretch of the Brule's called the flowage. Used to be one of the streams the loggers used to get the logs out until it was damned up for the town's electric power plant some years ago. The dam's a couple of miles down from the property. That creates the lake-like effect on this stretch. This part of the river's got Bass, Northerns, Walleyes, and Muskies."

Those were welcome words. I said, "What're the property dimensions? How big is it?"

"520 feet by 220 feet, the 220 fronts the river."

"What're you asking for it?"

"Ahhh," he hesitated, then said, "$24,000, but you guys could get it for $22,000 if you move on it soon."

"Beautiful piece of property. We'll think about it." I said.

"Do that. I'm in the phone book, the Bait Shop number," he said, and we drove back to town.

The next afternoon after fishing, Nat and I returned to the property to consider it more closely. We arrived about five o'clock p.m. The sun was still high in a nearly cloudless sky, the wind light and nonintrusive. Good time to go exploring, I thought. We left the car where Carl had parked the day before.

As we got out of the car, Nat said, "Let's go all the way down to the water and see if what Carl says is true."

"Okay, but remember it won't be trout water," I said.

We entered the woods and soon arrived at the place where we stopped the day before. Beyond this point, the property dropped off sharply. The descent continued to the water's edge. Although the steep angular terrain was strewn with deadfall and large rocks, many of which were covered with green moss, we made our way to the river without difficulty. Above us, leaves formed a mostly dark-green roof but open spaces existed among the trees. These allowed sunlight to penetrate and illuminate patches on the fern-covered forest floor.

In no rush, we took our time, stopping frequently to look and listen. As we descended, I observed the trees more closely than the day before and noted the continued abundance of maples, so prominent along the access road. The woods my son and I encountered that day repre-sented a typical "Northern Hardwood" forest, one that had last been logged eighty or ninety years before. Besides sugar maples, the woods included basswood, white ash, big-tooth aspen, and yellow birch trees. The tallest and most prominent among the several non-maples appeared to be the narrow, tall ash trees.

While I moved slowly toward the water, I made a point of listening to and observing the bird life. As I did, I recalled a line from Thoreau of similar forest bird life making him "suddenly sensible of such sweet and beneficent society in nature."

It delighted me to see and hear the birds I had hoped and expected to be present. Some of the most impressive and colorful sightings that afternoon included a crow-sized Pileated Woodpecker and its smaller, misnamed cohort, the Red-bellied Woodpecker, a male black and white Rose Breasted Grosbeak, a Purple Finch, a Yellow Warbler and two Acadian Flycatchers. The varied sounds and songs impressed me as well. These included a "weeping" Crested Flycatcher, a repetitious Red-eyed Vireo, and a lyrical Veery Thrush.

When we reached the river's edge, both the vegetation and the bird life changed. Bushes, scrawny saplings, small balsam firs, and a cherry tree with its unique characteristic longitudinal lines displaced the majestic hardwood trees of the forest above. Water birds, including a rattling Belted Kingfisher, honking Canadian Geese, mournful Loons and silently swooping Tree Swallows replaced the forest's other feathered creatures.

Throughout our descent, a flock of half a dozen Turkey Vultures circled in the sky above us, seeking their deceased fodder. As a bird lover, I couldn't have wished for anything more beautiful or inspiring than the show we witnessed that afternoon. Our evaluation walk had taken us through a wild, pristine spot, similar no doubt to the Canadian woods I fantasized about in my childhood Canadian trapping plans.

Standing at the water's edge, Nat spoke for both of us, "God, this is beautiful, fantastic, Dad. Better than the St. Lawrence!"

"Yeah, more peaceful, wilder, no ocean-going yachts, no speed boats, no loud water skiers. Made for nature lovers like you and me. What a blessing," I said.

Nat nodded.

The Brule River we viewed complemented the woods. We looked out over a stretch of smooth, dark flowing water that extended about three hundred yards to the opposite shore. The view downriver stretched for a mile or so, upriver not as far because the river curved to the north. As we eyed the river's several directions, the sun, located behind us, cast its golden glow on the river's surface. The intensified sunlight also highlighted the dense, virginal forest and rock-strewn shore across from us.

As we stood taking in the spectacular view, a pair of Loons flew over calling to one another in their forlorn fashion. That brought me down to earth and I said to Nat, "The opposite shore's not Wisconsin, but part of Michigan's Upper Peninsula."

"You mean part of that same UP as in the bumper sticker that says, "Pray for Me I Married a UPPER?" he said.

"Yeah," I laughed. "That's right."

"Okay, Dad, let's head out. Time to get some food."

"Right you are," I said. I'd seen enough.

We turned away from the water and started back toward the car. About half way up the slope, I stopped and called out to Nat, who was off to my right about ten yards and ahead about that same distance.

"Nat, come down here. Got something you should see."

"What Dad? I'm tired."

"You gotta see this," I said.

Turning toward me, he came down and said, "What is it? Better be good."

When he reached me, I pointed to the ground at a pile of what looked like dark brown processed acorns without stems and said, "Take a look at these."

"So, what is it?" he said.

"Those, my boy, are moose droppings. Remind me of my hunting days in Northwest Ontario."

"So it's moose shit. Big deal. So what?"

"Listen Kid, you don't get moose turds unless you've got moose and you ain't got moose unless you're in the real wilds. We got ourselves a piece of God's wilderness here," I said nodding with pleasure.

Looking back from today, I believe the moose droppings, those symbols of the wild, sealed the property deal for me. Later that evening at the restaurant, I elaborated more on the subject of the place's potential as a fishing and hunting site. I convinced my son we should purchase our lucky discovery. The next morning, we went to see Carl to close the deal.

When we entered his store, a smiling Carl said, "Well if it ain't the boys from North Dakota. You back for more flies or something bigger?"

I cut to the chase, "You still willing to sell us that chunk of woods for $22,000?"

"You bet. Be perfect for a couple tough outdoor boys like you lads," he said with a laugh.

Two days later, my son and I met Carl and his wife Mille in Iron Mountain at a real estate office to consummate the deal. With the purchase completed, Nat and I returned to North Dakota, I to start the fall semester at Minot State University, my son to get his belongings together in preparation for traveling to Ann Arbor, Michigan to begin graduate studies at U of M. For me and Nat, the 1995 trip to Florence had turned out to be a God send.

From that time on, I have been spending much, if not all of my summers, at the cottage on the Brule. There Reggie honed his intrinsic Labrador Retriever water skills. Like my other Labs, he loved retrieving tennis balls and dummies from the river. Just as Jason had at the island, Reggie loved swimming with his family. He didn't swim for the long stretches that Jason did, but Reggie swam with enthusiasm and obvious enjoyment.

When number two son Robbie would visit, Reggie would accompany him down to the water and share his swim. The same held true for my other older children. Incidentally, my children from Shannon all swam on the varsity swimming teams at Western Reserve Academy, so Reggie had competent companions in the river. Whenever someone put on a bathing suit, Reggie would perk up. He knew what to expect.

Reggie and Rob after a dip in the Brule

At the place in Florence, Reggie also developed his socializing skills, not only with humans but with other dogs as well. His first serious canine companion was the neighbor's female French Wirehaired Pointing Griffon named Rowdy. Reggie was three when he met neighbor Rowdy, who belonged to the couple Dan and Karen Wieske, who would become some of my best friends ever.

Hailing from football town Green Bay, a hundred and twenty miles to the south, the Wieskes had been living in their Brule River summer cottage for the two summers prior to my arrival. They bought their place for the same reason I did mine—they were fly-fisher people. How lucky could I be! We hit it off from day one.

The same held true for my Reggie and their puppy Rowdy. Reggie's treatment of the much smaller, younger dog and his ability to relate to Rowdy indicated how he would relate to other canines as well. That seemed fortuitous because a year after my divorce from Ann, I became involved with another woman, this time a dog-loving lady who had her own canine family.

Reggie romping with the Weiske's Rowdy

I met Julie, the dog woman, at Minot's Air Force Base in the fall of 1996 while teaching my Western Civilization history course there. Divorced with a ten-year-old daughter, Julie, a brash, brown-eyed, full-figured, loud-laughing, attractive brunette had decided to give up her contracting/carpentering business, return to school and get a teaching degree.

Intelligent, diligent, self-assertive and committed, Julie did very well in my course. After she finished, our friendship blossomed into a serious relationship. Fifteen years younger than I, she had abundant energy that I found attractive. The down side to this meant she often had difficulty relaxing or concentrating on single issues. Her impatience inspired her to engage in new and different ventures more often than most. Nevertheless, her energy and sense of humor made her a fun person to be with, at least initially.

We married in the late summer of 1997. She, her daughter and their two dogs moved in with me shortly thereafter. Both Julie's dogs, Buggsie the Chiwawa and Weenie the miniature Dachshund, were fun-loving, affectionate little beasts. When I introduced Reggie to them, they appeared terrified. Their unfounded fears soon disappeared. Reggie adopted both immediately as bosom companions and fun playmates.

Several years older than and not nearly as frenetic as Weenie,

Chiwawa Buggsie played less with Reggie than Weenie. Buggsie preferred to watch the antics of the other two when they played rather than get engaged.

Reggie would notice Weenie chewing on a toy or a rawhide bone. He would amble over to see what she had. Weenie would growl and try to find a place where she could keep the bigger dog from latching onto her prize. Reggie would follow and chase if necessary.

Eventually Reggie would grab the coveted piece. Weenie would react by growling and chasing in turn. She would jump at the thief trying to dislodge whatever he had taken from her. So much bigger, Reggie could fend off her jumping and snapping retrieval efforts by simply turning his body away.

All of this frustrated the little beast. Often, she would persist until near exhaustion. With her playmate panting, Reggie would then graciously return Weenie's toy. Both members of the show wagged their tails throughout. It amused me to watch the dog disparities have so much fun.

Reggie with his pal Weenie

Reggie related to larger dogs as well as smaller ones and puppies. His large dog companionship dated from the Julie period as well. During our time together, Julie exhibited many different interests. At one point, she decided she wanted to raise Labrador Retrievers for sale. To realize her plan, she contacted a breeder in Jamestown and purchased a female Lab puppy. Because she intended to make some serious money by raising and selling purebred Labrador pups, she did not have the dog spayed. On the day she went to buy her puppy, I accompanied her.

The yellow puppy we eventually picked was a self-assured, confident, boisterous little dog. We named her Clio, a name Julie let me choose. I have much more to write about Clio in a future chapter because I would inherit the dog. In many ways, Clio was the opposite of Reggie, especially in relation to Julie's other little dogs. Clio loved to play, but she played too intensely.

In the end, Clio's roughhouse playing with Julie's little darlings distressed Julie so much she pawned the dog off on me. In other words, I received Clio by default (more on that in the next chapter). Since Julie and her daughter resided in the remodeled basement while I occupied the upstairs, the move was not difficult. The dog had only to move up a level. Once completed, the move provided Reggie with a new pal that would keep him on his toes. As it turned out, Reggie enjoyed adopting and adapting to the little girl devil.

Reggie's ability to get along with so many different dogs amazed me then and still does. Thinking back, I can come up with only one instance where he growled at another dog. Second wife Ann and I were camping in Theodor Roosevelt National Park in western North Dakota. Reggie had to be about a year old, a nearly mature dog probably in the summer of 1992.

The growling incident didn't involve a fight or anything violent. A free roaming, larger dog wandered into our tenting area as we prepared supper, no doubt seeking to find out about the menu. He wasn't a recognizable breed, but a mixture. As I recall, the visitor seemed neither aggressive nor obnoxious, just curious.

When the dog appeared, Reggie with his neck hair raised, ran toward him and growled, no snapping, no fighting, just a run-of-the-mill growl. From Reggie's growl and my yelling "scat doggie, scat, run along now," the intruder got the idea he wasn't welcome and trotted off. That was it. I smile when I think about Reggie intimidating anything, let alone another canine.

Reggie's social skills and manners made him an especially attractive traveling companion. After my three elder children graduated from high school and went off to college, Reggie remained the sole family member in my Minot home.

I took the dog with me as often as possible whenever I left the house, whether on a run to the grocery store or the much longer journey to Wisconsin. He regularly accompanied me to my office at the university as well when I worked there in the evenings. I had a dog bed stowed away behind my file cabinet for that purpose.

At the time I drove a used, extended-cab Chevy pickup truck which suited nicely both my outdoor activities and my Wisconsin construction needs. Wherever I drove, the dog never rode in the back seat but rather in the front next to me. In our travels from Minot to Florence, a seven-hundred-mile journey, Reggie kept me awake and helped me pay attention to the road.

On one of the drives east, I recall a memorable gas stop in Grand Rapids, Minnesota on Highway 2 that illustrated Reggie's involvement. It occurred during the afternoon on one of our late May runs to the Florence cottage. I got out of the truck and proceeded to fill up the gas tank. It took several minutes and Reggie was getting tired of driving. We'd been on the road since dawn and he also needed a stop to do his business. When I finished the gassing up, I went into the station to pay. Reggie hawked me the entire time. As he watched, he moved over from the passenger seat to the driver's area.

I was at the counter paying when a young woman came into the station and said, "See the black dog in that truck, he looks like he's the driver."

I heard her and couldn't help responding, "Yeah, and he's a very impatient driver. If he's gotta wait too long, he'll blow the horn, telling me to get my butt back to the truck."

Both the girl and the guy behind the counter laughed. I paid up and started to leave. When Reggie saw me coming out the door, he moved from the driver's spot to the passenger side of the front seat. Although a small Lab, Reggie's size still made the move a tight squeeze.

On this day, his buttocks brushed the steering wheel and hit the horn hard enough to cause it to blast. He'd done that several times before. It always made me laugh. I found it especially funny on this occasion because it verified the prediction I made in the station. That represents one of the few times, I might add, when my predicting anything actually came true.

If Reggie, the traveler, surpassed both Jason and Boomer in that capacity, his hunting skills couldn't compare with those of his predecessors. At least that's what I believed in the beginning. Unfortunately for Reggie, his first four or five years corresponded to a time for me of limited hunting activities. By then I had no longer much interest in hunting waterfowl. I did hunt upland game birds on occasion.

To hunt effectively pheasants or sharptail grouse, the two most common North Dakota upland game birds, you need a good dog to flush the birds from cover and then retrieve the ones downed. Both pheasants and sharptails will run on the hunter, so walking them up as a lone gunman presented some serious problems. Some do hunt these birds without dogs, but it's much more difficult and correspondingly less fun I believe. As I've aged, the dog's role in bird hunting has increased. In fact, I think for most pheasant enthusiasts having a dog or dogs out in front constitutes the real essence of the hunt's fun.

Reggie hunted pheasants with me a few times. I don't remember much about those hunts, probably because they were rare. On those outings he didn't hunt with the skill or enthusiasm manifested by the pheasant Labs that would follow him. With Reggie, one pheasant hunt has remained in my memory though. We were hunting on private land in North Dakota's south west semi-Bad Lands country. In North Dakota, the term semi-Bad Lands refers to rugged, dry, and uneven topography. The landscape has numerous rock formations, or bluffs.

Generally, farmers and ranchers in that part of the state concentrate on livestock production, most often cattle but some sheep and on occasion even elk. Cultivated fields of corn or wheat do exist, but far less often than in the eastern portion of the state.

Despite the environment's harshness, pheasants survive in the southwest in good numbers. To hunt them in this landscape, however, requires more work than would be true for the east's cornfields or cat-tail sloughs. In the south west, vegetation reflects the rugged terrain closely; thorny bushes, small struggling trees, and parched vegetation exist in soil drier and less fertile than that characteristic of the Red River Valley.

On this particular semi-Bad Lands hunt, Reggie and I worked the creek beds and the sides of bluffs with significant vegetation. As I recall, Reggie flushed a rooster from one of the dry creek beds and I shot it. The bird fell in a clump of thorny bushes. Reggie saw the bird drop and I yelled, "Fetch it Reg, fetch it."

Reggie ran to the bushes, looked at the dead bird, and stopped. I urged him again to fetch it. No response. I repeated the command. He refused to go into that thorny trap. Apparently too many prickly things. I said some unflattering things to him. Still nothing. I couldn't shame him into risking the thorns.

In the end, I fetched the rooster myself by crawling into the bushes on my hands and knees just far enough to reach the bird with a stick and maneuver it out. It was a battle, I thought, clearly beneath the dignity of a real hunting dog's master, but I did it. That was my last pheasant hunt with Reggie.

A couple of years after the pheasant fiasco, I decided to take six-year-old Robbie duck hunting. One of my students told me about a great duck slough on his parents' land. According to him, it stretched about two acres in length and was surrounded by wheat fields, attractive fodder for local ducks and migrating ones as well. The birds would rest in the slough during the night and midday. In the early morning and late afternoon, they would fly out to the fields, returning to the water after feeding.

To do the hunt, I needed some Mallard decoys, which for some reason I had not given away when I moved out of Winnipeg to go to law school. Also, I still had the necessary duck hunting cloths that I'd used in the past to disguise myself in the cattails. For my little boy, I had camo cloth to cover him. To make the hunt more comfortable for Rob, I took an aluminum deck chair. He and the chair I draped with the camo material in our makeshift blind.

We arose at four-thirty a.m., each ate a bowl of cereal, and then headed out to the hunting spot, some 20 miles south of Minot. A full moon accompanied us out of town. As we drove, my boy fell back to sleep. We arrived at the hunting place a few minutes before the sun began to appear.

In the darkness, we walked out to the slough about 100 yards off the road. I got Rob set up in his chair on the edge of the cattails. With my chest waders on, I waded out and arranged the decoys in the traditional U-shape. While I organized, an agitated dog ran back and forth, trying to cope with his enthusiasm. Settled comfortably in his chair, Rob again fell back to sleep.

As dawn broke, the birds started to move. We could hear the ducks whistling overhead before we could see them. The first ducks zoomed toward the decoys about a half hour after sun up. Then the action began. I hunkered down and watched the ducks set their wings to land on the water.

As the first group came into the decoys, I shot three times. One duck fell amidst the decoys. Reggie, who was standing on the edge of our hiding place, saw the duck hit the water. He was off before I could yell "fetch." He swam straight out to the bird, grabbed it, turned about and swam back. He delivered the duck to me as if he'd been doing it for years.

Over the next hour and a half, the ducks continued to come into our decoy set. By nine o'clock we had our limit of six ducks, five Mallards, three of them greenheads, and a drake Gadwall. Reggie had fetched all six, even the ducks that weren't dead. In fact, several of the cripples he had to pursue a considerable distance before grabbing them. He executed all of his retrieves on the water. His performance impressed me throughout. My dog was a hunter, a water dog, a true Lab! I felt some serious guilt pains for ever doubting his hunting doghood.

Although Rob slept during the period before the ducks began coming into the decoys, he awoke when the shooting started and stayed awake until we finished. When we had returned to the car and started for home, I said, "Well, what'd you think. Like duck hunting?"

"Yeah, it's fun," he said.

"How so?"

"Watching the ducks come into the decoys," he said.

"Yeah, beautiful how they set their wings, sail in, and drop amongst the decoys. What else'd you like?" I asked.

"Fun watching Reggie get the ducks."

"Yeah, he was good. Did what he was supposed to do, like a good Lab. You mind getting up so early today?"

"No, it wasn't bad. But you sure missed a bunch of shots," he said.

I laughed. "Touché, you're right. Wasn't shooting too good today. Maybe because of your snoring."

"I snored? Was it bad?" He looked at me with his brow wrinkled.

"No, just kidding. Bad shooting had nothing to do with you. You were a very good hunting companion."

"Dad, when can I learn to hunt? You teach me?"

"You bet, little Buddy. Get you started in a couple of years. You were good today being quiet, sitting still. A big part of hunting."

"It was fun. Can we do it again?"

"Absolutely. Few more times this season. And when you get to be sixteen and have a driver's license, you can drive and I can sleep. Deal?" I said.

"Yeah." And Rob laughed.

That afternoon after we had returned home, Robbie drew a picture with colored crayons depicting the hunt. The drawing's action elements included a black dog running toward blue water, a hunter shooting upwards, and a duck falling out of the sky. All these features were illuminated by a big yellow ball at the picture's top. That was the moon, Robbie insisted.

This picture I later framed and hung up in my office at the university. It remained on the wall next to my desk until I retired in 2010. Throughout those years, it always inspired beautiful memories of my lovely black dog and equally wonderful little boy.

Reggie's performance that day compared favorably to what Jason had done in Manitoba. Reggie wasn't as big as Jason nor as strong a swimmer, but Reggie proved himself to be solid. Perhaps Reggie would have had more trouble with those Lake Winnipeg waves Jason mastered, but in the more limited North Dakota sloughs he retrieved every bit as effectively as his illustrious predecessor.

Much to my surprise, Reggie appeared to love duck hunting nearly as much as Jason had. Too bad for him that my fondness for duck dinners had declined so dramatically! In its own way, Reggie's service as house pal and travelling companion rewarded me as much as Jason's role in hunting Manitoba waterfowl had.

Reggie's sweet temperament, his most outstanding characteristic, inspired me throughout his life. It even influenced me when away from him. The best example of this comes from a trip to Germany I made in the summer of 2001.

At that time, I was doing research on German immigration to Canada. I started working on that subject during my time at the University of Winnipeg back in the 1970s. My law school stint and time practicing law rudely interrupted that kind of scholarship. However, I always enjoyed doing historical research and publishing my findings, so it seemed natural for me in Minot to pick up where I'd left off the decade before. Specifically, in the new century I committed myself to writing a book on German immigration to Canada from 1850 to 1939. To realize this goal, I traveled to Germany to research the relevant emigration records there.

In the summers of 2000 and 2001, I flew to Germany to visit archives in Berlin, Hamburg, Bremen, Koblenz, and Munich. The Staatsarchiv in Munich I found especially helpful, researching there in both 2000 and 2001.

When I visited Germany, I always tried to stay in private homes—that is, rent from local people. Renting a room in a private home cost considerably less than a hotel room and I found it more fun because I got personal attention and could talk German with my renters. Fortunately, in Munich I rented from a pair of especially solicitous and friendly elderly sisters. For my rent, I received a room to sleep in and breakfast the next morning. My ten days with them in 2000 worked so well I came back the next year. By then we were friends.

The two ladies worked each day and as a result left the home before I arose. Since the archive opened at nine o'clock a.m., I didn't arise much before eight o'clock a.m. By that time my hosts had already departed for work. Before leaving, they would leave coffee and German pastry in the dining room for my breakfast. On several occasions, they served me supper as well. For my second visit in 2001, they even made special arrangements because they'd rented their guest room to a Swiss lady. For me, they fixed up a bed in the study. That worked perfectly well.

At one of the suppers with the ladies during my 2001 visit, I talked about my dog Reggie. (Germans are especially fond of dogs. They're even allowed in most restaurants!) Naturally, I described him in glowing terms—sweet (suess), beautiful (schoen), a lover (Liebhaber) of his family, and non-aggressive (nicht angriffslustig). When describing his non-aggressive nature, I used the phrase "fast ein Feigling." The phrase means "almost a coward." I wasn't particularly happy with the term "Feigling," but they got the idea of him being not an attack or guard dog.

To continue the ruse, I told the ladies I wanted to get a sign for Reggie that I'd seen several times in Munich while walking about the city. The coveted sign had three German words on it—"Vorsicht bissiger Hunt." When I identified the desired sign and explained why I wanted it, they laughed. In English the sign translated as, "Beware vicious dog."

The sign conversation from my 2001 visit took place on the evening before I returned to the United States. At that time, I asked the sisters if they might try to find a copy of the "Bissiger Hund" placard and mail it to me in North Dakota. They agreed to try. I left them money to purchase the sign and send it on.

A month or so after I returned home, I received the sign package from them. The note accompanying it explained that they could not find the "Bissiger Hund" placard but they did find something like it. The eight-by-twelve-inch sign they sent read: "Vorsicht freilaufender Hund. Wenn der Hund kommt, flach auf dem Boden legen und fuer Hilfe warten. Wenn keine Hilfe kommt, viel Gluck." The translation goes like this: "Free running dog. If the dog confronts you, lie flat on the floor and wait for help to arrive. If no help comes, good luck!"

That greeting now adorns the entryway to my cottage in Florence, Wisconsin. Every time I enter the place and see it, I think of my kind German lady friends, my beautiful Reggie and how if he came upon you and found you lying of the floor in trepidation of being bitten, he would have licked your face and said, "For heaves sake, what are you afraid of? Don't be afraid. Get up. I love guests. Life is beautiful."

As mentioned above, Reggie had other dog companions in the home besides Julie's Weenie and Buggsie in the form of Clio, the yellow Lab puppy. At the time Julie bought Clio, I also purchased a puppy from Scott Snyder's Black Hawk Kennels.

My acquisition in 2000 at the time Julie got her Clio was a six-month-old chocolate Labrador puppy I named Sherman. He moved right in with me and Reggie. Again, as noted, at that time Julie and her daughter plus dogs Clio, Buggsie, and Weenie lived in the basement of our house. My dogs and I lived on the first floor. Reggie got along with my new puppy as easily as he had adjusted to Julie's dogs. His ability to adapt to almost any change seemed amazing then and does even more so now.

A happy Reggie bounding through the flowers

By the time Sherman and Clio resided with me in 2001, Reggie had become an old dog. He lived for another year after that, until he was almost 12. In the spring of 2002, I had him put down. I decided on this for several reasons. To begin with, he had become increasingly lame and his vision had deteriorated. When I took him and the other dogs out to fetch tennis balls, Reggie couldn't see well enough to mark where his ball landed. In addition, he began to lose control of his bladder and bowels. I resolved to have him put to sleep only after much introspection and sadness.

I remember the day vividly. I took him to the Minot Veterinary Clinic east of town. All the way out to the clinic I cried. Being his usual sweet traveling companion, the dog had no idea of his fate. When we arrived, I tried to stem the tears. I tied a rope to his collar and walked him into the clinic.

The young woman at the counter knew my mission because I called for the appointment. I led the dog in and gave the rope to her. I couldn't speak. I couldn't be present for the fatal injection. I turned about and left immediately. I cried again all the way home. It took several months for me to cope with the full impact of Reggie's death.

Since I started this chapter describing Nat's bringing Reggie to me, it's not entirely illogical to begin my concluding remarks with another

Nat reference. Here's what Nat wrote me when I recently asked for his thoughts and comments on Reggie.

> "I loved our little black Reggie, but I did not share as much time with him as I would have liked. He was gentle, sensitive, affable—a lover, not a fighter. He would cringe at the thought of disappointing you and would bound with glee if he recognized approval. He was deeply devoted to you. When you went to Europe for a week and left him with me in my apartment in Michigan, Reggie was a wreck! When my roommate would enter the room, Reggie would roll over on his back submissively and pee. He missed you fiercely and was lost without your beacon in his life. His great passion was being a good companion—to his master, to other dogs in the house, to all who crossed his path. He was a kind and gentle soul."

Younger son Rob echoed Nat's comments. "On the topic of Reggie," Rob wrote in his dog email to me, "I think what I remember most were his 'butt runs' around the back yard, him being in the basement because he had dirty feet, and how sweet he was. He truly did not have a mean bone in his body. He was one of those dogs that didn't need any sort of reprimanding because when he did something wrong he would be so sad about it that you couldn't even be mad at him."

Looking back from the vantage point of the present 2017, I'll add just a few more words to what my observant sons expressed about Reggie. As I conjure him up, I think of Erich Fromm's comments on love.

According to Fromm, real love among humans is defined by the phrase "I need you because I love you" rather than "I love you because I need you." Reggie loved me and my children in his devoted way, I sincerely believe, because he needed us to love. I've never had a dog so beautiful in this regard.

Reggie reminds me of the dogs James Herriot, the English veterinary, wrote about so successfully. Reggie could easily have been one of Herriot's subjects—a creature that made the life of his master more meaningful, more joy infused, and more complete through love and devotion. I also think Reggie would have been a good companion for Saint Francis. As with the Saint, Reggie had dedicated his life to love. I'm convinced if I had a cat in the house, Reggie would have loved it as well. That he'll be at the bridge when I arrive goes without saying, and I anticipate he'll break into a butt run the moment he recognizes me.

CHAPTER FIVE

CLIO (AKA QUEENIE)
(DAUGHTER OF ZEUS AND MUSE OF HISTORY)

My Three Musketeers

"If you don't own a dog, at least one, there is not necessarily anything wrong with you but there may be something wrong with your life."

— Roger A. Cares

"Jonathan, Jonathan," Julie yelled. Dressed in a blue sweat shirt, grey sweat pants and brown bedroom slippers, she appeared at the top of the stairwell leading from the basement apartment where she, her daughter and their little dogs resided. It was seven-thirty a.m., early April 2001. I was in the kitchen in my bathrobe fixing breakfast.

"What is it Julie?"

"Gotta talk about Clio," she said.

"What about?" I said.

"Can't have her downstairs."

"Why not?" I said, frowning.

"Her crazy behavior, can't handle it," she said, her voice almost hysterical.

"What crazy behavior?" I said.

"Beating up on the little dogs. It's driving me nuts."

"What'd you expect? She's a puppy," I said, pouring raisin bran into a bowl.

"She's just too aggressive."

"She's not mean or vicious. Just a puppy for God's sake," I said as I took milk out of the fridge.

"Are you listening to me? She's a brute, intimidating Weenie and Buggsie all the time."

"Yeah, I am. Welcome to life with a Lab puppy," I said, getting a soup spoon from the silverware drawer.

"Stop what you're doing and listen. This can't go on. You gotta help me. Take Clio upstairs. I'll pay for her food," she said, her tone desperate.

I stopped and turned toward her. "Food's irrelevant. Why'd you get the dog? Had to know what a big-dog puppy would mean."

"I didn't. Will you take her, please, please?" she said, the second "please" with her best seductive smile.

It worked. I couldn't resist. "Okay, bring her up."

Julie's acquisition of Clio was a story in itself. It came about, so she claimed, from a discovery that raising and selling purebred Lab puppies could be a fast and sure way to substantial money. During the time she developed her plan to purchase a Labrador puppy factory, I remained totally in the dark.

Then one day she announced, "Jonathan, I've decided to buy a female Lab puppy for breeding purposes. Spent the last week contacting breeders who've got puppies for sale. Found one I liked down near Jamestown. Told him I'd be down this Saturday to see what he's got.

Interested in coming with?"

I thought for a couple of seconds and said, "Yeah, be fun to pick a puppy."

As the next chapter explains, I not only helped her select her new imagined source of wealth, but ended up buying a puppy for myself. That dog, a chocolate Lab I named Sherman, would welcome Clio's moving in with us.

Clio adapted to the transfer upstairs with a vengeance. The move meant she had playmates her own size, if not her mischievous disposition. What she'd been doing to the smaller dogs downstairs, she now practiced on Reggie and my chocolate Sherman with relish and verve. Although larger and older, Sherman was still very much a puppy himself and not intimidated by his new playmate. Rather, he enjoyed her rough and tumble-foolery.

Although the play elements, that is, the leaping upon, the mock-biting, the lunging or crashing into were all physically rough, the spirit of the tussles remained light-hearted. In all the bouts, both tails wagged vigorously. The problem was they seemed to be going at it all the time. Clio, I concluded, had some kind of genetic energy imbalance that explained her crazy need for non-stop play.

Eventually, her rambunctious behavior began to wear me out. I tried to discipline her with harsh words; I spanked with rolled up newspapers. Neither effort had any effect.

After a couple of weeks of this, I went downstairs at suppertime and told Julie, "I can't handle Clio. She's a nightmare. Wrestling with Sherman non-stop, even bugging Reggie. She's doing to me what she did to you. Want you to take her back."

"Tough shit!" she said. "We got a deal, remember? She's your dog now. No way I'm taking her back. You wanna get rid of her, go ahead."

No seductive smile this time. I walked back upstairs trying to figure out what I should do. I kind of liked the dog despite her irritating behavior. If only she'd calm down.

A few minutes later, Julie appeared and said, "Jonathan, I'm sorry about Clio being such a pest. I'll help you build a kennel in the kitchen big enough for both Clio and Sherman. That'll limit their horseplay. Keep the action out of the rest of the house."

"Okay, we can try that," I said, not knowing what else to say.

The kennel helped, but it didn't really solve the problem. Clio continued to make constant chaos in the kennel area and beyond. In desperation, I called Scott Synder, the man in Jamestown who sold Julie the yellow devil. After I introduced myself, he said, "What's up Jonathan. You looking for another dog?"

"God no," I said.

"So why the call? Having trouble with the chocolate pup?"

"No, he's fine. Great dog. Something else," I said.

"You sound troubled. What's the problem?" he said.

"Julie's puppy, the yellow dog. Calling about her. That dog's driving us crazy."

"How so?" Scott snapped. I could tell from the sound of his voice he was getting irritated.

"On a rampage all the time. So crazy with Julie's Chiwawa and miniature Dachshund, she foisted the dog off on me."

"What's foist off mean?" Scott said, his impatience increasing.

"Julie claimed she couldn't take the bullying and chaos any more. Told me to take the dog."

Scott said, "What'd the dog do? Attack or hurt the other dogs?"

"No, just plays rough continuously, intimidates the smaller dogs."

"That's a Lab puppy thing," he said.

"Told her that. But the dog's doing it now to my dogs. I'm having the same reaction as Julie."

"So what do you want from me?" Scott asked. I could imagine him rolling his eyes.

"Would you take her back?"

Without answering my question, he said, "Sounds like she needs discipline. Did you or Julie punish the puppy when it acted up?"

"Don't know what Julie did. I spanked her with newspapers."

"Sounds pretty weak. Either of you punish her regularly so she knew what she was doing wrong?"

"Apparently not," I said.

Scott continued, "I know Julie wanted to use her to breed puppies. What'd you want from the dog? Why'd you take her on?"

"Planned to hunt her."

"Whether a breeder or hunting dog, it still needs discipline," Scott said.

"I trained my first Lab for waterfowl hunting only. Don't know anything about training for upland game. What'd you suggest?"

"I train hunting dogs for both waterfowl and upland game regularly. Many of the dogs I sell return for training. It's a 3- to 4-month process here. For especially hard to deal with dogs, I do force breaking. That's a tough routine but effective for problem dogs, ones overly aggressive or non-responsive. That sounds like your puppy. What's her name?"

"Clio."

"I'd be happy to train Clio. Can guarantee she'll be obedient after she completes the routine here. Teach her basic discipline and obedience, as well how to retrieve and hunt. An independent, enthusiastic dog can be a great hunter if trained properly. You should think about it. Don't want to bother, I'll take the dog back. Up to you," Scott said.

"I sorta like the beast despite her behavior. Realize she's only a puppy. Just trying to have fun when she plays, even if it's rough."

"Mull it over, Jonathan. Let me know what you decide. I'll do whatever you want. Don't want unhappy buyers of my dogs," Scott said and our conversation ended.

For the next couple of days, I considered Scott's "force breaking" idea. When I called back, we talked for half an hour about the details of his program, its nature, cost and length. In the end, I told him I was ready to go with the force breaking. We set up the schedule for May through August 2001, four months for Clio to learn how to behave as a civilized hunting dog. I'd grown fond of my devil girl despite her antics. Had my fingers crossed. Hoped she'd benefit from the training and become another Jason.

In late May 2001 on my way to the summer place in Florence, Wisconsin, I dropped Clio off at Scott's Black Hawk Kennels. She remained there for the next fourteen weeks. After returning from Florence in late August, I called Scott and arranged to pick up the dog.

As I recall, it was a Saturday afternoon. Less than a minute after I pulled into his yard and got out of my truck, Scott came out of the house to greet me. A thin, medium sized fellow wearing a baseball cap and knee-length rubber boots, he smiled and said, "Jonathan, you're right on time. How ya been? Have a good summer? You in Wisconsin the whole time?"

"Yeah, love the woods and the trout fishing but happy to be back in North Dakota, ready to chase some pheasants. My crazy dog didn't wreck your summer, did she?"

He laughed and said, "No, not quite but she's a feisty little brute for sure. Let's go get her. I'm anxious to show how much she's learned over the past several months. She's in the kennel. Follow me."

Located about 50 yards behind Scott's residence, the kennel consisted of a one story 8-foot-high, 15-foot-wide, and 36-foot-long central building extending north and south with eight runs on both its east and west sides. The individual dog runs were 4 feet wide by 12 feet in length. Both the sides and ends of each self-contained run were partitioned off by 6-foot-high chain link fencing.

The runs themselves were concrete, with draining troughs at the front and side to carry away the water used in cleaning them. The central covered building, which looked like an elongated garage, had a section for storing dog food and other tools as well as separate, four feet by four feet individual housing units off the external runs on both its east and west sides with sleeping mats for the dogs.

As we approached the kennel from the east, six black and yellow dogs, all Labs, out in their runs watched our progress toward them. They appeared excited at our approach. One of those canines looked to me like Clio. She had the same color as my puppy but was quite a bit bigger than the dog I'd dropped off. I said to Scott, "Is that yellow dog in the third run from the right my devil girl?"

He nodded. "Yep, that's your educated and newly civilized beast. Ain't she beautiful?"

"Much bigger than I thought she'd be," I said.

"Yeah, she's matured physically a good deal here. About full size now. Good size for a hunting Lab. Big enough to handle North Dakota sloughs and lakes," he said.

"She's magnificent," I said.

When we reached the kennel, Scott said, "Thought we'd take her out and put her through her routine before anything else. Want you to see what she can do."

"Great. Lead the way. Can't wait to see her perform."

"If you don't mind," Scott continued, "I'd like to work a second dog same time we do Clio, not together but in separate sessions. That okay?"

"Sure, be fun to watch both dogs do their stuff."

Scott let the two dogs out of their runs and had them jump into the back of his pickup, which had half a dozen units for transporting dogs. With the dogs loaded, Scott drove out into the country several miles and pulled into the entry way to a harvested grain field with a cattail slough in it. He got out and opened Clio's cage. She jumped out.

"Jonathan, I'm gonna do the obedience work first, then show off her retrieving skills. Okay?"

"Great. Go for it," I said.

For the obedience show, Scott had Clio heel at his left knee while he walked in a circle, sit on command, and then stay in place while he walked away with his back to the dog. When 15 yards away, he stopped and turned. After a short pause, he gave the command "Here!" and Clio bolted to him. When she reached him, he said "Sit." She did. He barked "Heel" and she moved behind him and assumed the sitting position next to his left knee. During the obedience work, Scott carried a four-foot-long black rod in his right hand, which I assumed to be his enforcement tool.

When he finished with the obedience session, I said "What's the rod for?"

"It's my 'whopping stick'. Absolutely essential. Makes obedience possible. Wouldn't be without it," he said.

"Why?" I asked.

"When you whack an unruly or disobedient dog, you get results. Has a serious sting to it. Don't know any dog that can tolerate it. Use it a few times and the bad dog gets the point. Follow?" Scott said.

"Yeah, where'd you get it?" I asked.

"Any farm or ranching supply store outlet has em. Actually, my switch's a sawed-off version of the normal cattle prodding rod ranchers use to herd their cows. You should get one. Clio knows exactly why it's used."

For the retrieving display, Scott dropped the whopping stick and picked up a fetching dummy, a 14-inch canvas covered, tube-like object with a 16-inch cord attached to it. With the cord, Scott could twirl the dummy above his head to get enough momentum to hurl it a good distance. When Scott picked up the dummy, Clio perked up. While he swirled and then threw, Clio remained sitting adjacent to his left knee in the heeling position. She watched it sail out and land. Although trembling with excitement, she held her position.

Scott said "Fetch" in a loud voice and the dog took off. When she reached the dummy, she grabbed it and raced back to Scott. She sat in front of him and at "Give," she rendered up the dummy. To clarify the hold and release system, Scott took the dummy out of her mouth and then pushed it back in giving the command "Hold." A few seconds later, he said "Give." Clio released the dummy to him.

After several land retrieves, Scott threw the dummy into the slough. The dog saw where the first toss landed and when he commanded "Fetch," she bounded to the water and dove in. In a matter of seconds, she had the dummy back to him. The next throw Scott pitched into the cattails, where the dog couldn't see it land. He sent her off. When she arrived at the edge of the slough, Scott blew his whistle. The dog stopped, turned and looked back. Scott raised his right arm above his head and then signaled with it to the right. Clio saw the arm move, heard the command "Fetch" and moved into the cattails in the direction where the dummy landed.

Several minutes later she emerged from the dense vegetation with the dummy and raced back to Scott. For the lesson's coup de grace, Scott went back to his pick up and returned with a dead pheasant. He had the dog sit next to him, threw the pheasant into the slough and commanded fetch. Clio returned the bird with the same enthusiasm she had the dummies.

With a satisfied look on his face, Scott said, "What'd you think? Like what you saw?"

"Yeah, the dog's a star. She loves it. You've done a great job."

Scott lit up a cigarette and said, "Glad you're pleased."

We talked a bit about what I should do once the dog was back home with me and he finished his cigarette. Then he said, "Now let's do Roy, the black dog. He's a year older than Clio. Has had force breaking too. As you'll see, he's not Clio but he'd make a good dog for somebody. Gotta find a buyer for him. Costing me too much to keep feeding him. Don't mind, do you?"

"Not at all. Bring him on," I said.

For the second session, Scott skipped the obedience instruction and ran Roy through the dummy fetching routine. A solid black Lab, taller and longer than Clio by an inch or two, Roy possessed a solid body, neither too thin nor too fat. His torso, legs, and muzzle all appeared nicely proportioned as well. When Scott tossed the dummy and commanded "Fetch," Roy did not leap at the opportunity as Clio had, but moved at a pace and speed about a third of Clio's.

The juxtaposition of different enthusiasms was dramatic. It seemed as if the camera that had recorded Clio's work had been switched to slow motion for the black dog. Roy obeyed his master but, I thought, appeared to doing so out of fear of retribution. He fetched very slowly.

He obviously disliked (maybe hated is a better word) the whole routine. A beautiful, timid, shy beast, Roy's passiveness and gentleness, which appeared to be the exact opposite of Clio's go-getter disposition, impressed me nevertheless.

A year later when my younger daughter Sarah expressed interest in getting a Lab, I called Scott to find out if Roy were still available for purchase. He was, and I bought him for Sarah. She and the dog hit it off immediately. Roy became devoted to Sarah. I'd never seen a dog so attached to any human (except maybe Reggie to me). He hung on her with rapt attention, following her about the house, waiting for her at the door when she returned home from work, riding next to her in her vehicle when she travelled. Roy's mistress returned the love and concern.

For Sarah, Roy seemed like a gift from God. I remember only too well her heart-rending sobbing telephone call at four-thirty a.m. from New York City where she was visiting a friend the morning Roy suddenly died from stomach cancer complications. Despite Sarah's suffering, I was happy she'd had her bosom pal for so long. Sarah and another Lab from Scott's kennel will appear later in the final chapter of these dog stories.

The Clio that returned to me in August from force breaking school was a different animal than the crazy puppy I enrolled in May. Over the summer she grew a good deal—added weight and acquired the figure she would have for the next ten years.

In size, Clio exceeded Reggie but not Sherman. She had a medium yellow coat, darker than the most white Labrador versions but about average for yellows. Of course, this changed as she aged and became increasingly whiter, especially in her face. Clio possessed a nicely shaped head about average size, not too pointed, not too blunt. In short, she was a handsome dog, not New York Kennel Club perhaps, but very respectable for me.

"I'm ready to hunt now, boss. Let's get those pheasants!"

If her physical features were not exceptional, her personality characteristics were. Socially Clio got along with other dogs. If Roy and Reggie had been shy, retiring, or modest, Clio embodied opposite traits.

Although neither aggressive nor hostile, she was confident, competent and cocky. Clio never seemed to doubt herself as far as I could tell. She would look you straight in the eye. When she did, her eyes seemed to sparkle. She was a tail-wager with a vengeance. She wagged even in her dreams—thump, thump, thump, in the middle of the night.

From the onset, she played the alpha dog in my household and enjoyed doing so. When I added a black female in 2005 to my Lab family, Clio's status didn't change. To borrow a phrase from Alexandra Horowitz, she remained throughout her life with me the head of my "benign gang."

Clio never exhibited hostility toward humans. She never played the watchdog when visitors came to the door. In fact, I remember Clio only ever barking at chow time. When I started to fill the dog bowls with food, she would lose her usual cool and jump and bark. Depending on my mood, that could be quite irritating.

Socially, Clio, the alpha dog, led my other dogs but not in a bullying fashion. She could play with them competitively and still be buddies. I found this to be particularly true at my summer place in Wisconsin.

One of Clio's favorite activities, and this applied to the other dogs as well, was fetching tennis balls from the Brule River down in front of the cottage.

On a good day with a light wind, I would take Clio and Sherman, and later Diana, down to our dock and throw tennis balls for them to retrieve from the water. They competed with each other to see which one could swim the fastest to reach the ball. As a young dog, Clio normally beat Sherman or Reggie to the floating object. That wasn't a problem for the race's loser or losers because I'd throw another ball or balls for the dog or dogs without one.

Clio loved competing even if it meant losing to younger sister Diana, who when mature became the gang's fastest swimmer. All the dogs could and did share in the fetching exercise happily, huffing and puffing and, I believed, smiling at the romp's end.

Unlike some of my Labs, independent Clio did not dote on me but seemed satisfied just being herself by herself. At night as a young dog, she slept in a kennel in the upstairs apartment. Later, I dispensed with the kennel and let her choose her sleeping spot. Normally, that was the living room rug or some other place removed from me.

Clio snuggled up for the night amongst my antiques

Over the years, most of my dogs slept on dog beds in my bedroom, but not Clio. She would enter the bedroom only in the morning just before feeding time, say seven or seven-thirty a.m. Unlike Boomer, she would not bark at me to force me out of bed. Instead, she would stick her wet nose in my face or, if I turned away, do the same to my neck. She might even put her front paws up on the bed and nudge me. By that time, she'd won the battle. I was up and putting on slippers in preparation for feeding her and the other gang members. I'm still amazed at how well Clio knew how to read me and to do the necessary to get her way.

If Clio's nonsensical barking and jumping at feeding time seemed irritating and undignified, her commitment and success as a hunter made up many times over for this domestic flaw. In fact, of all my Labs I think Clio was the best, most talented hunter. She did it all exceptionally well—pointing, flushing, retrieving, quartering, and following commands.

Most often,when I took only one dog hunting, I chose Clio, for she was the best. I don't mean to imply by claiming best for Clio that Sherman couldn't hunt effectively. He did, but not as effectively as his yellow sister. In the following passages, I'll try to convey something of just how skilled she was. But first, I must digress to describe where in North Dakota I took my Clio and the others to chase the wily Ring Necked Pheasant.

For the period from 2001 to 2011, the time when I hunted most effectively, the center for my hunting ventures was Minot, a good-sized city (by North Dakota standards at least) in the north central part of the state. During that decade, I hunted most often south or west of town but good areas existed in the northeast and northwest as well. Where I hunted depended on weather, of course, but also on time.

Many of my choice spots were close to Minot, which meant I could teach morning or midday classes and still hunt a bit in the afternoons. If I had a one o'clock lecture section, I could do that class, leave the university shortly after two o'clock, go home and change, load the dogs in the truck and drive to Max, North Dakota (25 miles south of Minot) and be in the field by three-thirty. If I did this in October, I'd have about two hours to hunt. Thus, I could be home again in Minot by six-thirty.

Besides the fields and sloughs around Max, other spots equally convenient existed east of town. The Velva area, for example, was only about 25 miles from my home, represented one of these. When I planned to hunt for the day, I normally drove a bit further, but not more than 100 miles, an easy drive within an hour and a half or two hours at the most. If I went for the day, I could hunt the more distant and extensive locations south of town, such as the refuge at Lake Audubon or the shores of Lake Sakakawea, both less than 100 miles distant.

Physically, the areas I hunted tended to be characterized by mixed farming, more cultivated crops and less grazing land than was the case in the south western semi-bad lands already discussed. The Minot area and its surrounding countryside lent itself to successful corn, soy beans, sun flowers and wheat cultivation, all of which served as excellent fodder for pheasants.

An important part of this landscape was the availability of water. The lands around Minot, no matter which direction one headed in, shared the common feature of cattail sloughs. These bodies of water surrounded by cattails functioned as effective cover for pheasants.

Some of the sloughs, such as the ones adjacent to Lake Sakakawea, could be extensive, extending often several hundred yards in length. The larger sloughs normally required more than one hunter to be hunted effectively. In the more common, smaller cattail bodies, the pheasants could not run ahead so easily and thus avoid flushing as in the larger sloughs. Generally, I avoided the bigger sloughs in favor of the smaller, more finite cover where the dogs could do their flushing and fetching routines more effectively.

Clio with Sherman and Diana
after a successful wheat field slough hunt

When Clio and I would make a lunchtime or early afternoon hunt to Max, for example, we would stop at a Cenex Station at the south edge of Minot for gas and a bite to eat before hunting. After getting gas, I'd go in and buy two ham and cheese sandwiches—one for me and one for my hunting partner. I'd get myself a lemonade to go with my sandwiches. Clio's water was in the truck for later.

When finished with our sandwiches, we'd head out. I'd be in a semi-euphoric mood and start singing for the dog, "Jon and Clio gonna shoot some roosters today; Jon and Clio gonna shoot some roosters today..." I don't know what the dog thought about my silly singing, but it amused me in the same way my singing to Rob had when he was little and I carried him to visit Reggie in the basement. The singing and sandwiches with Queenie set the right mood. We were about to have fun. I knew it and so did my hunting pal.

As noted, Clio possessed acute hunting skills. To start with, hunting for her always represented an adventure. She pursued the hunt all out. Her enthusiasm at times could even be life threatening, especially in the early season when the temperatures in the field were in the 60s or 70s. Several times in her first years' early seasons, Clio's intense effort precipitated the condition known to veterinarians as EIC or Exercise-Induced Collapse. When this happened, Clio's back legs would literally cease functioning.

She might try to continue to follow a scent but could only move forward with her front legs. She had to drag her back legs. This frightened me. When it happened, the dog had to be forced to stop moving, lie down and catch her breath. If we were near a slough, I would pick her up and carry her to the water and set her down in it. After a few minutes, she would cool down and recover her normal movement, but I had to watch her closely to prevent serious harm.

In her enthusiasm, however, there was always method. She pursued from a single purpose—she sought pheasant scent. In this seeking, she developed her skills naturally without having been taught.

Her most obvious natural skill lay in quartering. The dog had been trained by Scott to stay close to her master when hunting but not taught how to quarter, which involved running back and forth from left to right or right to left repeatedly in front of the hunter. By quartering, the dog covered more territory and did it more effectively than if she'd pursued a straight line out in front.

Of my several dogs, Clio mastered this technique better than the others. Quartering made the flushing process more effective. If, while quartering, Clio caught a hot scent she'd follow the scent directly. More often than not this would lead to a flush. If she were on a fresh scent, her apparent heightened interest would notify me that she was "birdie." I'd perk up and follow her more closely in anticipation of a bird taking flight.

If the bird being pursued stopped and hunkered down, Clio would halt her pursuit and point. In pointing, she would freeze and stare at the spot where she thought the bird was hiding. I loved this routine.

When Clio went on point, I would maneuver into position as close as possible to the dog. Once ready, I'd command "Get the bird, get the bird!" The dog would look at me and then do what I called her "coyote hop;" that is, propel herself with all four legs locked stiffly in a hop-like gesture onto the spot where the bird was supposed to be holding. Normally, that forced the prey to fly and provided me with an ideal shot. Some of my other dogs, most notably Sherman, managed this trick, but the real master among the gang was always Clio, my yellow Queenie.

Because of both her devotion to the job and her skills at carrying it out, Clio became my special hunter. Between 2003 and 2009, I occasionally made diary notes of my hunts. In these, I frequently commented on Clio's passionate efforts to find and flush birds and her spectacular retrieves. Here are a few Clio snippets from the diaries.

DIARY NOTES: TUESDAY, OCTOBER 21, 2003

Made a short afternoon hunt with Clio. Sparkling day, beautiful example of Indian Summer in N.D., almost no wind, blue skies, sun shining, 60-65 degree temperature. One of those days you can smell the earth, the fertility of the land. Couldn't have asked for anything better.

Headed to Makoti, 40 miles southwest of Minot to see if we could find some birds near the old fishing hole there. Remember hearing pheasants crowing last time we fished there in August. Turned out to be a great place to hunt. Five minutes after we started in the CRP (Conservation Reserve Program) field adjacent to the water, the dog put up a flock of maybe 15 birds, all Hungarian Partridges. Shot several times. Flock shot I was so startled.

Amazingly, I hit two birds. Both came down in the lake. Clio in the water almost before I knew I connected. Long swim out to make the fetch. I couldn't see the quarry on the water but she did. Brought back the first, quickly dove back into the water and fetched the second. Beautiful, colorful little birds. Were Clio's first Huns ever. First for me that season as well. Dog was amazing.

DIARY NOTES: WEDNESDAY, OCTOBER 13, 2004

Took Clio and headed for Max and Audubon. Left home at two o'clock p.m. Started hunting south of Max in the big slough off county road 6. Very windy and no wheat like last year. All the harvested fields had been planted with soybeans. In an hour of hard work, we managed to put up only one hen.

Left the Max area and drove south east to Audubon (North Dakota State Refuge on Lake Audubon). That's open from the beginning of the (regular pheasant) season. About 200 yards from the parking area, Clio got birdie.

We were hunting into the wind. Her quartering was tight and effective. Followed her into the tall grass off the trail and out came a rooster. Bang! Bird down. Clio fetched it. Continued to hunt up to the unharvested wheat (The North Dakota Game and Fish Department plants forage crops each year at Audubon for the refuge's animals and birds.) Was already four-fifteen. Hunting time getting short. On our approach, I noted birds moving into the wheat.

Shortly after we entered the wheat field, Clio put up a rooster. I shot twice, knocking it down. She went for it. When she reached the bird, it jumped up and flew away. Its flight was spasmodic; it appeared to fly into a Russian olive tree on the lake shore.

We pursued and spent several minutes looking for it in the area around the tree. No luck. Just as I was about to quit searching, Clio found the bird in the water. It had landed in the lake. She brought it to me. We started back to the truck. Had two birds but it was time to quit.

On our way out, a mere hundred yards from the vehicle, Clio got birdie again. Flushed a couple of hens. My heart stopped with each noisy flight. Then a rooster exploded from the cover no more than ten feet from me. Startled, I shot twice, missed both times. A few swear words followed. We continued heading out. When we were within 25 yards of the truck, Clio stopped and pointed. I said "Get the bird! Get the bird!" She did her hop. Out burst yet another cackling rooster! This one I nailed. Third bird! We had our limit. Fantastic hunt. Dog was absolutely spectacular. Tired and sore but superb! Gotta love that doggie!

DIARY NOTES: MONDAY, NOVEMBER 8, 2004

Clio and I alone again, went south and east of Max. Good day. Overcast, not much wind and best of all, not too cold. Proceeded to do some exploring, find some new sloughs. Walked a familiar railroad bed that I used often to access sloughs on its west side. Today wanted to see if any good sloughs existed to the east. About a half mile down the tracks, noted a small slough a hundred yards off to the east in a field of harvested sunflowers. Just what I was looking for.

We hoofed it out to the new spot and started our usual circling action, with me on the edge of the cattails and Clio in the cover. Not more than five minutes after Clio entered, she flushed a rooster. It flew out of the cattails over me and I shot. Bird down in the sunflower field. Called the dog and she fetched it. After this, we finished the rest of the slough. Nothing more came out. Checked out another smaller slough in the same field. No luck. Decided to return to the truck the way we came in.

On the way back near the truck, Clio picked up a hot scent in the tall grass on the edge of the railroad bed's west side. She followed her nose past our parked truck, over our access road and into the ditch on road's other side. From the ditch, she flushed a rooster. It flew across in front of me heading towards the big slough to the west of the railroad tracks we had just walked. I shot and it came down. The dog fetched it. She's superb—driven dog. Could I ever duplicate her? Be hard.

DIARY NOTES: WEDNESDAY, NOVEMBER 16, 2004

Hunted down near Max after my noon class. Took Clio. Beautiful day again—bright sun, a few fluffy clouds, barely any wind, quite warm for mid-November. Again, intended to hunt the old reliable sloughs west and east of the railroad tracks. About a mile from highway 83 on the dirt road into our destination, a rooster got up from the ditch next to the road and flew in front of the truck for about 15 yards before sailing off to the right.

Sitting in her usual seat in the front, Clio saw the bird. She freaked out, became almost hysterical, barking and whining. "Let me out, let me out, let me get it," she seemed to be saying. Couldn't help laughing at her hysterics. The brazen rooster flew into the next slough close to the road—a slough that had recently been partially burned over.

Both dog and I saw where it landed. I stopped the truck, reached into the back seat to get my shotgun, and grabbed some shells. Intended to exit the truck first before letting Clio out so I could load the gun and be ready to shoot. Assumed if she got out before me, she'd ruin any possible shot by flushing the bird before I was ready.

Real battle to get out of the truck before the dog. She wanted out my side. With one hand, I pushed her away so I could exit. She refused to cooperate. Scott hadn't taught her car manners! She wanted out, period.

After I had my shotgun and started to exit, she climbed onto me. Her front paws were in my lap, her body in my face. I leaned into her and pushed her away with my right arm as hard as I could. For the few seconds she was off me, I managed to get my door open and one leg out of the cab. I started to put a shell in the gun. Clio doubled her effort and forced her way past me. She jumped out and dashed into the ditch on the way to where the bird had landed.

Hustling, I tried to follow, made it to the edge of the ditch where my foot caught on something in the weeds. I tripped, fell flat on my face. Clio's rush flushed the bird. As I got up, I did see our rooster landing in a small patch of unburned cattails about 40 yards to the west. Wind out of the northwest. I managed to keep Clio close to me as we sneaked down the road and approached the bird's cover from the south. When we reached the cattails, Clio picked up the scent and flushed the bird. I shot it and she retrieved it. By the time she had the bird back to me, I had forgiven her bad manners. Smiled all the way back to the truck.

Shortly after that near disaster, we walked the cover along the railroad tracks next to the big slough and Clio put up a rooster not more than five yards from me. I shot and missed all three times. Some swearing but again I noted where the bird landed. We circled to the east and came into the slough in the general area where the bird had settled down.

Took Clio less than five minutes to get the scent and force a flush. This time I was on and the bird dropped. We continued to hunt the big slough for the next hour but to no avail. Called it a day and headed home. Both of us were tired but we'd gotten a couple of birds and had much fun. The battle with Clio getting out of the truck amuses me as I write. She's something. Always a new twist. Sure can be a devil but love her to pieces.

DIARY NOTES: MONDAY, NOVEMBER 22, 2004

Went to Audubon on its opening day. Couldn't get away until eleven-thirty. Started to hunt at one o'clock p.m. Walked east for thirty minutes with Clio on a leash trying to get as far away as possible from the parking lot and other opening-day hunters. Apparently, the boys had really shot it up in the morning. "It was like ants out there," one hunter I met in the parking area told me.

After our getaway walk, Clio and I started hunting on the edge of the lake. Shortly after starting, Clio put up a rooster in heavy saw grass/willows cover. I shot twice and hit the bird with the second shot. The rooster came down in the willows. Despite the heavy cover, Clio had no trouble fetching it.

Wind was 30 mph from the west. About fifteen minutes later, further to the east and north on the lake shore line, she put up another bird. Same story. I shot twice and hit the bird on the second time. It came down and started running. Clio saw and chased. It tried to fly but she caught it before it could get off the ground. Great retrieve. A few minutes later she went on point. She was saying, "It's here, it's here, get ready."

I did. When she did her hop, I was ready and knocked the rooster down with my first shot. Landing in the water about three feet from shore, it managed to get back to shore and start running. Clio saw it.

She had to climb down from the ledge about ten feet above the lake where we were when I shot. In five seconds, she made it to the shore and began racing after her prey. She ran about 50-60 yards before she caught up to the bird and grabbed it. Great job again. Great flush, great retrieve. Remarkable dog. Wonderful hunting companion! Three birds shot at, three birds in the bag.

Will try Audubon again on Wednesday with Sherman. Was horrific walk back. Thirty-five to forty minutes into a 40 mph wind. Still suffering from the exertion as I write. Thought I was going to have a heart attack. But great hunt, great day.

DIARY NOTES: MONDAY, NOVEMBER 24, 2008

Opening at Federal Audubon, was there early. So, it seemed, were half of N. D. rooster hunters. Birds down in numbers. Started the day missing two easy shots. Rushed them. Gun functioning well though! Finally shot one. Clio got it. She was my only dog again this day. Hunted for about an hour. Got frustrated and went back to the truck.

Talked to US Wildlife Warden in the parking lot. He suggested I hunt south and east. Stopped for breakfast at Tottten Trail, then drove to the spot he'd recommended. Hunted for about an hour with Clio putting up only one shootable bird. I missed. Gave up on the new place and went back to where I'd started.

Queenie on a frozen fetch

Only three vehicles of the original 20-plus left in parking lot. Started walking the road east as in the past. Clio was tired and hanging close. She pointed three birds off the road, two hens and a rooster. I shot the latter. Clio had no trouble fetching. Little further on, she pointed another rooster that I didn't shoot at. Too close to the lake and its thin ice. No bird worth losing my Clio on thin ice.

About an hour later we headed back to the truck. Clio was too tired to go into the heavy sloughs so we returned via the lake edge and worked down wind. Halfway to the truck she suddenly stopped and pointed. I yelled "Get it, get it." She did her hop and up came a rooster. I shot; it dropped. She found it in the cattails, a big older bird with a beautiful tail. Three birds finally. Day started poorly, ended in euphoria. Clio again magnificent. She put up every bird she scented. Pointed all day. Marvelous dog.

As noted in the previous accounts, each hunting season opener on the federal Audubon site caused considerable interest among North Dakota pheasant enthusiasts. Those who hunted included not only locals, but a good number of out-of-state people as well. Between 2003 and 2009, more often than not, one or both of my sons shared the Audubon openers with me.

For my younger son Rob, the Audubon experiences represented his pheasant baptism. There were two phases to this. On the state preserve, the Game and Fish Department staged an opening season for youth hunters at the beginning of October, one week before the regular season began. In both his 13th and 14th years, I took Rob and the dogs for the youth openers.

During the youth-week hunt, adults might accompany the youngsters but not with guns. When Rob hunted, I took Sherman and Clio along to assist him. The dogs and I would push the birds to Rob. He'd post 50 or 100 yards ahead of us. We'd work the cover back toward him. That worked nicely. Not particularly edgy or gun wise, the early season birds flushed as planned, close enough for him to get lots of shots and experience.

Rob learned the shooting skills he used at Audubon during his summer visits to my place in Florence. I based his lessons on an impressive video I'd seen on television. The instruction included four distinct stages, the first three done with a BB gun.

For stage one, I set out eight pop/beer cans on tie rods about eight to ten feet apart on the edge of my parking area in Florence. Rob and I would stand ten to fifteen yards from the semi-circle of cans and I would tell him which one to shoot at (Orange can on the far left, blue can in the center, green can on the right, etc.). He'd have to raise the BB gun and shoot in a single gesture.

I instructed him to shoot with both eyes open and aim the gun as he moved in the direction of the designated can. No hesitation, just a smooth motion to fix on the target and shoot. We practiced this for several weeks, sessions for fifteen minutes or half an hour, sometimes more than once a day.

As Rob practiced, he became more and more confident. After several weeks, he could hit most of the cans he shot at. You would know when he connected because the BB striking the can made a distinctive ping. When the pinging became regular, we progressed to stage two. That involved shooting not at stationary cans, but ones thrown into the air—cans I threw for him.

We started with big juice containers, like quart V-8 cans. When Rob could move the gun, follow the can's flight and make more shots than he missed, we moved on to stage three, the smaller dog food cans so common in my house. At the point where Rob could do to the smaller cans what he'd done to the larger ones we pressed on to stage four, shooting at clay pigeons.

I have a trap for projecting clay pigeons and Rob had his own shotgun, a 20 gauge pump gun I gave him the previous Christmas. In Florence that summer, Rob and I went out to the local trap shooting range and practiced. We did this a number of times before he had to return to his mother's place in Minot. When he left Wisconsin that summer, he had learned how to handle a gun and shoot. He was ready to hunt with a gun. Only one other condition needed to be fulfilled. He had to take the North Dakota Hunter's Safety course which he did in September 2006.

By the October opener, he was licensed to hunt. He'd been with me as a walk along on many hunts when younger, so he knew what to expect from me, the birds and our essential accompaniment, the Labs. As his older brother Nat does, Rob appears in my diary on numerous occasions. A couple of examples follow.

DIARY NOTES: MONDAY, NOVEMBER 27, 2006

Went to Audubon Federal Reserve with Rob. Cold day, bitter wind. To start, we walked for fifteen minutes to get away from other hunters. Had Clio with us. Birds seemed to be everywhere. Made my first two shots, then missed several before finally downing a third.

At first, Rob had trouble getting on the birds and making his shots. But he got a double at the bottom of his self-deprecation. Raised both our spirits. We left at ten-thirty a.m. with five birds. As we departed, Rob said, "Audubon is awesome." My kid did well, stayed with it.

DIARY NOTES: SATURDAY, OCTOBER 6 AND SUNDAY, OCTOBER 7, 2007

Pheasant hunting year started with the youth hunt at the North Dakota Audubon Reserve so had Rob as the sole gunner. Took Clio, Sherman, and Diana with us for both days. On Saturday, Rob shot five times and hit three roosters. On Sunday, he shot three times and downed three birds.

He's gained much confidence and skill. I'm proud of him. Very much enjoyed seeing him succeed. Large number of birds. Bodes well for the coming season. Six birds for the kid. No lost ones. Great retrieving by the dogs. Much fun was had by all of us, dogs and humans.

Clio's hunting career lasted almost ten years. In that period, she succeeded not only in the field but also as a homebody and member of the family. The obedience Scott Snyder instilled in her remained throughout her mature years. She became a pal to me, my children and the other canine members of our gang.

Throughout she played her alpha dog role not obnoxiously, but with confidence and aplomb. Sherman, her elder brother, had no trouble deferring to her and her younger sister Diana likewise followed her lead. Together these three dogs constituted my version of *The Three Musketeers* with Clio as d'Artagnan.

Rob and Labs after successful Audubon hunt

The end to both Clio's hunting time and her normal life began in the fall of 2011, the year of Minot's flood, an event that forced me to move 70 miles south east of Minot out to Mercer, North Dakota.

By the summer of that year, Clio had developed a serious respiratory problem. She wheezed constantly and lacked energy. The wheezing seemed to grow worse in Florence. As the young woman at the boarding kennel in Wisconsin put it, "Clio could not sneak up on any person or beast because you could hear her coming from a long way off."

When I returned to Mercer that fall, one of the first things I did was make an appointment for Clio to see her regular veterinarian, Dr.

Michelle Merwin, at the Minot Veterinary Clinic. I called on a Friday and had an appointment for the following Monday.

Dr. Merwin, a calm, competent, attractive, middle-aged brunette greeted me in the reception area that Monday morning pleasantly. "Jonathan, haven't seen you for a long time. How've you been? How're the dogs? Your puppies were some of my favorite victims. Have missed them," she said with a smile.

"Thanks. Dogs and I have missed you as well. Haven't been in to see you because of the flood. Lost my house. Had to move to Mercer," I said.

"Oh, I'm sorry to hear that. Terrible what the flood did to Minot. Where's Mercer?" she asked. "Never heard of it? You still in North Dakota?"

"Yeah, Mercer's 70 miles southeast of here. Town of about 80 people. Only business is the local bar. Beautiful area though. Real plus is the abundant pheasant population."

She laughed and said, "I see you brought Queenie with? What's her problem?"

"Serious one, I fear. She seems really sick. Having trouble breathing. Sounds awful. Had this problem most of the summer."

"Bring her in. Let's take a look," she said. We moved into one of the small examination rooms.

"Let's get her up on the table," she said. We lifted Clio onto the examination table. Dr. Merwin ran her hands over the dog. She could hear the dog's loud, forced breathing. She turned to the counter next to the table and picked up her stethoscope. Bending over, she listened intently to the breathing, moving the scope from the dog's side to its front.

After what seemed like a long minute, she stopped and took off the scope. I said, "You know what's wrong with her? Why's her breathing so difficult?"

"Not absolutely sure, but it sounds like she's suffering from laryngeal paralysis," she said.

"What's that?" I felt sick.

"Sounds like one or perhaps both of the flaps that guard the opening to her lungs are not functioning properly. Hence, the breathing's so difficult."

"What can be done to fix that?" I asked, my dread mounting.

"Only remedy I know of is a sophisticated operation that involves tying back one or both of the affected flaps."

"You do that operation?"

"No, I don't and I don't know of any other vet in North Dakota who does. Your best bet is to take the dog to the University of Minnesota Veterinary Medical Center in Minneapolis."

"That's the only option?" I said, shaking my head.

"Yeah, I'm afraid so. Sorry." Both her voice and eyes told me how serious the dog's condition was. I said good bye, took Clio and headed back to Mercer.

I followed Dr. Merwin's advice and called the U. of M. Veterinary Medical Center that afternoon and arranged for Clio to be examined. The next day, Clio and I drove to the Twin Cities where my son lives. I stayed with Nat during the process. On October 11th, the dog was examined and admitted to the hospital.

In the laryngeal examination, the vets observed the cartilage flaps (arytenoids) that opened and closed to allow air to pass to her trachea. They found "weak paradoxical movement" where the cartilage flaps only partially closed when she breathed out. This confirmed the existence of laryngeal paralysis. The next day they performed the "tie back" operation that used sutures to pull and tie back the left arytenoids, opening the air way on that side. On October 14th in the morning, a weak and passive Clio was discharged from the Medical Center. We returned to Mercer that day.

When I picked up the dog, one of the vets, a young man involved in the operation who looked to be no older than thirty, filled me in on the operation and gave me explicit instructions on how to treat her and, most importantly, how to feed and water the animal.

"Dogs with laryngeal paralysis in general," he began, "are at risk of getting foreign material into the airway and lungs. Greatest risk from this condition and surgery is aspiration pneumonia."

"What's that?" I asked.

"It's when fluids and material enter the lungs and cause inflammation and disease. Clio's larynx has been altered and she'll have to relearn how to swallow safely in this new arrangement," he said.

"You mean she's got to relearn how to eat?" I said, shaking my head.

"Basically, yes. If she ingests food or liquid into her lungs, she risks dying. You must be very careful with her."

When the conversation ended, he gave me a pamphlet describing what dangerous behavior patterns to watch for, how to exercise her, what kind of food to start her on and how to serve it. I took my Clio and set off for North Dakota. Although his words nearly traumatized me, I was determined to follow the exercising, feeding, and watering guidelines to the letter. And I tried.

For the first several days she seemed to be coming back to life. But progress was slow. Her energy level remained very low. As recommended, I tried soft food rolled into meat balls; I provided her with small, frequent waterings. I watched her closely for any coughing in particular.

The threat of aspiration pneumonia hung over my head like the proverbial sword of Damocles. Clio seemed to have good days, then ones not so good. Just when I began to think she was improving, she'd cough as if she'd ingested something she shouldn't have. When she coughed like a human who had something caught in his throat or like one with water in the lungs, I'd pick up the phone and call the vets.

Over the next six weeks I took her to see vets three times. The first visit was to a veterinary hospital in Bismarck. There she was hospitalized for several days and put on antibiotics. When I picked her up, she seemed to be somewhat better but she still looked and acted as if she were sick, moping, without her old effervescent spirit.

Once home, she'd improve for several weeks until there'd be another relapse. This time I took her to my regular vet in McClusky, the next town to the east of Mercer. Again, more antibiotics were prescribed and applied. These didn't work. The dog became more lethargic, vomited frequently and then refused to eat. I feared for her life.

The dog that used to jump and bark in an excited way when I started to prepare her food now just sniffed the offerings in an uninterested way. She wouldn't eat. The water she drank she vomited up in large brown pools. I began to panic. Back to the vets in McClusky. Getting the dog to see the doctor was a task in itself. Too weak to climb into the truck on her own, I had to pick her up and put her in the vehicle. Same problem at the vet's. I had to carry her into see the doctor.

After a very short examination, I got the straight talk. Dr. Kitto, the vet who examined her, said, "This dog has severe pneumonia. She's dying. She's miserable and suffering. Jon, she should be put down. That's the humane thing to do."

As I listened to him, I began to tear up. I muttered, "Best that we end her suffering. Go ahead. Put her down."

Dr. Kitto said, "I'm sorry, but she's had a good life. You're doing the right thing."

That was one of the hardest decisions I've ever had to make, even harder than saying goodbye to Reggie. I cry about it as I write. My poor sweet Clio never learned how to eat in a new way! After she was put down, I had her body cremated and her ashes returned to me.

All three of the staff of McClusky, North Dakota's Sheridan Animal Hospital, including Dr. Kitto, signed the condolence card they sent me after she passed. For that I am eternally grateful. Those kind souls recognized the depth of my grief. Clio's ashes will go with me in my coffin.

Defining the meaning and significance of Clio's life for me is not an easy task. Like my human children, she was special and unique. As I sit here and try to sum her up, to balance the negative and positive elements, I can honestly say the only negative elements I can conjure up were her puppyhood enthusiasms. Her incessant play and teasing did both irritate and frustrate me. But, as noted, these youthful extremes were eliminated by her training with Scott Synder. From 2003 until her tragic death, she fulfilled all that I expected of her and much more.

I've described in some detail Clio's remarkable ability as a hunter, her flushing and retrieving skills in particular, but Clio was much more than a hunter to me. She served as an inspiration as well. I admired her qualities as a cosmic being as much as I admired her skills as a dog in the field.

Clio expressed and embodied attributes that were more than canine ones—they were, in fact, universal qualities. The elements in Clio that I especially admired included her sweet temperament, confidence, self-assuredness, determination, enthusiasm, acceptance of discipline, ability to learn, and her loyalty and devotion to me and my family.

In many ways I envied her, wishing I could have expressed in my life what she so consistently manifested in hers. She thus functioned as a model for her canine family, but also as a model for her devoted master. When I cross the bridge, I'm sure Clio will be there waiting for me. And if I know her, she'll be instructing Jason how best to line up the other Labs and make sure their tails are waging appropriately to greet me in style.

Although I've been partial to Clio in so many ways in this chapter, that doesn't mean I didn't love the other Labs who lived with my Queenie, including the most prominent one, her big, brown brother Sherman, subject of my next chapter.

CHAPTER SIX

SHERMAN
(AKA SHERMIE, MY BIG BROWN HONEY BEAR)

Sherman sniffing his pal Robbie's bug jar

"He (Black Lab Izzy) always leaned against me, returning my love but revealing and explaining nothing—nothing but affection, connection, faithfulness."

— Jonathan Katz

I secured my second chocolate Labrador Retriever in the spring of 2001 at the same time Julie bought Clio. Again, I never intended to purchase a dog when I accompanied my third wife to Blackhawk Kennels, but only to help her pick one.

While Julie studied the members of Scott's two-month-old litter, I noticed two larger, older, chocolate puppies in an adjacent kennel.

The dogs sat sitting shoulder to shoulder, noses almost touching the kennel's fence, watching intently as Julie and I scrutinized the younger dogs. They appeared forlorn, or maybe jealous, at the attention the puppies were receiving. I probably read too much into their expressions but I thought they were begging, "Take me, take me!"

Succumbing to their visual pleas, I walked over to Scott, who was with Julie and said, "Tell me about the two brown puppies over there." I pointed at the chocolates.

"What'd you want to know? They're available. Make a nice addition for the yellow pup," he said, grinning.

"Didn't come down to buy another dog, but they're gorgeous."

"From the same litter. Six months old. Larger one's a male, smaller female. I'll let em out if you want. Julie's busy. Give you something to do," Scott said.

"Okay, why not?" I said.

Scott let the female out first. He had her run around a bit, made her sit for me, be petted. He threw a couple of dummies which she fetched successfully. Then I got a look at the male. Scott ran him through the same routine as the sister. The female appeared as a sweet, gentle pup, somewhat timid and hesitant, the male less so.

When he'd put the male back in the kennel, he said. "What do you think? Interested?"

"I might be. How much for the male?" I said.

He cited the price. I thought for a minute or so. The figure seemed fair, not much more than the dogs Julie was viewing. I decided then I needed another dog. The rationalization came more easily than I imagined.

Simply put, I decided in the ten minutes I watched the two brown dogs show off that Reggie needed a buddy his own size. Julie's little dogs weren't enough. The bigger puppy would be perfect for Reggie. The more confident, secure male would complement him nicely. Both of Scott's impressive dogs would have sufficed as good companions. I could easily have adopted both. However, that option would have complicated matters too much.

I knew Julie wouldn't object. With her new puppy, she'd still have more dogs than I. The neighbors concerned me more. With the two new puppies, Julie and I would have five dogs in our house. I didn't know what the neighbors would think. Hoped for the best.

I named my new dog Sherman after the Civil War Union general. Thinking back, I can't remember exactly how I came to that conclusion, but it makes sense now and probably did then as well. As a teenager, I developed an interest in Civil War history, being particularly fond of Civil War historian Bruce Catton's books including *Mr. Lincoln's Army*, *U. S. Grant and he American Military Tradition*, *Stillness at Appomattox* and *This Hallowed Ground.*

My Civil War fascination, I discovered, had a family connection as well. From my mother Hilda Fletcher Wagner, I learned how the war had affected her family. It turned out that my great grandfather, my mother's father's father, had fought for the North as a member of the Grand Army of the Republic.

During his service, he'd been wounded in combat and later received a GAR (Grand Army of the Republic) pension. His devotion to the Union cause also took the form of naming his eldest son after General George B. McClellan, the commander of the GAR. My mother's uncle George, the older brother of her father Charles, bore the full name of George B. McClellan Fletcher. So maybe there was some genetic role in my dog's name selection!

In writing this, another influence occurred to me. One of my classmates at Western Reserve Academy told me a story about his big brother Sherman. When the parents were travelling in the South with their new baby Sherman, a native lady, admiring the child, asked the baby's name. When the mother replied "Sherman," the woman questioner became upset.

She said, "Not a good name around here. In fact, it's the most hated name in the South!"

I, who attended Maine's Bowdoin College where a faculty wife,

Harriet Beecher Stow, wrote *Uncle Tom's Cabin*, found the name attractive, not hateful. As far as I could tell from my Catton readings, the general was a bright, tough, determined campaigner. Great name for a dog! I only hoped my Brownie could live up to it. Even more importantly though, the dog had no objection to the name.

The six-month-old puppy matured rapidly in my company. At maturity, he weighed just over 90 pounds. In size, he distanced himself from both Clio and Reggie. Sherman's body was not so much heavy as muscular. He was not only impressive in size, but in color as well. Sherman developed a rich, dark brown coat that matched the best of the chocolates I've ever seen before or after him. In short, Sherman had an impressive physique. To me, he seemed always a beautiful, regal animal.

Nevertheless, Sherman had a physical flaw. He had a touch of epilepsy. By touch, I mean he exhibited symptoms of a mild form of the disease. He manifested his lesser version of canine epilepsy in a fly-snapping routine, a form of epileptic fit.

When experiencing a fit, he went into a kind of trance and began snapping at imagined flies. He would point his head upward as if he were being circled by insects and he would snap at his tormentors. The fit would last for several minutes and end with him licking his feet. After five minutes or so, he became his normal self again. He experienced these fly-snapping incidents about once a week.

Shortly after I noticed this odd behavior, I took him to see a veterinarian. The vet I consulted, a friendly, efficient young man named Dr. Ron Thunshelle, who'd played soccer as a youth with my daughter Sarah, identified the fits I described.

"Jon," he said, "What you describe is not that uncommon. It's a form of mild epilepsy."

I was shocked. "So what does 'mild epilepsy' mean?"

"It's not totally debilitating. Can be harmless if it doesn't get worse. Fits become more intense, you'll need medication. But right now, from what you describe and what I see, don't be too worried," he said.

"What are the chances of it worsening, Doc?"

"Don't know for sure. Think it's fairly common that the mild condition remains so. Depends on the animal," he said.

"I'll keep my fingers crossed, hope for the best. Got big plans for him as a pheasant hunter. Hope those aren't in vain," I said.

"I'm a hunter, can relate. But I wouldn't worry too much now. Just go ahead with your plans," he said.

As I started to leave, he said, "Oh, before I forget, please don't breed the dog. Too much epilepsy as is. It's one of those diseases we can do something to limit. It's transmissible. You understand?"

"Yeah, too bad. He'd make a great stud. Makes me sad." He nodded as if he understood.

I said, "Good bye" and left. I feel that sadness even today as I write. Of all my dogs, I think Sherman would have made the best parent, not only because of his physique, but also because of his character.

Sherman's social skills derived from his personality. To begin with, he was gentle and he loved being petted. He loved human company and he got along with children and adults equally well. My younger son Robbie experienced Sherman's attention most often among my children and the boy loved the dog.

Sherman's sweet personality made him a good playmate for mischievous Clio. Another positive social capacity, Sherman's confidence contributed to his generally calm, laid-back, and cool behavior. His ability to comply or get along made him able to adjust to other dogs. That included not only the canine companions in his family, but the dogs of other hunters.

Sherman was also compliant. He followed orders normally without a fuss. His ability to "go with the flow" meant he had no problem with Clio's assertions as alpha dog. It didn't matter to him if she sat in the pickup's front seat and he was relegated to the back. During feeding sessions, he waited patiently as a second or even third recipient. The same held true in tennis ball fetching sessions. Sherman would let Clio fetch the first ball. He didn't mind holding off his fun until the second or third ball. Precedence didn't consume him.

In his patience, Sherman exhibited confidence; he seemed satisfied in being himself, a lovely trait I admired and wished I possessed to the same degree. Nevertheless, on occasion Sherman would not follow Clio but act on his own. For example, he would not let Clio take a bird he was fetching away from him. He had to bring it in himself. On occasion, that meant both dogs would be fetching the same rooster. I always found that amusing. Not a pushy, aggressive dog, Sherman nevertheless knew how to stand up for himself.

Over the course of his life, Sherman developed one idiosyncrasy that none of my other Labs would duplicate. He became our master beggar. In his begging routine, he reminded me of my former clown Boomer, who'd created that especially irritating howl-bark routine to get me out of bed. Sherman's begging was less melodramatic and more subtle. When he wanted a dog biscuit or another goodie, he'd come over, sit down in front of me and stare. The staring represented his way of telling me he had a serious request to make. After a few seconds of this, the real show began. He'd shake his head from side to side. Then he'd move his front legs back and forth, left to right, right to left. Together the movement of head and legs became a kind of dance. His eyes sparkled as he performed. The look on his face always amazed me—expectation, love, and joy mixed together. The dance would last for a few seconds, then stop. After a short pause, he started over. The dance-stop, dance-stop routine would continue until it paid off and he got his cookie. The dance cracked me up.

Although I knew he wanted a cookie or tidbit, I always felt the dance was more for me than for him. It seemed he knew it amused me and he liked that. Sherman's dance may sound a bit like Grogan's *Marly Mombo,* but there was a difference—Sherman never brought anything physical for me, such as Marly's cat poop gift. For me, the gift in Sherman's dance was more spiritual; he danced love and peace, two more sublime legacies.

During Sherman's early years, I was married to Julie. During that time, Sherman adjusted not only to her dogs but also to the physical move that I, Clio, and Reggie made to accommodate the wife. Sherman came to me when I occupied the first floor of my home. At that time Julie, her daughter, and the two little dogs lived downstairs in the basement.

Acceding to Julie's wishes, we switched living levels in the spring of 2001. My dogs and I descended to the basement, while Julie and her family moved up to the first floor. I agreed to the move to enable Julie to begin a major remodeling project on the house's upper levels. Sherman had no problem with the switch; neither did Clio or Reggie. For me, the move meant less space and light but also less hassle than if we remained above.

Although Julie and I lived on separate floors, we remained in contact without difficulty. An event that originated on one of my pheasant outings illustrated this intimacy. I can't recall the exact date but it was, I think, in mid-season (late October or early November) because I don't remember it being cold. Clio, Sherman, and I hunted that day near Makoti, North Dakota.

We had worked a good-sized slough and Sherman, who was a tiger in such cover, found a skunk. I didn't see the confrontation but I knew it the moment he emerged from the cattails—he stank of skunk. Nothing much I could do in the field to help him, so I put Sherman in the kennel in the back of the pickup and headed for home. By this incident, I knew how to deal with skunk smell. I had the necessary hydrogen peroxide at home that I lacked when, years before, Boomer had his skunk run in.

When we arrived back in Minot that evening, I put Sherman on a leash and led him into the house via the back door. We just started down the stairs to the basement when I heard a loud yell—Julie's voice.

"What the hell! Skunk smell! Get it out of here. Get it out of here."

She hadn't seen us come in and I didn't think she'd heard us either. But she certainly knew we were present.

Dressed in her working clothes, black gym pants and a grey sweat shirt, she came to the top of the stairs and said, shaking her head, "It's the dog, right?"

"No, no it's me. I was petting this little skunk bastard. Told it I was gonna take it home to meet your dogs. So it sprayed me."

"That's bullshit. It's the dog." There was a pause. "It better be."

"You're right," I said laughing to myself. "Shermie got blasted."

"So get him out of here."

"The smell's only temporary. I got the antidote."

"Yeah, right. Get him out of here, take him to the garage," she snapped.

"I can't wash him in the garage. Need the shower. Give me ten minutes. If the smell isn't gone by then, I'll take him out."

"If it isn't, both you and the dog can spend the night in the garage. I won't have that smell in this house," she said and slammed the basement door.

Shaking my head, I took Sherman directly to the shower and washed him down using a mixture of dish detergent and hydrogen peroxide. The smell disappeared and the crisis passed.

Not long after our skunk conflict, Julie launched her extensive remodeling project on the upper portion of the house. It included work on the first floor, but also renovation of the attic. The more dramatic changes affected the latter. Originally a tight, empty space between the floor beams and the rafters holding up the roof, Julie's alterations turned it into an autonomous apartment.

The changes included a new stairway from the ground level back door up to the attic. The former attic space itself she framed out into new rooms, including a living room and bedroom. To increase the living space and light, she had two dormers added to the roof.

All of these additions involved more than simple carpentry. The roof dormers required cutting significant holes in the roof and adding on new major constructs extending outward. For the newly framed areas, new plumbing and electrical wiring were installed. Julie, a skilled carpenter, worked on the framing and flooring renovations. For the plumbing and electrical work, she hired professionals.

On the main floor that I occupied previously, Julie introduced major changes as well. For example, she built a second staircase at the front of the house to access a new laundry space in the basement below.

Also on the main floor, she remodeled the two original bedrooms by opening up the exterior walls to provide more square feet for the two rooms. That required not only new work on the walls and floors, but also extension of the external roof.

After about a month had passed and the real extent of the work became apparent, I asked "Why are you doing this? Do we really need a remodeled attic?"

Julie said, "So my mother can move in. She'll be in sometime next week." Having spoken, she turned and walked away.

In the summer of 2003, Julie and her daughter did not accompany me to Florence as in the previous three years. When I asked her if she planned on coming to the summer cottage, she said, "I can't. Got too much to do here. Simple as that." Julie kept her word. She remained in Minot the entire summer to complete remodeling the house.

For my part, I went to Florence at the end of May. Nathaniel and his family, plus my daughter Johanna and younger son Robbie were all present for significant visits, so the Wagner family enjoyed a kind of reunion. I fished with my neighbors the Wieskes, enjoyed my dogs and their water antics, and continued to work on finishing the Florence cottage. In short, the summer without Julie was a busy and enjoyable one.

In mid-July, I received an evening phone call from Julie. "Jonathan," she said, "got a great business deal for you. I'm finished with the house. It looks great. But I think it's too small for all of us. I've found a much larger place not far away that's more comfortable, more attractive. Would make a better place for all of us. It's got twice the square feet of the old place, even with the finished attic. We could make a palace out of it. Old place's just too cramped."

"How about costs? If it's so much grander, it's gotta cost a lot more," I said.

"Cost's not a problem. Got people interested in the old place who'll pay our price. If they do, we can buy the new property outright. Be an even swap. Won't be inconvenient. Won't cost any more. You'll love it. Within walking distance of Minot State," she said.

To this day, I don't understand why I went along, but I did. I arrived back in Minot at the end of August and headed directly for the new place, which was, as I had been assured, close to the university. I found it easily enough, an imposing green building on University Avenue, four blocks west of the university. It was indeed significantly larger than the old place. I pulled into the parking space in front, went to the front door and knocked.

Dressed in blue jeans, a sweat shirt and brown work boots, Julie answered the door. Startled when she saw me, she pulled down the dust mask on her face and said, "What are you doing here?"

"I live here. Don't I?" I said as I entered the building and looked around.

"No, not now. It's not ready for you."

"So what am I supposed to do?" I said.

"No idea. That's up to you."

"Where do you expect me to live?" I snapped back.

"This is your space when it's ready."

"My space? I can't live in this," I replied.

"Well, that's your problem, not mine. You're home too early."

The space she described as my new digs represented the front two thirds of the building where we stood. The look about my supposed new home shocked me.

I saw a single room. In the open space's rear, Julie had piled my furniture and belongings, the possessions moved from the old house. My alleged residence had no bathroom, no toilet, no bedroom and no kitchen. Moreover, it had no yard for my dogs.

As I learned later, the building served for years as the local hardware store. The part intended as my future home constituted the area where the hardware materials had been displayed. When Julie purchased it, the building did have a finished living space located in the building's rear, which the previous proprietors occupied. Julie and her daughter had already taken up residence there.

Realizing I could not live in this place and still work at the university (or remain sane), I left and went to find a motel where I and my dogs could reside until I located another house. I found such a motel and for the next three weeks we resided there.

During that time, I went to the university during the day and looked at homes in my free time. I considered several different houses, finally selecting one, two blocks from my former place.

As soon as the deal was closed, I got a couple of colleagues to help me move my belongings from the former hardware store to the new place. Julie didn't know of my decision to purchase another home. Several months later, I filed for divorce. No objections from the third wife. The divorce became official in May 2004.

When I think back to the time when my marriage to Julie dissolved into chaos, I often wonder how I managed to survive. Trying to find a place to live, teach my classes, and look after my dog family at the same time seems today almost an impossible task. My children from Shannon all supported me. Their support was crucial, but they all lived far away. I think my ability to survive the crises owed nearly as much to my dogs as to my own efforts or the support from Nat, Johanna, and Sarah.

My Labs represented the family that supported me in person, who exhibited love and affection for me each day. Their presence enabled me to persevere, to bounce back, and to recoup my life. In this process of recovery, none of my dogs contributed more than my peace-loving, secure, calm Sherman. Of all my dogs, he showed the least stress; he took the dramatic changes in stride the most easily. For Clio and Reggie, the adjustments required living in a motel room for three weeks were more difficult.

No sweat Sherman, up close

Continuously nervous, they didn't seem to know what was going on; they couldn't relax. Sherman, on the other hand, as I recall, exhibited no signs of stress. He acted his usual self; his message seemed to be "easy does it, relax, be cool, no sweat." In his laid-back behavior and calm moods, he showed me more than his fellow dog roommates how to get through it. For that survival assistance, I am both grateful and amazed to this day.

The new home I bought, a modest two bedroom, one bath house, worked out well. It had a large unfinished basement and a substantial back yard. Over the next several years, I remodeled the basement to include a bathroom, a study, and a guest bedroom for visitors like my son Rob.

Half of the backyard I had enclosed with a chain link fence and then finished off with concrete. The fenced in area functioned as my dog run and a place for the dogs to do their business. For the next eight years, this house served as my residence in Minot. It constituted a convenient and comfortable place for me and my Labs until the disastrous flood of 2011.

Sherman with me and his fellow gang member, Diana

By the time the 2003 pheasant hunting season opened in October, I was ensconced in my new place and ready to hunt. Likewise for both Clio and Sherman. I've already discussed Clio's merits in the field, so now it's time to consider the skills of her big brother.

Sherman may not have been the equal of Clio in quartering, but his fetching and flushing skills were close to the level of his yellow dog partner. He did surpass her in one capacity though—he was stronger in hunting heavy cover, particularly the most dense cattail formations. This superiority derived from his greater size and strength, for he was the toughest of my dogs.

It also reflected his determination. Sherman persisted when the going became most difficult. At times when Clio or Diana hesitated to dive into heavy cover, Sherman never refused. I developed great admiration for this determination and his commitment to persist regardless. My hunting diaries from 2003-2009 include numerous references to Sherman the hunter.

Sherman retrieving a Sharp-tailed Grouse

DIARY NOTES: SUNDAY, OCTOBER 19, 2003

Robbie (10 years old at the time) and I started early. Went to Unruh's place (south of Golden Valley, North Dakota in the state's south west). We hunted in Unruh's west section near the barn. I dropped Rob off at the south end of a multi-rowed, immature tree wind break. I planned to loop around and position myself at the north end of the tree rows. Left Sherman with Rob, took Clio with me.

Before leaving to take up my post, I told Rob to count to three hundred. Then bring Sherman toward me, that I'd be at the other end of the little trees. I also told him to weave between the tree rows and make as much noise as possible. Sing, talk to the dog, babble. Just be heard. Told him he'd scare the pheasants and make them run toward me. Maybe I'd get a shot or two.

He did as told. I could hear his singing and his "Sherman do this, Sherman do that" as he advanced toward me. When he was about half way up the tree rows, two hens burst out of the cover heading east. Shortly thereafter, a rooster flew north right over me. Bang! One bird down.

Clio immediately fetched it. A minute later, a second rooster flew out, this time bending west. Bang! Second bird down. Again, Clio retrieved. Fantastic! Robbie did a great job. Kept Sherman close and did exactly as he was supposed to do.

DIARY NOTES: THURSDAY, OCTOBER 30, 2003

First time this week I could get away. Day not promising. Evening before we got about five inches of snow. Clogged the roads and slowed travel down. But I remembered my hunting friend Jim Miller's line about the best hunting coming after fresh snow. So I decided to see if his contention was true.

Went to Velva (20 miles south east of Minot). Roads were bad, but 4-wheel drive and patience made it easy. Left at noon and started hunting about one-thirty p.m. Dogs and I worked sloughs exclusively because that's where the birds were supposed to be, and they were. Jumped a rooster right away in the first slough but I wasn't ready. No shot. Then several hens flushed. Finally, a cock flew off to the right and I shot it. Both dogs saw it drop and both retrieved it. Clio had the head, Sherman the body!

About fifteen minutes later in our second slough, another rooster got up but it was quite far out. I shot twice. The second shot put it down. Not dead. It began to run. Called the dogs out of the cattails and we pursued into a pasture with three skittish horses. Thought the bird would try to get back to the slough. Sherman thought differently.

Circling in the pasture, he stopped suddenly before a snow drift and stared at the snow. Clio came over and joined the point. When I reached them, I said, "Get the bird, get the bird." Sherman poked his head into the drift and grabbed the bird from where it had buried itself. He had it figured out.

Returned to the slough and pushed it west. At its narrowest part, one after another hen pheasants or immature ones flushed. Finally, one with color flew. I shot it. Sherman retrieved. We had our three birds. Fantastic, easy hunt. Birds were in the cattails just as Miller had predicted. Home at four o'clock p.m.

DIARY NOTES: MONDAY, NOVEMBER 5, 2003

Left after class at about one-thirty p.m. Was very cold and windy. Bright sun, however. Went to hunt some sloughs south of Max. Snow was quite deep and the going tough. Started hunting into the wind, heading west. For the first five minutes, thought I would have to turn back because of the potential wind chill danger. However, persevered.

Walked the entire half mile of the south side of the main slough. Put up a solitary hen. On the north side heading back Clio and Sherman seemed birdie. Finally, Sherman flushed a rooster off to the left, almost behind me. I shot and down it came. Bird started to run. Both dogs raced after it. Clio got to it first, then Sherman joined in. Dual retrieve! My efforts to call Sherman off failed. Retrieve made me laugh.

We found nothing more heading back to the truck. Drove over to a smaller slough, one that had been good the year before. Very heavy cover and the snow made walking difficult. However, there were fresh pheasant tracks. We kept working the slough. Finally, Sherman put up a rooster and I shot it. Sherman's retrieve. He did a great job in the heavy cover. We quit at four-thirty, home by five-thirty. Glad we went.

DIARY NOTES: THURSDAY, DECEMBER 19, 2003

Exam week. Finished grading most exams so decided to hunt. Went to Audubon first. Saw no roosters and only a couple of hens. Abandoned Audubon, headed to Max. Hunted some likely spots but again no luck.

At about three-thirty, driving homeward, saw three roosters feeding on grain in a stubble field. When I stopped the truck, they flew into a nearby slough. Not posted so we moved over to it and started in on the cattails. On the first sweep the dogs put up one rooster. I shot it; Clio fetched. Coming back, Sherman pointed. I yelled, "Get the bird, get the bird."

He moved in and flushed a rooster. I missed the first shot but connected on the second. It dropped and started running immediately.

Feathers near the spot where it dropped. I followed the tracks into a clump of cattails. No tracks that I could see coming out the other side. I called dogs and said my usual "Get the bird, get the bird."

Clio came over and sniffed. Not interested. Same for Sherman. I believed the bird was hiding in the snow or beneath the bent over cattails in front of us. Dug into the snow with my foot to show Clio where the bird was. She wasn't impressed. Ditto for Sherman. He began circling and working a few yards off to the south. I spent the next several minutes holding to my certain spot, trying to get the dogs to see the light.

Irritated, finally gave up. Walked the 10 yards over toward Sherman. Still believed the bird had to be where I originally thought it was. As I approached, Sherman pointed. I moved in next him and repeated "Get the bird, get the bird." He punched his snout into the snow beneath the cattails he'd been pointing and grabbed the rooster. Sherman's day. Humbling experience for me! Wonderful dog.

DIARY NOTES: MONDAY, NOVEMBER 19, 2007

Had a couple of hours after my doctor's appointment so decided to hunt. Headed to Audubon. Had all three dogs. Hoped there'd be fewer hunters than after the opener (on November 12th). Arrived at three-thirty so didn't have much time. Dogs put up a bird in the slough on the way to the grain field, I shot and missed.

Winds were strong. Ten minutes after starting on the field next to the grain dogs put up another rooster. One shot. Bird dropped. Sherman fetched it. After flushing several hens, Sherman pointed a bird on the lake shore. He jumped; it flushed; I shot it. Bird number two.

Nothing more so we started back to the truck. By then it was almost quitting time. At four-thirty in the saw grass ten yards from our vehicle, Sherman pointed again. Bird up, bird down. Number three. Great day to be out. Great day for all the dogs but especially for Shermie. He held his points. I gave the command to go and he flushed the birds. Magnificent job!

Sherman with a Limit on a boulder

Some pheasant hunts in North Dakota did not go as smoothly as those just described. Pheasant hunting had its risks, as well as its obvious benefits. Sherman and his partner Clio experienced with me the most trying and dangerous hunt of my entire life on December 1st, 2005.

On that day, we travelled to hunt the Federal Reserve at Audubon, which had been especially productive that year. We left Minot at one-thirty so the hunt was to be a short afternoon one. I figured we could get in about two hours of hunting before the closing at four-thirty.

Shortly after we left town, it became obvious that this outing might be problematic. Outside the city, the weather was worse than in town with strong winds and blowing snow. Looking back, I admit we shouldn't have risked hunting. The old cliché about hindsight was correct.

We arrived at the reserve about two-thirty p.m. No other hunters were present. That should have told me something, but didn't. Sherman, Clio and I hunted the sloughs close to the parking area for the first half hour with no success. I expected the birds to be holding tight and they were.

The wind was blowing at 30 mph at least and it contained snow. We walked a good deal east into the area of the refuge that contained the best large sloughs. There we found the birds. I made my first three shots. Two of those birds had been pointed, one by Sherman, the other by Clio. By three-thirty we had our limit and started back to the truck.

That's when the trouble began. We had walked not only eastward, but also in a southerly direction to reach the sloughs with the birds. When we started back, the weather seemed to have worsened with stronger winds and more snow. Furthermore, it had begun to get dark.

About this time, I realized I wasn't sure of the truck's location. The landscape at Audubon is flat, but only partially so. Much of it is rolling. From some portions of the refuge, the adjacent lake is not visible. That was our situation. As I struggled with deciding which direction to take to reach the truck, I realized I wasn't sure. Maybe I couldn't locate the truck. Darkness had descended upon us.

Thinking about the risk involved in getting lost almost caused me to panic. I knew I had little time left before total darkness and understood then that getting lost would be a disaster, truly life threatening since the temperature had dropped well below zero. Serious risk from wind chill existed. In short, the sub-zero temperature plus the wind made freezing to death a real possibility.

I knew the nearest town to the refuge was Cole Harbor three miles to the south. It was possible to see the distant lights of Cole Harbor from where we were in the refuge. Thus, we set out to go there to seek help.

We spent the next hour walking south into the wind toward the town. The trek into the punching wind was not easy. The dogs kept up well. Reaching the edge of Cole Harbor, we looked for an inhabited house. The first several houses had no one at home. My concern deepened. I was exhausted, shaking from the cold and terrified. Finally, we found a small white bungalow with lights on. I went to the door and knocked. A blond young man dressed in blue jeans and a red tee-shirt opened the door.

I said to him, "Please help us. Need to get in out of the cold."

Looking shocked and concerned, he responded without hesitation. "Come in, come in. What happened?"

I said, "I've got two dogs with me, can they come in too?"

"Of course, of course. What happened?"

Once inside, I explained, "We were hunting the Reserve. Got turned around. Wasn't sure where my truck was. Getting dark fast. Didn't want to risk trying to find the truck. Decided to come over here."

"Probably for the best," he said.

Still shaking from the cold, I said, "Didn't realize how far it was."

"Yeah, it's a long way, especially on a night this cold. Dangerous to be out tonight."

"I know now. Could you give us a ride over to my truck? I need to get home."

"Don't have a vehicle right now, wife's got it. But I'll call my father-in-law who does. You sit down and warm up. I'll put my dog in the kitchen so your dogs are okay where they're at."

"Thanks. I need to sit down. Nerves are shot."

"Go ahead. Where you from?"

"Minot," I said.

"Long way away on a night like tonight."

"Sure is," I said.

"You're okay now, relax." He went into the kitchen and made his call. A couple of minutes later he returned.

"Got you a ride. It'll be here in a few minutes. Just take it easy."

"Thanks. You don't know how much I appreciate your help."

"I can imagine. Want some coffee?"

"Yeah, that'd be great."

Ten minutes later a red four-door Ford pickup pulled into driveway. My host said, "That's my father-in-law. Go ahead on out. He's expecting you."

I thanked my host again and called the dogs. They followed me to the truck. When we reached it, the driver, a white-haired man with glasses, smiled and signaled from the driver's seat for me to open the truck's back door. I did.

Speaking over his grandson, who sat next to him, the driver said, "Get in the back seat with the dogs. You'll all fit."

Once we were settled in, he said, "Okay, where's your truck?"

"At the first parking area when you come in from highway 83. I'd guess about two miles into the reserve," I said.

"I know the place. Hold on. We'll be there in no time."

As we got under way, the elderly fellow said, "I'm Fred. My partner here is my grandson, Georgie."

The boy, who looked to be about seven or eight, had on a heavy blue parka with only his face showing. When his grandpa introduced him, he turned toward the back seat so he could see us and said, "Hi, you got nice doggies. What's their names?

I said, "The yellow one's Clio, chocolate's Shermie."

He looked at the dogs and then said to me, "How come you went hunting when it's so cold?"

I said, "I guess because I'm not too smart."

"That was dumb, wasn't it?" he said.

"Yeah for sure, but your Dad saved us," I said.

"Good, my Dad's nice," Georgie said.

"Okay, that's enough Georgie. Let our guests relax," Grandpa-driver said.

"So is your Grandpa, Georgie," I added.

"Yeah, he is," Georgie said.

Five minutes later we were at my truck. I put the dogs in my vehicle, started the motor, got out and went over to our rescuer and said, "I don't know how to thank you for this. We're most grateful. Can't tell you how much."

He said, "Not a problem, glad to help. Now you drive straight out to the highway. I'll follow to see you get off alright. Okay?"

I said, "I will. And thanks again, the both of you."

He and his grandson followed us out to the main highway leading to Minot. Only when I was well underway heading north did he turn south to return to Cole Harbor. Forty-five minutes later, Sherman, Clio, and I were home safe. Our nightmare was over.

That experience, the worst one I'd ever had as a hunter, was truly frightening. The snow, the wind and the wind chill combined would have killed us, I am certain, if we got lost trying to find our truck. I thank God for getting out safely.

The next weekend when Rob came to visit, we bought two Christmas baskets of fruit and candy, drove down to Cole Harbor and delivered the first basket to the young man who brought us in out of the cold and the second to the elderly fellow who had ferried us to our vehicle and made sure we were safely on our way home. I'll never forget those good Samaritans and the help they rendered that cold, miserable day.

When Clio and Sherman were in their prime during the period from 2003 to 2010, I estimate we harvested at least 50 roosters a season and some years more. We had a lot of pheasant dinners at the Wagner household.

Although denser than chicken, pheasant is just as tasty and versatile as a main dish. I've cooked pheasant in many different ways—baked, broiled, in stews and soups, on the grill outside, and inside on top of the stove. One of my favorite ways to cook and serve pheasant is as chili. Over the years all my children and many guests have experienced my pheasant chili and found it tasty. For that reason, I include here the chili recipe I've employed for the past decade.

PHEASANT CHILI (PREPARATION TIME 1-1/2 HOURS)

Ingredients

- 4-5 pheasant breasts
- Salt

- Pepper
- Chili Powder
- Garlic Powder
- 24 oz. Tomato Sauce
- 24 oz. Stewed Tomatoes
- 1 Large Onion
- Green Pepper
- 1 8 oz. package Frozen Corn
- 2 15 oz. cans Kidney Beans
- 2 15 oz. cans Black Beans
- 2 15 oz. cans Chili Beans
- 1-2 tablespoons Sugar
- 1 tablespoon Red Pepper Flakes
- 3 tablespoons Cooking Oil

Wash and clean 4-5 pheasant breasts, then cut them into grinder size pieces. Remove any shot that may be in the meat. Cut off and discard the discolored or black portions of the breasts.

In a meat grinder, grind up the pheasant pieces. In a large cooking pot, place 3 tablespoons of cooking oil. When the oil becomes hot, put the ground pheasant in the pot and cook until the meat turns light brown.

Salt and pepper the meat as it cooks. Dice the onion and add to the cooking meat. When the pheasant is brown and the onions translucent, add the beans, corn, tomato sauce and stewed tomatoes.

Now comes the seasoning and this is personal. It will differ among cooks. I like my chili hot so I tend to be generous with the seasoning.

- 2 tablespoons Chili Powder
- 1 tablespoon Garlic Powder
- 1 tablespoon Tabasco Sauce
- 1 tablespoon Red Pepper Flakes
- 1-2 tablespoons Sugar

After combining all the ingredients, I cook the mixture for fifteen minutes and taste. At this point, I adjust the chili's spiciness by adding more Red Pepper flakes or Tabasco Sauce. I usually include additional sugar to reduce the acidic level. All of this is personal and you will have to experiment to find the right taste for you. If you like more garlic, by all means add more.

Once the taste seems appropriate, I'll cook the chili for thirty to forty-five minutes at a burner temperature between low and medium low, stirring occasionally. Then the chili is ready for consumption.

The batch as described is substantial, too much in my household to be finished off at one sitting, so I normally freeze any leftovers. Freezing works well. Often, I will freeze five to ten plastic dishes for fast lunches or quick suppers. After making chili many times over the years, I still can't tell the difference between the frozen and non-frozen end product. Freezing allows me to dine on my favorite game bird long after the pheasant season has past.

Finally, besides being tasty, this is a healthy meal. All those vegetables, virtually fat-free meat and so little cooking oil makes it ideal dieter's fare. Add a nice salad to accompany it and Weight Watchers would salute you.

In Sherman's last years of hunting, specifically 2010 and 2011, I had to watch him closely. His hearing had declined so the whistle that worked for years to guide him was less effective. In that time, I tried to avoid hunting large fields or sloughs for fear of him becoming disoriented and perhaps lost.

His strength and endurance gradually declined as well. He tired more easily, even in cool weather. I hunted him for short periods in 2011 when I had to leave Clio at home. Two months after I put Clio down, I decided to do the same to Shermie.

My sweet, big brown dog did not suffer from respiratory difficulties as Clio had. What ultimately did Sherman in was the intensification of his epilepsy. As noted, his epileptic fits involved snapping at imagined insects and leg licking. The latter became the more telling in the end. Sherman licked his feet for long periods and at different times of both night and day. He licked and licked.

He had trouble sleeping; he seemed unable to find a comfortable place to lie down. Whenever he did settle down, he would do the licking routine. Finally, I decided the discomfort and torment should end. In June 2012, I took him to my veterinary in McClusky and had him put to sleep. As with my other Labs I'd put down, I cried going to and coming from the animal hospital. Again, I could not bear to see my precious friend die. I left before the fatal, final injection.

To my survey question about which of the Labs my children favored the most, Sherman received the most votes, three of four to be exact. Here are some appreciative words from Rob.

> "Papa...My favorite Lab was Sherman. I loved that gentle giant. He was such a teddy bear. I loved those nasty cold hunting days when all the birds were in the heavy cattails, because Sherman really got to shine. He would be the only dog big and strong enough to handle that brush. I liked to see him be the star for a day or two every now and then.
>
> I also think I became closest to Sherman because he would sleep in my room in Wisconsin (during Rob's summer visits). When I was a little uneasy about sleeping in the woods out there, I would just listen to his slow, deep breathing. I found it calming.
>
> I could reach down into the dark and pet him and he would always return with a couple of thumps of his thick brown tail on the hard wood floor. Those times that I petted him in the dark were some of the only times when he wouldn't come back looking to get more petting. I felt like he somehow understood that pats on his back weren't for him this time, but for me."

Rob's sister Sarah had these thoughts for Sherman.

"Shermo was my favorite. I have two very distinct memories of Sherman: his utter joy at launching himself into the air, whether to land in a pile of snow or, more preferably, in the river. I always thought Sherman should have entered one of those dog jumping contests you see on sports channels. The other memory is of his love for snuggling.

Mind you, Sherman was huge...85 or 90 lbs. He was a leaner—he'd sit his butt down next to you and just ooze into your legs. Or, when he was greeting you, he might do what JoJo coined, "the juggle," that is, his jump and snuggle. That meant he'd jump up on you—very, very gently—almost wrap his two front legs around and again, sort of slid down. It was adorable!"

Why was Sherman so popular among my children? I think the answer lies in his love for them, but also in his expressing, as Sarah noted, that devotion gently. As his "juggle" act illustrates, he enjoyed being affectionate, but his love was never rough nor rambunctious. The picture of Sherman in Robbie's lap sniffing the boy's insect-collection jar beautifully describes that gentleness, the softness of the dog's affection.

To borrow a phrase from author Jonathan Katz, Sherman was indeed "relentlessly affectionate, a happiness generator" but he always expressed that love and joy gently. Laid-back, Sherman bestowed his love in a cool fashion, as a big, beautiful, peaceful dog. In doing so, he embodied for me the ideal of a canine "Sweet Spirit."

Besides his gentleness, Sherman had other virtues and positive attributes as well. He was almost as easy to control as Reggie. He certainly was the dog family member least likely to overreact. When I think of Sherman, I recall the quote from Richard Wolters that a Lab should be more than a house pet or hunting companion. A Lab should also be a good citizen.

Jason at the island watching me run

Jason at the island chasing ducks away

Crazy Boomer restrained by his buddy Nat

Boomer fetching at the island

Reggie at the welcome sign in Florence

Puppy Reggie in Nat's dorm room at Carleton

Three Musketeers with Sherman in the middle

Sherman sniffing Rob's insect jar

Clio with Dad and brother Rob after a successful hunt

Clio asleep amongst my antiques

Jonathan Wagner

Concerned Diana fenced in

Auntie Diana and niece Toula after a successful hunt

Segen on the deck in Florence with Sarah

Toula saying hi to Dad with her eyes

Daughter Sarah's Saint Roy

Daughter Johanna's angel Gus and his dependent house-mate

Sherman played all those roles and did so with success. He wasn't as good a swimmer as Jason; he wasn't as good a hunter as Clio; he didn't make me laugh the way Boomer did; he wasn't as devoted to me as Reggie. Nevertheless, Sherman was a good swimmer, a good hunter, and most of all, a good companion and good citizen.

Sherman knew best how to fulfill the obligation of fitting into both his human family and his canine group. He never objected to sharing the truck's back seat with Diana so Clio might have the front. Finally, I think Sherman was physically the most beautiful of all my Labs. Even more importantly, he was a marvel to have as company.

When I think of the Sherman legacy, I almost naturally think of the immediate aftermath of my third marriage's end. During that intense time of strain and uncertainty, Sherman, the master of relaxing and coping with stress, taught me how to avoid being hysterical—to be calm, to believe that things would work out.

To cope adequately with my despair, I needed to have patience, acceptance, and the belief that adversity could be overcome. Sherman's behavior provided the necessary lessons; his example helped me learn enough of them to survive. My recovery benefited not only him but also his canine siblings. For those gifts, I remain most grateful.

If the legacy of James Herriot's Tricki Woo were alive, one might imagine the following scenario among my dogs. Sherman would contact Clio and Reggie and suggest they send a birthday card with notes of appreciation to Robbie on his tenth birthday. They would all agree that it would be a great idea. They would entrust Sherman to carry out the deed, which he does with great pleasure.

It didn't happen of course, but if it had, Sherman would have been the logical choice to deliver the card and greeting. He was, after all, little Rob's favorite. All my children loved the big brown honey bear because he always seemed to return their love with interest. We all miss him to this day. I trust he will be present with his pals Reggie and Clio to greet me when I show up at the bridge. In doing so, I think he might even try to embrace me with one of his wonderful "juggles."

CHAPTER SEVEN

DIANA (AKA DIDI)

(GODDESS OF THE HUNT)

Diana with her Dad

"I have found that when you are deeply troubled, there are things you get from the silent devoted companionship of a dog that you can get from no other source."

— Doris Day

In the spring of 2005, two years after Reggie departed, I decided I needed another black Lab to complement my yellow-Clio and brown-Sherman dog family. I called Scott to find out if he had any available puppies. I got lucky.

He said he had a litter ready to be weaned and adopted which included several black puppies. That weekend, I travelled to Jamestown to view the litter, one spawned by Tessa, a litter mate of my Clio. When I arrived at Scott's place, I had the same experience as in the past— enjoyment playing with the puppies and the usual difficulty in making a final choice. After at least an hour of witnessing the antics of a throng of little dogs, I chose a bright, curious, confident-looking black female. I paid Scott and took my puppy back to Minot. In the truck on the way home, I named the new family member Diana, after the Classical Goddess of the Hunt. It would be several years before my new black Lab would live up to her name but in the end, she surely did.

Diana represented not only my second chance with a black Lab, but also my fourth acquisition of a Labrador at the two-month-old puppy stage. In the past, I followed the Wolters house breaking routine of keeping the puppy tethered in the basement to a place designated for the dog's first few months.

With my new black puppy, I used instead a small kennel as the place for the dog to sleep and stay in my absence. Her initial kennel conformed to the size for small dogs and cats. Borrowed from my hunting pal Jim Miller, I kept it in the kitchen. Diana's daily routine included the majority of the day and night in her kennel, but she would have numerous chances outside of it to play, eat, and go potty. Her breaks were nevertheless relatively short. House rambling would occur only after she matured enough to know when and where to do her business. Once she learned that, she'd be allowed to roam freely about the house.

This system worked well. She never urinated or pooped in the kennel. If she did, the theory had it, then she would have to sleep in her own waste and dogs didn't like doing so. Once she outgrew the first kennel, I put her in a larger one. With this system, the only waste from

Diana I had to deal with appeared in the dog run which she shared with Clio and Sherman.

Diana grew rapidly, becoming a bit larger than Clio, but not as big as Sherman. She had a typical dense Lab coat. Her head was smaller and more pointed than most Labs, but that did not detract from her general appearance.

In fact, of all my Labs, I think she used her head most effectively. She had the most intense, telling way of looking at me. If Boomer had his clown look and Sherman his dance glare, Diana employed a yearning, soft, pensive look that I believed conveyed her special fondness for me. I called it her "shadow" stare.

Diana at the grill watching me cook

When Diana reached eight months and had become house broken, she was allowed out of the kitchen into the rest of the house. From her first opportunities beyond the kennel, she liked to lie at my feet, often even on them. As a mature dog, she maintained this puppy-time habit. Jon Katz, the well-known dog author, had such a Lab. He labeled it his stealth dog—"I have a shadow, a pal and companion, a stealth dog who appears and disappears, but remains within a few feet of me... always there," (Katz, Izzy, and Lenore, p. 16).

I couldn't describe Diana's need for proximity any better. She loved to ride beside me in the car, stretch out next to me as I watched television, follow me about the house, and lie under the dining room table as I ate. The same held true when I sat in my study at the computer. I had to shut the bathroom door on her to get privacy if I wanted to defecate in peace!

I found her need for proximity both amusing and endearing. Neither Clio nor Sherman, with whom Diana spent many years together, ever exhibited this physical bonding with me that my beautiful black Goddess of the Hunt did.

If Diana's physical characteristics weren't exceptional, her social ones were. Like Reggie, she was a very sociable dog that got along with her housemates, and other dogs as well. She deferred to Clio, in particular, right up to Clio's death. Following the alpha dog seemed to come naturally.

In Clio's last years, Diana hunted with her yellow sister and if Diana found a downed bird, she would stand over it until Clio came to make the retrieve. Such deference and respect for one's elders seemed to me almost biblical.

The only time I can think of when Diana exhibited hostility or aggression occurred on a hunting trip with Nat, when his chocolate Lab, Grady, confronted her with his hair up and a ready-to-go-at-it attitude. Grady's an interesting beast, and among other things, one of the friendliest Labs I've encountered. Nat's younger daughter, Clare, loves Grady. Grady reciprocates by letting her dress him up in human clothes and play house with him. When she takes a bath, Grady lies next to the tub, apparently there to make sure she washes properly. At the same time, Grady can be somewhat socially stunted, particularly around female dogs. His pushy, in-your-face attitude in that context is mostly braggadocio, but it does illicit strong reactions sometimes from other dogs. For females, he attempts to impress them by peeing on them.

A couple of times he tried this on Clio. He didn't succeed, but nearly did. The one time he looked as if he might get his wish. I yelled at him, "Get away, get away." Grady didn't listen of course, so I had to go over and push him away with my foot.

Elder son, Nat, embracing his two Labs

I told Nat, "If Grady pees on one of my females, I'll kick his butt all the way to Canada."

Nat said, "Grady wasn't trying to pee on her. Just marking his spot."

"No, no," I said, "he tried to pee on Clio. By God, if he succeeds, he's gonna have a real sore rear end. That's a promise."

Nat laughed, "You're exaggerating, Dad."

I shook my head. "Just keep an eye on your marker," I said and left it at that.

Later that day, when Grady tried out his peeing act on Diana, she stared at him, showed some teeth and growled a deep one as if to say, "You do that again, I won't kick your butt to Canada like my Dad says, but I'll tear your God-damned head off." After that, Grady left her alone. That day my respect for Diana rose considerably. I laugh now when I think about that sweet tête-à-tête.

Besides her social skills, Diana possessed serious athletic ability, making her perhaps the most athletic dog I've ever owned. Even as an elderly lady, she was quick and fast of foot. Diana manifested her athleticism in several ways, the most dramatic being her tennis ball retrieves.

At the summer cottage in Wisconsin, she competed with both Clio and Sherman for years. When I threw a single ball into the water and the three dogs went for it, inevitably Diana reached the missile first. Her body, sleeker than either Sherman's or Clio's, slid through the water with greater ease.

On land, she excelled as well. It didn't matter what the retrieving exercise, dummies or balls, Diana could out-pace the others in reaching the thrown object first.

Always for Diana, ball retrieving brought joy. In Wisconsin I had a neighbor Dave who lived down the road and had a chocolate Lab. His dog, Rosco, loved to retrieve as well. Dave played the game with his pal every day more than once.

He had an unlimited supply of used tennis balls given him by his tennis coach brother. So every time Dave went out on his ATV, to visit neighbors or just to run the dog, he took multiple tennis balls with him. Normally, he stopped several times during any ride to throw balls. Rosco loved the routine. Fortunately for my dogs, Dave's largess created a spat of tennis balls in the woods that Rosco missed or couldn't find.

The existence in the woods of numerous tennis balls inspired Diana. Whenever I walked her or took her for an ATV run, she turned the excursion into a tennis ball hunting trip. As we moved down the road beyond my drive, she was on the lookout for something Rosco had missed.

Once she found a ball, it belonged to her. She wouldn't share it with the other dogs—she most emphatically wouldn't let the other dogs take it from her. Clio always tried but in this instance, Diana refused to oblige her alpha gang mate. It amused me to watch her evade Clio's efforts to snatch her prize.

Diana and her tennis ball antics always remained the same. Our walks and rides became not just exercise sessions, but serious fun-time periods and her playfulness, her *joie de vivre*, became contagious. The other dogs joined in seeking to find new balls before Diana did. All this made our exercise outings enjoyable for both me and my canine companions. It paralleled the pleasure we all shared in the field chasing pheasants.

If, in her love of play, Diana was not unique among her cohorts, her inclination to express herself in sound was. Of all the dogs I have owned, Diana stood out as the most vocal. To begin with, she was a barker.

She barked when people came to the door, when we passed a pheasant at the side of the road; she barked at the people who parked next to me when I went grocery shopping. Some of the sounds she made I had never heard from a dog before. The best example of these (or worst might be a better word) occurred when I was at home about to go hunting or in the truck driving to a hunting place.

My dogs know when I intend to hunt. All I have to do is put on hunting pants or boots and they know what's coming. All of them, from Jason to Diana, got excited when they sensed an impending hunt. Only Diana, however, made serious noise to complement her excitement.

When we entered the truck to start the day's outing, she would make a variety of noises expressing her excitement. Essentially, she whined—not occasionally, but steadily. She could fill a vehicle with her noise and it could be abrasive and irritating. I'm pretty tolerant and sometimes she was better than others. But there were times when it became so annoying, I would stop the truck, take her out of the cab and put her in the back where I couldn't hear her.

Just how irritating her incessant whining could be Nat expressed cogently on a trip we made several years ago. We had just started out and Diana's excitement accelerated to the point of whining, crying and shaking at the same time. I tried to quiet her down but to no avail. After about ten minutes of her excessive excitement, my son, a pretty laid-back guy and not one prone to use profanity, couldn't stand it any longer. In a loud, angry voice, he shouted, "God, damn it! Shut up!" I stopped the truck and put Diana in the back.

Her performance that day for Nat didn't compare to what she did for me on a number of occasions as a two-year old or younger. On some of my hunts to Audubon in her early years, I left her at home in the kennel and took only Clio or Clio and Sherman. She hated that and emphatically voiced her discontent. In expressing her disapproval, she didn't whine or yip. She didn't ululate, howl, or yowl. She didn't bark. She screamed, squealed, and shrieked. Her protest didn't stem from her chest, deep down—it issued from her head. The sound was truly God-awful and uniquely horrible: pain, anger, disappointment, grief, hysterical protestation, all lumped together. She sounded as if I had cut off her ears or tail. Her cries of pain were not only ungodly but depressing. My sweet black dog knew how to convey her disappointment, her awareness of betrayal, her consciousness of abusive neglect.

I've heard wounded rabbits scream when Satchel caught up to them; I heard pigs squeal when being slaughtered, but never anything like Diana's shrieking at being left behind in her kennel while I took the other dogs off to hunt. Her protesting was meant to cut to my heart and it did. But it wasn't enough.

I wouldn't go back on my decision to hunt with the other dogs for three hours. I knew Diana's deliberate exaggerations; I knew she wouldn't die; I knew she'd live to hunt again with us. I just hoped the neighbors or any passing animal rights activist hadn't heard what I had. If they had, I believed a call to the police or the humane society would have been forthcoming. Thus, in leaving I made my disappearance as swiftly as possible, hoping her sounds remained with me and no one else.

Diana may have had some slow or low times in her early hunting career, but by the time she was two-years-old, she'd received a proper education and some practical experience. As far as training goes, I sent her to Scott as I did with both Clio and Sherman. Much more tractable than Clio, Diana didn't require force breaking. Under Scott's tutelage, Diana learned basic obedience and retrieving skills and returned to me ready to hunt.

During the 2006 pheasant hunting season, I included her in most of my outings. The diary I kept over the years 2005 to 2009 has a number of entries beginning in 2006 that describe Diana's hunting enthusiasm and skill. A few representative comments follow.

DIARY NOTES: TUESDAY, DECEMBER 19, 2006

Hunted with Leo Brunner and Jim Miller's son-in law, Scott, an air force officer and dedicated hunter. Had only Diana. Wanted to give the other dogs a day off. We started at Garrison. No luck for me or Leo, but Scott got a rooster. Then went to Wolfe Creek. Same story, except this time Scott was shut out as well.

Finally, went to Mallard Island (in the Missouri River). Got there over the ice after a long walk. We split up with each hunting a different section of the island. Both partners had dogs so that made sense. Diana worked hard and stayed close. Finally, she got birdie.

Once she did, I had to run after her to make sure I'd be close enough for a shot if she forced a flush. She did. I was ready and shot, knocking the bird down. Bird started running. Dog after it. Just as she was about to grab it, the bird took flight. But only for a few yards. Diana tried again, same results.

On the third try, Diana leaped as the bird took off and snatched it in mid-air. Fantastic, acrobatic move! She brought the bird to me, didn't want to part with it at first but finally did. She was awesome in her running and jumping. Got to use her vaunted athletic ability to get that bird! Wonderful! She's getting the idea. Made a fuss over her after the flush and retrieve.

DIARY NOTES: SATURDAY, OCTOBER 13, 2007

Went to Max. Afternoon hunt. Splendid day, 60 degrees, sun shining, cloudless sky. Took Diana, let the other dogs have a day off. Hunted the old faithful slough adjacent to the railroad tracks. Dog put up half a dozen fledglings in the first 100 yards. No color, no shots. Another 50 yards and up went a rooster. Made a good shot. Diana fetched it nicely.

Thirty minutes later Diana went into the slough chasing a rooster that had flushed initially too far out in front of me to shoot. Took her five minutes to force the bird to fly. I shot it over the water. Dog swam out and brought it back. Then on the way back to the truck, she got birdie again, had a runner. I sped up. It flushed. Bang. Bird number three. That was our limit. Great hunt, dog worked exceptionally well. Made me smile. Home by five-thirty. Younger dog almost as good as her elders!

Diana with the October 13th Limit

DIARY NOTES: THURSDAY, OCTOBER 18, 2007

Got out of class at three o'clock. A few light, puffy clouds, sparkling blue sky, 60-degree temperature. Too beautiful a day not to hunt. Took Diana. Went to Logan (10 miles south of Minot) to see if birds were there as in the past. Had only an hour to hunt before closing time.

Diana put up four roosters in the time we hunted. I shot two, missed the others. Very poor shooting, think I rushed my shots. Didi seems to love to hunt as much as Clio and Sherman. Looking forward to using all three dogs when Rob will be with me this coming weekend. Today's trip worth it.

Diary Notes: Saturday, December 15, and Sunday, December 16, 2007

Went to New England (200 miles west of Minot) with Rob and Erick Klein (former student), stayed overnight in Dickenson. Incredible number of pheasants, never seen anything like it. Reminded me of the stories I'd read about South Dakota pheasant hunting. Almost too many birds. Problem for both Rob and me—which bird to shoot when four or five would flush at the same time.

Hunted sloughs that contained hundreds of birds. Rob shot three birds on Saturday and two on Sunday. He missed a bunch on Sunday and got down on himself but at the end of the day, he made two good shots that lifted his spirits. I shot poorly as well, missed too many easy ones. Shot one bird that the dogs could not find. Think it was because of too much pheasant scent in the cover. Very frustrating. I did manage to hit my first bird on Saturday and last one on Sunday however.

Best show of the weekend was Clio and Diana chasing down a wounded rooster. The bird was about 75 yards out when it dropped. Started running hard. Diana got to it first but overran it. Bird turned to the left. Clio overran it as well. Diana reversed and grabbed it. Clio piled into her and took the bird away. Clio brought it back. Great retrieve for both dogs. Fun to watch.

Beautiful weather both days. Also spectacular scenery, with a blue butte in the background for much of the hunt. Young Erick did a great job of lining up places for us to hunt. Between Rob and me we returned with ten birds—five from Saturday, five from Sunday. Doesn't get any better than this. Dogs hunted well, had fun. Magnificent hunt, great company, dogs and humans both.

During the 2012 pheasant season after both Clio and Sherman had departed, I had only Diana as my hunting companion. Although she had played second and third fiddle when the other two dogs were living, during that season she came of age. By then I had stopped my diary keeping, but I did occasionally take some notes after special days. The hunt on November 17th, 2012 stands out as one of these.

She showed she'd almost become the equal of her departed inspiration Clio.

On that Saturday, Diana and I hunted with my long-time fishing and hunting friends Jim Miller, Leo Brunner, and Gary Hiltner. Jim set up the hunt with a Thursday night call to me.

"Wagner," he said, "it's Miller."

"Hey, Jim, haven't heard from you for a while. What's up?"

"Calling about a hunting trip for this weekend. Hiltner, Brunner and I are planning to try a place down near Audubon. You interested in joining us?"

"Yeah, I would be. Where's the place?" I said.

"Private land, east of the state reserve. Owned by a neighbor of Hiltner's," he said.

"How close to Audubon?" I said.

"About five miles or so. Supposed to be a huge area with lots of birds unless Hiltner is lying. You never know with Hiltner," he said.

I laughed. "Love that area, lots of birds on the refuge this fall. Bet it's true what Gary says."

"So you're up for it?" Miller said.

"You bet. When and where do we meet?"

Jim filled me in on the location. We met at eight o'clock a.m. that Saturday and took to the field shortly thereafter. I think the reason Jim called had to do partly with the size of the area to be hunted.

It included several square miles of land with multiple harvested fields of sunflowers and wheat. As I recall, there were no pasture portions. It also had a great deal of water in the form of cattail sloughs. In short, it had fodder and cover in abundance for pheasants. Also, it had experienced only limited hunting pressure. The prospects for us having a bonanza day seemed highly likely.

The weather cooperated as well, with the temperature in the mid-30s, no clouds, and the sun bright. The sloughs were frozen hard. The ever-present North Dakota wind did not exceed ten to fifteen mph. We lucked out. We had an ideal hunting day at an ideal spot. Amongst the four of us, we had three dogs: Jim's, Leo's, and my Diana.

Jim worked the hunt's strategy out before we assembled. He talked to the landowner and been told where the best, most likely pheasant sloughs were. We began our hunt at about eight-thirty, working the east and west sides of a major slough, which extended a quarter of a mile running north and south.

Jim and his dog took the west side; Gary went ahead a half mile to post for Jim. Leo and I were assigned to walk the slough's eastern edge working northward. The three of us waited ten minutes until Gary got set up at the slough's north end where the water narrowed and ended. Leo's and my slough side was more extensive than Jim's with cattails several times denser than those on Jim's edge. To carry out our assignments, Leo walked the right side while I covered the slough's left edge. About 100 yards of cattails separated us.

With Gary posted, we began to move north. For the first 100 yards, Leo and I put up nothing. After about 50 yards, our side of the slough began to divide into two distinct bodies, one portion continuing north, the other bending left; that is, to the west. Leo stayed with the main body heading north. I moved to the left to cover the new configuration. As I walked, I lost sight of Leo. What I hunted increasingly became an independent entity, a separate branch of the main slough.

Diana worked the cattails 10-15 yards ahead of me. About five minutes into the new, lesser slough, she put up a rooster. I shot and it came down, but was not dead. It ran on the ice for a short distance before ducking back into the cattails. Diana saw it drop and pursued. I stopped walking and waited to see what would happen. Two or three minutes later, the dog came back with the bird. We continued.

Following the same small slough as it continued north, Diana put up another cock. I shot; the bird dropped, landing in the cattails. I had no idea whether it was crippled or dead. I stood still and waited. A little longer wait but within five minutes my gifted partner returned with the second rooster. Both Diana and I were on a roll! I was having a ball.

We moved forward up to the slough's end. At this point, the dog and

I started back to the west, hunting the north side of our lucky pheasant cover. This maneuver had us moving in the direction of Jim. As we made the turn, Diana flushed yet another rooster. I shot and knocked it down.

Again I held my ground and waited, this time for a full five minutes. I was about to blow the whistle to bring the dog back when Diana returned with the bird. I stuffed it to my hunting coat with the others and congratulated my super dog. I couldn't believe how well things were going.

We continued. The north side of our slough arm ended about 50 yards ahead where it rejoined the main body of water. In that 50-yard stretch, the dog flushed a forth rooster. I shot and hit it. The bird bounced off the ice, recovered, and started to run, hooking back into the cattails.

Diana emerged from the cover onto the ice just as the bird fell. She saw it and chased. A couple of minutes later she returned with the bird. Number four. Lucky for me I had partners, so I could exceed the three bird limit! Fantastic hunt. Ten minutes later, the dog and I rejoined the group at the north end of the big slough.

I met Leo first and he said, "Heard shooting. That you?"

"Yeah."

"How'd you do?"

"Unbelievably well. Blows my mind. Dog put up four roosters. I got em all. First for me," I said.

"Great," he said, "wish I'd been with you. Saw nothing, not even a hen."

As we talked, Gary appeared. "Who's been doing all the shooting?" he asked.

Leo said, "Jonathan, not me."

I said to Gary, "Best I've ever done. Got four birds. Dog was fantastic. Reminds me of the time you, friend Dave Presser, and I were hunting down near Turtle Lake and you shot nine birds."

Gary snapped, "I didn't shoot 9. It was 8."

Gary looked irritated. I meant my comment as a joke. I said no

..ore. Ten minutes later, Jim and his dog joined us. They had one bird. We walked to the truck Gary used to get to his post and then drove back to my vehicle. The four of us moved on to hunt another section of our benefactor's property. As I recall, the others got a couple of birds in the second place. I had no more shooting.

At noon, I decided to call it a day. My arthritic knees had started bothering me, so I left one of my birds with Leo and headed home. That evening, I talked to Jim and he informed me they finished with limits as well. That pleased me. Thus ended a great day for everybody, but an even more special one for my beautiful hunting partner Diana. I'm sure Clio would have been proud or her black protégée.

Diana's performance on that day with my friends illustrated one of her most prominent features—that is, her role as companion in sharing with me a passion we both loved. From her puppyhood, she enthusiastically identified with my hunting. Her hysterical protests at being left alone at home graphically displayed that. When we hunted, we were together in a common endeavor. But her commitment to me, to be my pal and companion, Diana extended well beyond hunting.

Over the course of her life, most of her time with me did not involve hunting or chasing game. At home, Diana always sought to be as close physically to me as possible. When I ate, she found a spot under the dining room table; when I watched television, she lay next to the lazy-boy I sat in. When I slept, she, as with my other dogs, was not permitted on the bed, but she solved that limitation by sleeping under the bed.

My antique bed at the summer place in Florence, Wisconsin had a metal frame that left a 14-inch space between the floor and the mattress. Ignoring the soft pillow-like doggie bed available on the adjacent rug, Diana opted to squeeze into the tight floor space directly beneath me under the bed. In the mornings, she often had to struggle to extricate herself from that confining choice.

Diana's companionship with its insistent sharing manifested for me her version of love. From my Labs in general, but from Diana most dramatically, I understood the relationship of such sharing love.

To want to be close to the person you love, to want to be doing what that person is doing, and to want to share in the risks and rewards of that combined effort illustrated a bonding that could only be described as love. Several of the Labs that preceded Diana, especially Jason and Reggie, exhibited some such love, but none more so than my beautiful, black Diana.

In mid-October 2011, Diana experienced with my lady friend Mary, me and my two other dog-family members an event that could have ended all of our separate lives. I'm referring to an automobile accident that occurred during a hunting trip south of Minot.

Before going into the details of the accident, I need to introduce Mary, the divorced mother of three impressive children, whom I first met in 2009 in Minot. A calm, laid-back, bright, attractive, brown-eyed brunette with an ironic sense of humor and an acute social conscience, Mary, a special education teacher by trade, has been, since we first met, a fun companion in activities both indoors and out. On most days she makes me laugh a lot, but not on the fateful day of the accident.

On that Saturday, Mary and I, plus the dogs, had been hunting pheasants south of Hazen, North Dakota in one of my long-term, favorite hunting places. It had been a magnificent, Indian Summer Saturday. All of us had had fun. We even had a couple of roosters to show for it.

As we drove home, passing Max, North Dakota on highway 83 around four o'clock in the afternoon a pickup truck, driven by a distracted young man, slammed into us. The collision was completely unexpected. I never saw the impacting vehicle before it hit us. I remember only Mary's panicked words, "Look out! Look out! They're not gonna stop!"

The driver of the colliding truck coming from the west had not bothered to stop or look before attempting to cross highway 83. The offending truck smashed into our front end on the driver's side. The collision crushed in the driver's door and bent the right front wheel in. The impact's violence also smashed the front and back windows on the truck's left side.

Both Mary and I had our seatbelts on, so neither of us was thrown through a window nor out of the vehicle. We suffered no cuts. Asleep on the back seat, Sherman was covered in splintered glass but unhurt. The other two dogs in the far back likewise asleep escaped injury as well. My truck was a disaster—the front end was a mess with the hood thrown up, the right front fender and wheel mangled.

Confused and dazed by the crash, I remained conscious but in considerable pain. Within minutes, the state patrol arrived and an ambulance followed. I remained stuck in the front seat until the help arrived. When the state highway patrol officer pulled in behind us, Mary stepped out of the truck and met him as he came over to view the wreck. The officer looked in from Mary's side and said to me, "Don't move. Help's on its way."

He turned to Mary and said, "What happened."

She replied, "The other truck drove right into us. We didn't have a chance. It never stopped at the stop sign, drove right through and plowed into us. It was horrible."

A few minutes later, the ambulance arrived with its two attendants. A third member of the team appeared a few minutes later in her own vehicle to assist the other two. In viewing the scene, the female member of the ambulance team stuck her head in the truck from the passenger side and said to me, "Where do you hurt?"

Still dazed, I said, "My left side, ribs and back."

She said, "Just hold on. Don't try to move. Have patience. We'll help you out. But don't move."

She reached into the cab and felt my pulse. In the meantime, the ambulance driver had gotten the stretcher out of the ambulance and moved it up next to the truck.

The female attendant said, "Relax, try to relax. Don't move. We'll get you out. Let us move you. You remain still."

I muttered, "Okay."

I don't remember much after that. Mary told me it took the ambulance people a good half an hour to check my vital signs, ease me gently out of the truck, strap me on the stretcher, fit me with a neck brace, and put me in the ambulance. Once in the ambulance, I was taken directly to Minot, the closest hospital. I assumed Mary was okay since she'd been speaking to me throughout the accident's aftermath.

As Mary told me later, most of that time I spent muttering, "Are the dogs okay? Are the dogs okay? How are the dogs? How are the dogs?" until the ambulance left.

In the hospital's emergency room, I was examined and ex-rayed. No fractures were discovered, no lacerations, nor serious abrasions, only a bruised back. With the tests completed, I remained in the hospital for several hours for observation.

After the ambulance drove off with me in it, Mary remained with my ruined truck and my three lucky-to-be-alive canines. While the state highway patrolman and the ambulance people worked the accident scene, Mary took Sherman out of the shattered-glass covered back seat and sat with him next to the truck in the ditch, trying to figure out how she and my dogs would get home. Fortunately, she had Jim Miller's phone number. She called Jim, who was at home entertaining hunting guests from the East. He answered her call.

"Jim this is Mary, Jonathan's friend. Calling because there's an emergency."

"What happened?" he said.

"We had a bad accident. A guy drove into us at Max. Jonathan's truck is a wreck," she said.

"Anyone hurt?"

"Jonathan was taken to the hospital in an ambulance to be checked out. He wasn't cut. Had back pains. I'm okay. Dogs are okay. We were very lucky. But, I'm stuck down here in Max with the three dogs. Could you come and get us? I'm alone. Don't know what to do. Don't know who else to call," she said.

"Yeah, I'll get you. Tell me exactly where you're at," he said.

"We were hit on highway 83 at the over pass at Max. The truck's in the ditch on the east side of 83. I'm calling from there," she said.

"Okay, I'll be down there shortly. Hang on."

Jim arrived with his truck 45 minutes later. After he pulled in, he got out, approached Mary and asked, "You still okay?"

She nodded. Jim walked over to look at the truck. "My god, what a mess. What happened to you guys? Were you speeding or what?"

"No," Mary said, "not at all. The kid who hit us was distracted by his buddies or something. Don't know what his problem was but he never stopped. Just drove right through the intersection and smashed right into us."

Jim shook his head and said, "What'd you want me to do about the truck?"

"Nothing, just get us home. Somebody else'll look after the truck," Mary said.

"Okay, let's go."

He put the three dogs in the back of his truck. Mary climbed into the cab. An hour later they were back in Minot. It had been nearly two long hours after the accident before Jim arrived to take Mary and the dogs home. During a good deal of that waiting period, the woman who arrived in her own vehicle after the ambulance appeared remained to look after Mary. She insisted on having Mary and Sherman sit with her in her car while waiting for Jim. Once back in Minot, Mary left the dogs at my place and proceeded to the hospital to check on me.

By the time she arrived at the emergency room, I was ready to be released—my only negative physical effect from the accident being a bruised back. Mary drove me home. We both realized just how lucky we'd been not to have been seriously injured or even killed. Amazingly, my dogs appeared unaffected by the whole affair. For his rescue of Mary and my canines, Jim earned my abiding respect and admiration. He proved himself to be a true friend.

My dear friend and companion Mary deserves the same encomium.

Since we first met, she's been a delightful accomplice with me in activities ranging from chasing pheasants to ice fishing, to attending the Antique Road Show, to picking Lab puppies. One of her most attractive features relates to the latter. For her ability to appreciate my dogs, I am more than impressed—I am indebted as well. Her role in seeing after me but also after my dogs in the accident that ruined my truck and endangered our lives illustrates just what kind of a friend she is.

Initially, my truck was towed to a repair shop where an attempt was made to fix the damage. In the end, that failed. After six weeks of wasted time and effort, the insurance company replaced my totaled vehicle with a new truck.

That same year in November and again December, my dogs and I returned to the field to chase more pheasants. The season wasn't a total loss after all, but it had been traumatic for sure. To this day, I thank God for sparing Mary, my Sweet Spirits Clio, Sherman, Diana, and me.

In April 2016, Diana, the last surviving member of my Three Musketeers, entered her eleventh year. From past experience, I knew I could expect to have her with me only for another year or two if I was lucky.

As she approached the end of her days, Diana had not lost her capacity to love, her ability to socialize, or her fondness for the hunt. Slowed a bit by declining energy levels, her enthusiasm for life nevertheless remained strong.

In this regard, she retained her skill as a noisemaker. Some of her most recent noise excesses she expressed when I donned my boots or overcoat in preparation for going out into the untraveled street in front of the house to throw tennis balls. I usually did this in the early morning when there would be virtually no traffic (Mercer, at present has 80 residents).

If I made the recognizable preparatory moves for a ball session, Diana would begin to whine, run about in mini-circles, jump and head for the garage door, the fastest way to the street. The hysteria would increase as I followed her into the garage and reached up on the shelf to grab the balls and the ball launcher.

At that point, Diana seemed to have gone berserk: barking loudly, squealing, ears perking at full attention, eyes sparking, tail wagging frenetically. She was, in short, ready to experience heaven. The whole process amused me. I always laughed as I stepped out the door and launched the first ball missile.

Besides her abilities to make noise and experience joy, Diana continued to be a sweet creature not just for me and other humans like my children or friend Mary, but also for an added fellow dog pack member named Toula.

My reason for acquiring another dog was simple—I would have a Lab continuation after Diana left me and Diana would have a younger dog to keep her company in her final years, just as her predecessors Clio and Sherman had enjoyed having youngster Diana as a pal. In short, I figured if I got another one of Scott's beautiful dogs it would be a win-win situation for me and my dog family.

Diana and new dog family member, Toula,
on the deck in Florence

Diana's response to the new dog was as expected. From the beginning, she treated the new, younger dog I named Toula as an appropriate elder family member should. Not long ago, when Diana and the new dog were sitting at my feet as I watched television, Diana began to lick Toula's face to groom her about the eyes.

To me, Diana seemed to be playing the mother-dog role, a touching testimony to her goodwill and capacity for accepting her new family member. At that moment, she reminded me of my beautiful black Reggie. Diana's grooming seemed to symbolize for me her sweetness—her capacity for loving. As I watched, I could not help tearing up.

The end of Diana's tenure with me came suddenly in the late summer of 2016. None of my other Labs except Jason left me so suddenly. When the terminal crisis arose, I was not prepared. Until nearly the end, I assumed she would be with me as usual for the upcoming pheasant season. My assumptions were based on ignorance, misunderstanding and false hopes.

Maternal Diana looking after Toula

In the late spring after the snow had disappeared in North Dakota, Diana tore an ACL (Anterior Cruciate Ligament) in her right back leg during one of our tennis ball fetching sessions. Because of the limp and apparent pain, I took her to the veterinary in nearby McCusky, North Dakota. I was told the usual solution for ACLs involved an operation, but that I might try something less drastic to start with.

The vet instructed me to be very careful with her, cease the fetching sessions, and get her swimming to work up the muscles in the affected leg. I tried to do what the vet suggested, but did not succeed. Her condition worsened. Not only her back legs remained problematic, but she also developed a breathing problem. Recalling Clio's breathing crisis, I took her to see a different vet to have the breathing issue dealt with.

In that visit, Diana was diagnosed as suffering from a lungs/heart problem and given medications to relieve both. For a week, I followed instructions and medicated the dog as told. The medicine did not help. In fact, the dog became lethargic and listless.

The leg problem worsened as well. It seemed even more threatening than the heart/lung issue. Because we had gone for the summer to the cottage in Wisconsin, I took her to my vet in Niagara, Wisconsin.

Diana's locomotion problem had worsened dramatically. She began to have trouble getting up. Both of her back legs became increasingly dysfunctional. If I managed to help her stand and get her to walk, she would stagger and collapse. She had lost control, not only in the leg with the ACL, but in the other back leg as well. When she tried to walk, she would do so with her right leg paw inverted. In human terms, it looked as if she were walking on her knuckles!

As the crisis worsened, she appeared to be in constant pain. When I tried to help her up, she would cry out in pain. In addition, as she lay on her bed, she could not control her bowels. Witnessing this suffering broke my heart. I decided to end it. I called the Animal Hospital in Niagara and made and appointment to have Diana put down.

To complicate matters, I found getting Diana to the hospital to be a serious problem. In Wisconsin that summer, I developed a back problem. It became very difficult or impossible for me to lift heavy objects. With my back hurting, I couldn't lift my 78-pound dog by myself into my vehicle.

On the afternoon of her appointment, I went to see if either of my closest neighbors could help me with the dog. Both of them were dog owners and dog lovers, but they were not at home. I began to panic. As a last hope, I walked over to the construction site down the road from my place to see if one of the men working there might help me. When I got to the site, I found two carpenters on their knees nailing on a ceiling frame.

By then I was crying. I took a deep breath and called out, "Hey, guys I got a crisis next door. I need some help. Only take five minutes. Will pay you for your trouble."

They both looked up and stopped hammering. The older guy said, "What's the problem?"

"I gotta take my dog to the vet's to be put down. Can't lift her into my car. Got a bad back. Could either of you guys give me a hand?"

"Yeah, sure," the elder man said. "Where are you?"

"I'm a hundred yards down the road, the red house," I said.

They both put their hammers down, stood up and started walking toward me.

"I really appreciate this, fellas. You don't know how much. Sorry to interrupt you," I said, trying not to sob too loudly.

"No problem. We needed a break anyway. Glad to help," the elder fellow said and smiled. His companion nodded agreement.

"I'll drive you down and back," I said.

"Nah, we'll take our pickup."

They climbed into their truck and drove after me to my place. They got out and followed me into my kitchen where Diana was lying on the floor. She didn't try to get up to greet the visitors, which she always did in the past.

"Beautiful doggie. What's wrong with her?" the elder guy asked.

"Can't walk, can't control her poop, in great pain," I said.

"How old is she? I got a Lab too, a yellow one," the younger fellow said.

"She's eleven," I said, again struggling to keep from breaking down.

I picked up the camping blanket I set on the stove to carry her and spread it out on the floor next to Diana. We slid the dog onto it. The two fellas lifted the dog, carried her to my car and set her on the back seat. She didn't move.

As they finished positioning her, I said to my wonderful, kind helpers, "I don't know how to thank you enough. I really appreciate what you have done."

The younger fellow said, "We're both dog people. We know what you're going through. Glad to do it. Sorry for the loss. Beautiful dog." They returned to work, leaving me to my duty.

I drove to the Animal Hospital in Niagara and left Diana there. She was put down that afternoon. I cried on the trip over. When I dropped the dog off, I could barely speak. Throughout the ordeal, the staff at the Niagara Animal Hospital exhibited kindness and sympathy in assisting Diana out of her misery. For that, I remain very grateful.

Two weeks after Diana's death, I called Dr. Bissen, the Niagara veterinarian, to get her opinion on what happened to Diana. She told me Diana had suffered from advanced intervertebral disk disease (IVDD). The malady had pinched the nerves coming off Diana's spinal cord which, in turn, had produced not only pain but also a lack of sensory and motor function in her rear legs. That explained why Diana had appeared to be walking on her knuckles!

Looking back, the whole affair now seems like a nightmare, intensely painful and tragic. The suddenness and the intensity of the crisis were worse than anything I ever experienced with a dog. Although it has been very difficult for me to describe the loss of my beautiful, precious black dog companion—the last of my vaunted Three Musketeers. I know I will see her again. She will surely be with my other Labs when I cross that bridge. And she will be the easiest Lab to pick out among marvelous pack. For Diana will be the one making the most noise, the one running in mini-circles, the one jumping and squealing with delight, the one barking at me to get my attention to remind me of our lovely past together and how much we loved one another.

CHAPTER EIGHT

TOULA

(FROM GREEK WORD FOTOULA, MEANING LIGHT)

Special friend Mary with Toula, two beautiful ladies

"We are absolutely alone on this planet and the forms of life that surround us, not one excepting the dog, has made an alliance with us."
— Maurice Maeterlink.

The acquisition of Toula has an interesting history behind it. In the beginning, it was unrelated to the deaths of Clio and Sherman, and rather had to do with the demise of my daughter Sarah's Roy.

I was profoundly moved when Sarah called me from New York City at four-thirty a.m. to tell me about Roy's passing. I was nearly as upset as she was about losing her dog. After I spoke to her, I thought she needed another dog and I resolved to see to it that she got one.

I gave her five or six months to work through her loss and then broached the possibility of a new dog with her. She was favorable. In early March 2010, I made another phone call to Scott Synder in Jamestown.

When I called, his wife answered. I introduced myself. She said Scott was out with the dogs. I asked her to have Scott call me back. Around noon, he did so.

"Jonathan," he said, "don't tell me you need another dog. Anything wrong with Clio or Sherman?"

"No, they're fine. I'm not calling about myself, but for my daughter Sarah. Her Roy's the reason for the call."

"What's wrong with Roy?"

"He died," I said.

"Sorry to hear that. What happened?"

"He collapsed and died in New York City about six months ago."

"Why?" he asked.

"I don't know the details but I was told he suffered a massive failure of internal organs, cancer I think."

"Sounds awful," he said.

"It was. She really loved that dog. I'm thinking she needs another one. You got any puppies ready to go?"

"Just so happens I do," he said.

"What've you got?"

"A litter of eight, only one's been spoken for so far."

"What colors?"

"Seven blacks, one yellow."

"I'm interested in the blacks, one just like Roy."

"Thought you were partial to yellows and chocolates."

"I am, but this dog's for Sarah. It's gotta be black."

"Well, you'll have a bunch to choose from then. When you coming down?"

"This weekend if possible. I'll have younger son Rob with me. Should have fun helping me pick a puppy. Saturday okay?"

"Yeah. We'll be here. About what time?"

"I assume around noon. Any problems, I'll call."

"Good, see you soon," he said, and hung up.

Despite snowy weather and some dicey road conditions, Rob and I arrived at the kennel on that Saturday at midday. During the drive, I explained to Rob what to look for and that, in our selection, sex didn't matter but color did, that our puppy choice had to be black like Roy. He agreed. He remembered Roy fondly and his sister's attachment to the dog.

Because of the weather, the puppies were in the basement of Scott's house, not in the outside kennel. After he led us to the puppies, Scott went upstairs and left us alone to scrutinize the doggies and make our choice. Our puppy observation, with its hand clapping, whistling, clicking noises, and turning the puppies on their backs lasted for more than an hour. As always, the choice was tough. We finally agreed on a little female that seemed perky, friendly, curious, and confident.

I went upstairs to notify Scott of our choice and to pay for the dog. After I wrote out the check and handed it to Scott, he said, "You sure you're not interested in a dog for yourself?"

I laughed and said, "No, no I'm definitely not interested."

"What'd you think of the little yellow pup?" he asked.

"Cute, seems like a fun little thing. Haven't room for another dog. Three are enough, perhaps too many. Couldn't possibly take on a fourth."

He said, "My wife really likes the yellow puppy and wants a good home for it. Told me to tell you if you take her, she'll give the pup a bath and tie a ribbon around her neck."

I laughed again and said, "That's a nice offer, but I can't oblige her. Tell her I had to pick a black one, but thanks anyway."

Rob and I returned to Minot that afternoon with our black puppy purchase. She rode in Rob's lap the whole journey, sleeping most of the time. When back home, I put her in the small kennel I'd bought for her flight to her new mistress, Sarah.

On the following Wednesday, I took the dog to the airport and sent her off to Greensboro, North Carolina where Sarah lived. She was to be my daughter's Easter present. Sarah received the dog the same day I sent it. My daughter was delighted. She named her new puppy Luna.

After a typically frenetic Lab childhood and adolescence, Sarah survived. Luna developed into a mature, mellow, loving friend. To this day, I'm pleased at how well Luna has related to my younger anthropologist daughter. Luna may not have been, Roy but she was close enough.

In 2012, roughly two years after acquiring Luna for Sarah, I called Scott once again. This call was about purchasing a new dog for myself. It was late May. I got through to Scott on the first try. "Scott," I said, "it's Jonathan up in Mercer."

"Jonathan, what's up? Good call or a bad one?"

"Good one, but a sad one as well. Don't know whether you're aware, but I had to put down both Clio and Sherman a few months ago."

"Didn't know. Sorry to hear that," he said.

"Old age got 'em both. The other dogs, Diana and Sarah's Luna are fine."

"So what's the call about?" he asked.

"I'm embarrassed to say, but I think I need another dog. Can't seem to live with only one."

"What're looking for? What you got in mind?"

"Basically, I want a dog to accompany my Diana in her old age. She's been lonely since Clio and Sherman passed. Not sure if it should be a puppy or an older dog. What've you got?"

"Some nice five-month-old yellow pups, four not spoken for."

"I'd like to come down, take a look. This weekend a possibility?"

"Certainly, just give me a time convenient for you. This Saturday, is that what you mean?"

"Yeah, that'd be good. I'm gonna bring a friend to help me choose."

"Okay. What time?"

"Mid-day as in the past," I said, and we hung up.

My pal Mary and I showed up the following Saturday. We considered the yellow five-month old puppies to begin with. They were all wild, fluffy, crazy, sparkling-eyed creatures. At the same time, Scott introduced us to an older yellow female he called Q, a mild, small, rather dark, almost red, adult Lab. She appeared a bit shy but very friendly.

While we were in the process of observing the possibilities, Mary said, "Jonathan, you realize a younger dog would require a lot more time and effort than Q. Be some advantages in getting her."

"I know, but I love those puppies. They remind me of Reggie." I said.

In the end, I couldn't make up my mind that day whether to take the older or a younger dog. So, we left.

Before we departed I told Scott, "Need more time to think things over. I can't decide today. I'll be back though for sure."

"No problem. Just give me a call when you're ready," he said.

Two weeks later we returned. By then I was leaning in favor of the older dog. On arrival, I asked Scott to fill me in on Q.

"I've trained her for both obedience and retrieving. Shall we see what she can do?" he said.

"By all means. Show me her stuff."

Scott proceeded to run Q through the same routine he'd shown me with Clio ten years earlier. Q sat, heeled and fetched on command. He showed off her retrieving talents by throwing a dummy into the slough on his property. It landed in the midst of a small cattail cluster about ten yards from shore. The dog had no trouble finding and bringing the dummy back. I was sold.

When he had finished showing off, he said "So what's the verdict? You want her?"

"She's a star. I'll take her."

"You know, you're getting the sister of Sarah's Luna. She's the little yellow puppy my wife wanted you to take when you bought Sarah's black puppy."

"Must be God's will or fate or something. I thought Q might be the same puppy, but wasn't sure. Means Diana is my new dog's auntie, right?" I said with a smile.

"Right on. She's Grace's puppy. Diana came from the same litter as Grace. They're family."

He patted me on the shoulder and said, "Good choice."

"You tell your wife since I did what she wanted me to do, my new puppy gets a bath and a ribbon."

Scott laughed. "She will if you insist."

"I'm kidding, of course. But you can thank her again for her foresight. I'm happy to have fulfilled her original wish. Fate indeed."

For the dog I took home that day, I'd already chosen a name. All I

Auntie Diana and niece Toula

needed was a female dog, and now that condition had been satisfied. The preferred name was Toula, derived from one of my all-time favorite movies, *My Big Fat Greek Wedding*.

Having taught Western Civilization for forty years, I found the film's Greekophile father ("There are only two kinds of people—Greeks and those who want to be Greek.") who forced his daughter Toula to answer questions about Socrates, Plato, and Aristotle before allowing to eat her breakfast cereal hilarious. I pledged my next female Labrador Retriever had to be a Toula. Furthermore, I considered my acquisition of the same dog Scott's wife had tried to get me to take two years before as almost divinely decreed.

Beyond the name, Toula would become unique for me in several other ways as well. To begin with, her color differed from all the Labs that had preceded her. Scott had described her to me on the phone initially as yellow—the same, I assumed, as Clio and Jason. But her color was not the traditional yellow.

Toula was much darker than either of my previous yellows. Toula's hue reflected a new strain among Labs that I was not aware of, a strain developed quite recently. She was more reddish than yellow. I've been told the red version of the breed has grown in popularity in America within the past 20 years.

Toula's second noticeable feature—her size—distinguished her from all her predecessors in my dog family, even from Reggie. By average Lab size, Toula was small, maybe a little over half the size of Sherman. Her snout resembled that of her aunt Diana in being more pointed than the average Lab. That, of course, reflected Scott's breeding tradition. My son Nat has seen Toula on numerous occasions but has, as of this time, refrained from labeling her another one of "*Dad's northern pikes*"

Toula's personality resembled Diana's closely. A fun-loving, sociable animal, Toula adapted to my household and home traditions easily. Although she had lived most of her two years in an outdoor kennel, she learned house-breaking in very short time. A couple of mistakes and appropriate reprimands and she knew what was expected.

Besides the fast house-breaking, she warmed up to Diana from the very first day she arrived. In this regard, she did what I hoped. She became a fast friend for my black dog, who I thought missed her departed mates Clio and Sherman. Other features besides social compatibility that Toula shared with Diana included her athleticism and speed.

Toula loved competition. This became apparent quickly in our tennis ball sessions. Toula could outrun Diana, as Diana had once outrun Clio and Sherman. Since this was so, I would throw two balls each in a different direction, the first for Toula and then the second one in the opposite direction for Diana. Toula would grab her ball and then rush back to see if she could get Diana's as well. In these sessions, I deliberately favored the older dog, an interesting twist given Diana's earlier role as my dog gang's number one jock.

My living room cohorts, Diana and Toula

Toula picked up a number of traditions from Diana in the house as well, one of them being her tendency to stay close to me, to follow me about and to sit at my feet. While I watched television, often I had two dogs crowding the front of my lazy-boy recliner. When I got up to go to the kitchen to get coffee or cookies, I had to step over two dogs, not just one.

When I wasn't at home, the dogs had free reign of the house. They were not allowed on the furniture and they respected that prohibition. They usually slept together in my bedroom. Unlike Clio or Jason, Toula slept next to my bed each night in close proximity to both me and her aunt. In short, Toula and Diana hang on me the way Reggie did. For a divorced man living alone, they were appropriate sympathetic companions.

Although neither Clio nor Sherman ever heard nor were influenced by Diana's crazy, hysterical protesting, Toula, who looked up to Diana and was much closer to her, picked up on some of Diana's distinctive vocal habits.

I first noticed this in our ball fetching activities at home in Mercer, North Dakota. Each day, weather permitting, I would take both dogs out to fetch tennis balls on the road in front of my house, usually in the early morning. As I put on my shoes in preparation for going out, Diana would get excited and begin to bark and whine. By the time we reached the street, the elder dog was barking loudly and continuously.

I don't know exactly when Toula picked up on her aunt's act, but she did. The younger dog doesn't bark as loudly as Diana did, but she does whine and jump up at me as I walk out the house holding the tennis balls above my head. After a dozen or so tosses, both dogs would be huffing and puffing, not barking. When the fun ended, I gave them a drink and a chance to lie down to recover from their frenetic exertion.

The noise making of the ball-fetching sessions would be eclipsed by another activity which generated equivalent excitement in both dogs. This occurred not outside, but rather in my vehicles and it relates more closely to hunting than the exercise entertainment. I discovered this particular noise activity unexpectedly. It developed out of the need to drive beyond Mercer to shop for groceries, visit a hardware store, or go to the library.

Mercer, the place where I settled after the 2011 flood in Minot, is a small village of about 80 souls. There are no businesses in town except a bar and small gas station. Thus, to get a loaf of bread, milk or dog food one has to drive a minimum of 25 miles and the drive in all directions passes through prime North Dakota farming/ranching country with its cultivated fields and cattail sloughs.

The drive passes through vintage pheasant country as well. On nearly every trip we undertook, we encountered pheasants, either in the road itself or on the roadside. This was especially true in the early morning or toward the end of the day. When driving to shop, I normally took both Diana and Toula with me. That gives them a chance to get out of the house. A change of scenery always seems to me a good idea for both humans and canines.

Early in her life, Diana responded to the sight of roadside pheasants by barking. Unlike so many of her other barking exhibitions, this never irritated me. I thought it kept her pheasant consciousness alive. Not a bad idea for a pheasant hound, could only help later on in the pheasant season I thought.

Toula picked up on Diana's pheasant excitement and barking from virtually her first exposure to it. Surprisingly, the sound and sight of two barking dogs with their noses pushed against the vehicle's windows didn't irritate me. Rather, it both pleased and amused me. In fact, it made me want to join the game. I did.

Human eyes, according to dog authority Alexandra Horowitz, are generally better than canine ones, at least at detecting stationary objects. I agree with her. The dogs missed a lot of birds that did not move. So my role in the game became to search out and identify any roadside pheasant not moving.

Once I located one, I'd cry "Lookie, lookie, a rooster brooster over there," and point in the bird's direction. The dogs would get excited and try to see what I did. If the bird moved, they'd bark. Most often, when I sighted a bird or birds along the road, I'd slow down, sometimes even stop so my playmates could bark at will.

Toula, who in this routine often seemed more intense than her auntie (never thought that would be possible), would even begin to scratch at the window, trying to get out and give chase. Because we turned this routine into a game we all loved, every time we went out in the car or truck the dogs were primed to play and expected Dad to do his bit to advance the game. I did my best to oblige them. The only time I wouldn't play "Rooster Brooster" was when late for an appointment or church.

I acquired Toula for my and Diana's companionship, but also as a future hunting companion. Although Scott had trained Toula to fetch, he had not taken her hunting. Thus, the whole hunting routine was new for her.

It took a season and a half for her to pick up on what was expected. To begin with, she needed to learn how to hunt wearing a hunting dog collar. All my dogs after Jason and Boomer have been subject to collar control—a transmitter sending beeps and brief electronic shocks to keep them close to me and tending to business.

Initially, Toula's enthusiasm had her hunting too far out in front. The first beeps were ignored, but the shocks and some accompanying harsh words intimidated her into compliance. She quickly learned to stay close and to heed the warning beeps. By the end of the first season, she could do most of what was expected of her.

Toula fetching a rooster

Like my other Labs, Toula loves to hunt and works hard at it. She was not intimidated by Diana and never deferred to her elder when a bird was downed. Rather, it became a fetching contest just like our tennis ball sessions.

In her first season, Toula retrieved only one pheasant, a hen some other hunter shot. I remember the retrieve because Toula was behind me and out of sight. When she showed up at my side with the hen, it came as a total surprise. She didn't understand, I think, why I put the bird in an adjacent tree and not in my hunting jacket.

In her second season, she retrieved nearly as many birds as Diana. They hunted well together, one working the left side, the other the right and both in front of me.

In summing up Toula, I can say I'm optimistic and pleased with both her progress as a hunter and with her ability to function as a family member. She hung close to her auntie and followed the older dog in going out, begging for cookies, getting in the car or truck to travel, and playing in the backyard.

In short, the two dogs were very compatible, closer than any pair I've ever had. Both are gracious when I have guests in the house. Toula exhibits the same sweet disposition as Diana—one which enjoys attention and being petted and fussed over by both strangers and master. Like Diana, Toula hunts easily with my other hunting companions who have brought their own dogs.

Toula may be smaller than most Labs, but her speed, enthusiasm, and commitment make her an excellent addition to the hunt. In brief, both Toula's hunting skills and her sociability conform very nicely to the grand legacy she inherits from the six Labrador Retrievers that preceded her into my life and heart. I expect great things from her for the next half dozen years in the field—if my knees hold out. If they don't, my red "Sweet Spirit" will continue as a model companion in my home.

When Sweet Auntie Diana passed, I knew I'd have to do for Toula what I did for Diana, that is, secure another living child-Lab for Toula to provide what Diana did so beautifully for niece Toula; that is, continue the love.

CHAPTER NINE

"Segen"

(German word for Blessing or Gift from God)

Segen with her new Dad

Two weeks after Diana was put out of her misery, I called my old pal Scott Synder in Jamestown again to inquire about a new Lab puppy to be Toula's and my companion. As usual, Scott graciously received my call.

"Scott," I said, "it's Jonathan out in the Wisconsin woods calling."

"Hey, Jonathan, long time since I've heard from you. How you doing? You couldn't be calling about a dog, could you?" And he laughed.

"Maybe," I said. "My beautiful Diana had to be put to sleep. Very sad process. I'm still grieving."

"Sorry to hear that. What happened?"

"According to my vet, she suffered from a disc disease pinching the nerves in the back. Her back legs wouldn't function. She couldn't walk.

Terrible pain and suffering."

"Oh, my God. So sorry. How old was she?"

"Eleventh year. Came on all of a sudden. I'm trying to cope. Thought I might try to get over her by finding another Lab puppy. Hence the call. Got any puppies ready to go?"

"Yeah, I do. You're in luck. First litter in five years for me."

"So, what've got?"

"Seven puppies at seven weeks, three females, four males."

"I'm looking for a black female to replace Diana. You got any of those?"

"Nope, no black females. All the females are yellows. But the males are impressive. Beautiful dogs. You should think about one of them. My wife has a favorite. She'd probably want you to take it. Should I ask her?"

I laughed. "She's done well by me in the past I know. Remember, Toula was her recommendation and that dog's been great. I might have to take a black, but need to see the yellows first," I said.

"Come on down then. None've been spoken for. Now's a slow time for me, good time for you to have the pick of the litter," he said.

"Okay, how about next Saturday? I'm in Wisconsin now, should be able to get back to North Dakota for that weekend."

"We'll be here. Just let me know the time you'll be coming. Okay?" he said.

"Yeah, I will. I'll be bringing my friend Mary again to help me choose. She's been a great helper."

Scott laughed. "Yeah, I know how she is. Not as wishy-washy as you. More rational. Got a good head for picking. Makes you choose the right dog."

"Yeah, you're right. Okay, I'll be in touch soon. Thanks." And I hung up.

The weather on the Saturday morning Mary and I visited Black Hawk Kennels was nearly perfect—no wind to speak of, bright sun shine, and temperature in the mid-sixties. Scott came out to great us shortly after we pulled into his yard.

"You both ready to do some serious dog viewing?" he asked.

"You bet, bring em on. We got lots of time," I said. Mary nodded.

"Before we go to the pups, I wanna show you their mother. She's in the east kennel part with the other adult Labs, most of them boarders," he said.

As we walked over to the adult-dog kennel section, Scott said, "The mother is the black dog in the third runway from the left. I'll let her out if you like."

"Don't think you need to do that. We can see her up close enough," I said and walked up to the gate of her run. She came up to greet me with her tail wagging. She was a rather small black Lab, about Toula's size but calm and friendly. She licked the finger I struck through the fence to touch her.

"She's a beauty," I said. "How old? How many litters she had?"

"Eight years. This is her third litter. She's been free of the puppies for the past two weeks. She may appear a bit worn out. Nursing pups is tough. Takes a lot out of a dog," Scott said.

I nodded. "Still looks good to me. What's her demeanor like?"

"She's sweet, friendly, easy-going, a really nice dog. Could have sold her more than once. She'd have gone fast if I'd wanted to," Scott said.

I turned to Scott and said, "Okay, where are the pups?"

"On the west side of the kennel," he said. "Same arrangement. Half a dozen separate runs. Easier on me and the older dogs to keep em separate. Adults would have little patience with the puppies and their constant jumping and horsing around."

We walked around to the west side of the main building and Scott opened up the several individual runs, letting the puppies out. He released all seven of the two-month-old dogs—three yellows and four blacks.

They were all about the same size: 10 inches tall, with 14-15 inch bodies ending in 6-7 inch tails. From ear to ear, their heads measured no more than 4-5 inches. They seemed larger than most of my previous

Lab puppies, maybe twice as large as the Reggie pup Nat gave me. The size of the puppies enabled them to run about at considerable speed and still be in control. It became quickly apparent that they knew what to do when let out—run about colliding with one another, knock each other down, or dash away to chase whatever inspired their interest.

Scott's yard from the west side of the kennel extended for at least 50 yards in three directions. In that space, the puppies could run together or break away to follow individual whims—to find a weed big enough to pull on, a stick to carry, or a sibling to chase.

For Mary and me, the seven dogs running about together created an amusing energy-infused panorama. It was difficult to follow a single figure in that chaos. After standing for a while trying to follow the circus, we decided to sit down on the grass and observe, hoping the puppies might be curious enough to come to us and visit. I tried to concentrate on the yellows, but I found that didn't help much. The black males and yellow females seemed to be chasing and wrestling with each other non-stop.

As noted, I came to Scott's wanting a female but also a black puppy. As I watched, that problem choice seemed to increase. I based my female preference on the belief they were easier to handle and train and, as a consequence, less hassle then a male. My most recent Labs, Diana and Toula, clearly influenced me in that direction. But I couldn't help admiring the black puppies.

Black, I thought, remained the premier Lab color. I yearned for a repetition of Diana, a black female, but that was not possible. As I sat, my frustration increased. I began to toy with the idea of getting two puppies, a yellow female and a black male.

"Mary," I said, "What do you think about getting two pups, a black and a yellow?"

"I thought you only wanted one, and a female at that," she said.

"I do. I mean I did," I said.

"Jonathan, you're not making a lot of sense. You know how much more hassle two puppies would be?"

"You're right, but I love the black ones."

"Okay, get a black one then," she said.

To try to simplify things, we asked Scott to put four of the pups back in their kennels, leaving the two yellow females and a single back puppy as the final picking field. Mary and I agreed the two females and one black seemed the least crazy acting of the bunch.

We watched them closely for half an hour. We picked them up. We made noises at them. We cuddled them. The decision was almost impossible. But I finally decided on a yellow. I knew realistically, that in terms of expendable time and energy, I could only do justice to one puppy and that had to be one of the two females.

I turned to Mary and said, "Which of the yellows do you prefer?" I couldn't choose. The two were equally beautiful.

"I vote for this one," she said, pointing at the smaller yellow. "I think it's the friendlier, milder one."

I agreed. We told Scott of our selection. I paid cash for the pup. We headed back to Mercer.

As we got underway, Mary said, "Jonathan, you have a name picked out for the pup?"

I said, "Not yet but I got a couple of possibilities. Wanna hear what they are?"

"Sure, this should be fun," she said.

"How about Eleanor or Ellie?"

"Eleanor, for a dog? That's weird. Never heard of that before," she said.

"Eleanor or Ellie after my favorite English teacher at Reserve. Her full name was Eleanor Roundy, an inspiring, confident, regal lady who taught my senior year American Literature course. For that class, we read poetry and fiction. A couple of novels I remember were Hemmingway's *For Whom the Bell Tolls* and Hawthorn's *The Scarlet Letter*. Both classics. To open class discussion, Mrs. Roundy would begin with this question: 'Boys, what's the conflict?' Never forget that. Used that line in God-knows how many of my history classes over the years. I thought I could honor one of my favorite teachers by calling the new dog Ellie. What'd you think?"

"Nice thought. What other possibilities you got?" Mary said.

"Okay. How about Renee? After the pop song. 'Just Walk Away, Renee.'"

"Jonathan, Renee's a dumb name for a dog, after a dumb song," she said, laughing.

"No it isn't. I like the idea of walking away. 'Let it go' as the psychologists would say. Let go, walk on, walk away. With that name, my dog would be above the usual canine pettiness. She would be transcending," I said.

I could see Mary shaking her head. I assumed she was rolling her eyes as well.

"Okay, how about the name "Segen?" I said.

"Where'd you get that? Never heard that name before. Has two syllables. That's a plus. Better than Renee. But what's it mean?" she asked.

"Ha, I got you! It's a German term."

"What's it mean?"

"Blessing, a gift from God."

"Hey, I like that," she said.

I did too, and thought it appropriate because my Labs have all been just that, blessings in my life.

Toula's initial reaction to the disappearance of her aunt Diana seemed to be uncertainty and confusion. She had never been in my home without the presence of her black aunt.

During all those years when I moved from one room to another, the two dogs usually accompanied me and when I did something out of the house, I usually took both dogs with me. In the car, Diana sat in the front. Toula took the back seat. After Diana's death, I think Toula seemed puzzled or hesitant, both at home and when travelling with me without a canine companion. That even included the time she loved the most—ball fetching.

When I procured Segen, Toula's uncertainty and confusion seemed to increase. Initially, the older dog spurned the new puppy, turning away and moving off when it appeared. If the puppy would run at her or after her with its tail wagging, looking to play, Toula would growl at Segen, warning her to stay away. She never bit the newcomer, but the growls sounded sincere. On occasion, I had to reprimand the elder dog.

The growling/threatening behavior lasted for about ten days. Then the tension seemed to dissipate. Gradually, a little at a time, Toula loosened up. She let the puppy jump at her without growling. The next step involved pushing back, dodging and even nudging Segen. Sometimes Toula would knock the puppy over on its back. If that happened, Segen would lie still as Toula sniffed her underside. The acceptance came slowly, but it came. They began to have fun together, running about and chasing each other.

During the third week, I started taking both dogs to the Florence Dog Park. On these initial visits, I threw balls only for Toula. In the fourth week, however, I began tossing balls for both dogs as I had done for years with Diana and Toula. Initially the new routine involved tosses for Toula at 30 yards or more; for Segen, the balls travelled from five to ten yards, a distance at which she could see the missile's movement and where it stopped. By the end of the third week, both dogs were retrieving their individual balls. Segen's mouth just fit the ball and she would run back to me, lie down at my feet, and try to chew her prize rather than give it up.

The whole exercise I found amusing and fun. Both dogs loved it as well. On the basis of what I saw in the first month of their cohabitation, I felt confident the two dogs would become close friends and allies, sharing their skills and love with each other and with me just as their seven marvelous Lab predecessors did.

Fenced-in fun time for both puppies

Once back in North Dakota, Segen's behavior has not changed. Since the summer, she has grown a good deal and her enthusiasm for life has increased as well. Because of her constant puppy chewing, she has had to spend most of her time in her portable kennel in the kitchen. When out of that confined context, she tries to make up for the restrictions by expressing exuberance in virtually everything she does.

When I let her out of the kennel, she dashes for the door to the garage and freedom. She exhibit's the same enthusiasm when I relegate her to the enclosed dog area next to the garage, where she hopes to find a ball or other play toy to grab and then get me or Toula to chase her. I can't remember any of my other Labs having had more such excessive exuberance.

One of Segen's favorite entertainments in that fenced off area is chasing and engaging in mock-battle with her larger family member, Toula. The latter reciprocates in the chasing, mock-biting, mauling, and knocking over routines. Although much smaller than Toula, Segen's efforts represent a real challenge for the older dog.

In the course of the romp and combat, both Labs race about, collide, tumble, and fall, with first Toula on top, then Segen. The amount of energy expended tires the combatants out after only a few minutes.

More often than not, Toula is the first to seek relief by running to me to let her back into the house.

But this exuberance always seems to be expressed in the right spirit: that is, with tail wagging frenetically and eyes sparkling. Such behavior conveys a happiness with life message. The overall impression I received of my new puppy was of a creature that would always be fun to be with because she was having such a great time, no matter how limited her context might be.

Lab-loving daughter Sarah with Segen and Toula
on my deck in Florence

Last fall, I left Segen with Mary for the day so I could go hunting with my buddy, Jim Miller. Later, when I picked Segen up, Mary remarked about the dog's effusive joy, her overall sense of fun, and how much she seemed to enjoy Mary and her daughter's company. In short, from everything I've seen so far, I think Segen will be a wonderful addition to the Lab tradition I venerate so highly. She will, I'm betting, continue that loving Lab legacy. She will live up to her name by blessing me with her presence as her seven Lab predecessors did so marvelously.

P.S. Segen made the same impression on my daughter, Sarah, when she visited me recently in Wisconsin.

CONCLUSION

THE LAB LEGACY

Jason watching me run

---

*"No matter how close we are to another person, few human relation-
ships are as free from strife, disagreement and frustration as is the
relationship you have with a good dog. Few human beings give themselves to another as a dog gives itself.*

— Dean Koontz, *A Big Little Life*

As noted in the Sherman chapter, my third and last marriage ended
in 2004. During the years that followed, I would be a single man living by myself with Labrador Retrievers as my house companions. In
those years, I continued my teaching career at Minot State University.
Although officially retired from full-time teaching in 2010, I have car-

ried on as an adjunct professor doing online courses. Looking back, those years appear as both peaceful and productive ones.

I have been able to keep my interest in history alive while devoting as much time as I wish to my other interests, including both fishing and hunting. Moreover, with the disappearance of conflict at home, I have been freed up to enjoy the family created from my marriages; that is, my three grandchildren and four children—my bookend sons, Nathaniel and Robert, and my two academic daughters, Johanna and Sarah.

I don't fly fish as much as I used to. My eyes are getting weaker and switching flies has become more problematic. Also, my arthritic knees make wading streams with slippery rocks and chasing pheasants more difficult than in the past. Nevertheless, I'm still active abroad and that activity more often than not allows me to enjoy the presence of my dog companions.

At present, I experience the joy of my memories and the actual presence of two dogs, Toula and puppy Segen, inhabiting my home and life as I write. At least one of them and sometimes both are with me when I travel out of the house for whatever reason, from grocery shopping to visiting friends. In addition to the antics and shared participation of Toula and Segen in my everyday events, I possess the vivid memories of the six beautiful Labs that preceded my present duo.

These recollections of the departed include both sadness and happiness. In my thoughts, I try to concentrate on the happy moments, the legacy that has uplifted and inspired my life.

As a way of bringing my memoir to a close, I wish to remember and honor what each of my seven unique Labs has meant to me, how they have influenced my life and view of the world, and how my coming to know them as special, sentient individuals has made me not only more aware of my world but also, I believe, a better human.

In short, I wish to put into words what my Sweet Spirits, those gifts from God, have embodied and meant for me and my life. Finally, I want to try to sum up their legacy beyond me, that is, describe how they have affected my children. I will start the discussion with my first Lab Jason, the wonderful pace setter for those that followed.

Although the president of the Manitoba Labrador Retrievers Club thought Jason ugly, I certainly did not. To me, his striking yellow coat and powerful physique overshadowed his somewhat distorted snout. To me, he always appeared physically beautiful. But even more importantly, his character as a dutiful dog and friend made him special.

Jason's ability to learn obedience I discovered first hand, more so than for most of my other dogs who received their training from Scott Snyder. Jason impressed me by taking instruction without rebellion, hostility, or indifference. His patience in accepting his role as house pet and my companion in the duck blind likewise earned him credit. I don't remember him as a particularly troublesome puppy or naughty adolescent.

From the onset, he exhibited good will and ready acceptance of his several assigned social roles—house pet, hunter, and babysitter. Indeed, Jason's most distinguishing virtue lay in his acute social skills, not only with other canines, but with humans of different ages.

As noted, Jason came to us in 1971 when my first three children Nathaniel, Johanna, and Sarah were infants. Thus, from his initial arrival as Shannon's and my dog until his untimely death in 1981, he played a major role not only with us adults but with our children as well. None of my later Labs would have such an advantage (or maybe disadvantage). Jason, I firmly believe, loved my children and felt at home with them.

As Johanna described so well in her St. Lawrence River sermon, Jason's swimming with the family represented physical enjoyment for him but it also constituted an act of sharing and participating with his family. In all his many activities with the children, he never showed irritation or non-acceptance. No snapping or growling was ever heard. The affectionate patience he extended to the children often exceeded that of their parents!

The children received no chastisement, admonitions or scolding from their yellow housemate. Jason never seemed uninterested enough not to join in their fun, to share his enthusiasm and energy with his family siblings. The long-term effects of Jason's closeness and interaction with Nat, Johanna, and Sarah influenced them profoundly.

It is no accident that all three of these children from my first wife, the ones who shared their first decade of life with Jason, are at present owners of Labrador Retrievers. Finally, Jason's social skills inspired me to continue to want to own Labs and I am, as my children are, very grateful for his bequest of love, interest, and companionship.

For Boomer, my second Lab, his life and times differed dramatically from those of Jason. Boomer's role in the family as a result differed as well. Chaos, change, moving, and divorce all made Boomer's ten years chaotic. My Law school stint, law practice, and return to academia as both a professor and administrator meant nearly constant change for the family and Boomer. As a result, he never enjoyed the opportunity to be babied, spoiled or even trained appropriately.

The absence of continuity and routine meant, among other things, that Boomer was more often than not on his own, able to do his own thing more freely than any of my other Labs. Boomer responded to this life circumstance in ways that often caused irritation and frustration for me and his family. But there was a positive side as well.

Despite the generally less certain and unsettled life, Boomer still exhibited many of the breed's admirable characteristics: he was affectionate, upbeat, intelligent, well-intentioned, and non-aggressive. He had the Labrador *joie de vivre* in abundance. These characteristics, as I noted, he shared with the Labs that would follow into my family. Nevertheless, Boomer managed to remain his own special self.

Much of Boomer's uniqueness, I recognize now, stemmed from his less structured existence. He was freer than the others to define himself. That represented his special advantage. Of all my dogs, Boomer was the only one to play the clown and he did so with effect. He managed to get away with being naughtier than the others. In addition, his naughty deeds more often than not were forgiven. He could do almost the unimaginable and survive.

I think he recognized this. He seemed to do his clowning with a smile on his face, as when he snatched the deliveryman's hat. Also, I think he recognized that he could get away with playing the clown, even if his audience didn't laugh. His sense for fun seemed to be a permanent state with him. He couldn't avoid playing the joker.

There are humans who suffer from the same condition or enjoy the same advantage. Over the years in a number of classes I've had Boomer-like students, that is, jokesters amongst my students. It amuses me today when I think of these characters. I'm referring to those students who would sit in class just waiting for an opportunity to say or do something that would get a laugh from their classmates.

Usually, these self-appointed comedians would be sitting in the back looking at me with barely suppressed grins, waiting impatiently for me to make an error or say something they could construe as a joke. If I presented the opportunity, they would fire off an amusing remark for the benefit of their cohorts.

Although, on occasion, irritating, they more frequently amused and amazed me. The lesson they promoted was simple—almost everything in life can be construed as ironic, ridiculous, or amusing. If you can laugh about it, you're on the right track. Boomer represented the canine version of this—laugh first and last. That's life.

If you're taking yourself too seriously, you're missing the point. The existence of such jokester students in my classes clearly helped me understand my magnificent clown dog.

Boomer's ability to make me laugh more than any other quality caused me to love him and venerate his memory. I think the joker feature in Boomer's career also influenced my children in the same way it touched me. All my children love to laugh; and they remember him fondly as having made them do so.

"Life," he seemed to be saying, "doesn't always have to be serious. Dogs and humans both need, at times, to lighten up." That was his major bequest to us. I and my children from Shannon are grateful to this day for receiving such a gift from our beautiful brown Labrador clown, our Boomerang.

Of all my Labs, Reginald, my first black Lab, contributed the least to my hunting activities and interests. He may have liked to fetch ducks, but hounding pheasants was not his bag. Despite his meager hunting contribution, Reggie ranks highly as one of my favorite Sweet Spirits because he was quite simply the "Sweetest of the Sweet."

That was Reggie's greatest legacy, one that endeared him to me but also celebrated and honored the breed's versatility. Looking back, I thank my lucky stars I had Reggie during those difficult times with my second and third wives. I'm convinced he was a major reason I managed to endure the stress and strain of those failed marital relationships without suffering a mental breakdown.

Indiscriminate in his largess, Reggie's sweetness extended to both humans and non-humans. All my children, especially younger son Robert, identified with Reggie. As my other three children did from Jason's presence, I think Robbie benefitted greatly from having Reggie as a pal growing up. The childhood summer months Rob spent with me in Wisconsin were ones he always shared with Reggie. I can't remember Rob swimming off the dock without Reggie beside him in the water. The acceptance Reggie had for Rob extended to the other dogs I added to the family.

First Sherman, and then Clio—Reggie welcomed both as brother and sister into our family pack. He suffered their constant puppy roughhousing and torment with aplomb. The same attitude and long-suffering behavior he exhibited toward Julie's little dogs, Weenie and Buggsie. In short, he was the consummate accepter, a model of adjustment. Non-aggression and happy welcoming were his hallmarks.

I loved telling my two German lady friends about Reggie constituting the exact antithesis to the "Bissiger Hund" stereotype, for it was surely true. In his soft-spoken, gentle, faithful and loyal ways Reggie represented the saint among my string of God-gifted, wonderful Labrador Retrievers. He taught me much about how to love and the benefits from doing so. To this day I miss his sweetness, his loyalty, and his love.

In terms of social skills, my second chocolate Lab, Sherman, was not far behind Reggie. The two male dogs differed not only in size, with Sherman being significantly larger, but also in confidence and self-approval. Sherman appeared much more secure than Reggie. He always seemed at home with himself, a very important characteristic and one I envied.

His self-satisfaction translated into calm and confident behavior. Thus, of my several Labs, he best represented Mr. Cool. I don't ever remember him having disputes with his family cohorts or with other canines beyond our pack. In the field he hunted with other hunters and their dogs without problems. He always performed as a team player.

As a hunter, Sherman left little to be desired. His nose was every bit as effective as Clio's. He pointed, he quartered, he persisted in tracking or chasing injured birds nearly as well as Clio, the team leader, did.

Sherman's star shown most brightly in the field when conditions were at their most challenging. He never hesitated to tackle the thickest sloughs, to take on the densest of these challenges. On occasion, Clio might hesitate, but never Sherman. This, his most serious side, Sherman juxtaposed at home with his dancing beggar's act.

In his sense of humor, he reminded me of Boomer more than any of the others. Gentle Sherman never used his size to force himself on the other dogs. He was the consummate team player, a dog who accepted riding in the back and not the front of the truck, a dog that waited to be fed until the others had received their share. As the photo with little Rob and his insect jar shows, Sherman was a gentle, loving giant. Of all my several Labs, I believe Wolters would have voted him my best citizen. He taught me the advantages of being both gentle and relaxed, two human qualities far too often absent in our hectic, present world.

Sherman's best pal, rival, and competitor, Clio possessed her own set of breed qualities and individual characteristics that made for uniqueness. Of my seven Labs, Clio functioned as the outstanding alpha dog.

From her first appearance in my apartment to share her puppy-hood, she played the boss—the canine who set the pace. As a puppy, her dominance meant more trouble than was true for the average youngster. Clio's dominance stemmed not only from her confidence and self-assurance, but also from her energy.

She led or dominated as if knowing from the outset that she would be in control, that she would set the pace. It seemed as if she could lead naturally. Her effort to get out of the truck before me when that rooster flew in front of us was symbolic. She should lead the other dogs, but also her master.

Despite this confidence and near arrogance, Clio learned how to obey. The lessons Scott drilled into her remained to the end. Of all my dogs, Clio was the one who obeyed the best. It was as if she recognized that leading and obeying were not mutually antithetical but complementary.

Despite this self-assurance and alpha posturing, Clio remained a sweet and loving spirit throughout. She both shared and dispensed affection for and with her canine companions. She did the same among her human family.

All my children thought highly of Clio as a pet and fellow family member. She remained Lab friendly throughout. Even when so sick at the end, she would try to wag her tail if you spoke kindly to her. She may have teased her dog cohorts, but never resented or bullied them. She fit into the family as a full-fledged loving member.

In many ways, I especially admired her because of her hunting skills and obedience, but also for her love of being with me as my companion. I shared ham sandwiches with her as I would have with Rob, Nat, or their sisters. I knew she would be grateful to me and appreciate the chance to be alone with me as sole hunting pal. In the end, like all the others, she was a lover. I can't now and don't want to ever forget her companionship in the field and at home.

As of this writing, Diana, the last member of my Three Musketeers, has left me. To the end of her days, she had not lost any of her capacity to love, her ability to socialize, or her fondness for the hunt. Slowed a bit by declining energy levels, her enthusiasm for life nevertheless remained strong. In this regard, she retained her skill as a noisemaker. Her late-life noise excesses were expressed most often when I donned my boots or overcoat in preparation for going out into the untraveled street in front of the house to throw tennis balls. I usually did this at mid-morning when there was virtually no traffic in my town with its 80 residents.

If I made the recognizable preparatory moves for a ball session, Diana began to whine, run about in mini-circles, jump and head for the garage door, the fastest way to the street. The hysteria increased as I followed her into the garage and reached up on the shelf to grab the balls and the ball launcher. At that point, Diana had gone berserk—barking loudly, squealing, ears perked at full attention, eyes sparkling, tail wagging frenetically. She was, in short, ready to experience ecstasy. The whole process amused me. Nearly always I was laughing as I stepped out the door and launched the first missile.

Besides her abilities to make noise and experience joy, Diana continued to the end to be a sweet social creature, not just for me and other humans like my children or friend Mary, but also for her fellow dog pack member, Toula. The longer she lived, the more I believed I made an inspired choice in selecting her as my second black Lab. Like Reggie, Diana taught me about those priceless gifts —love, loyalty, and devotion.

If Diana's book has closed, Toula's is less than half read. My little red/yellow girl has just mastered/learned what life with me is all about and she appears to be not only accepting it, but enjoying it as well.

Her presence in the house certainly makes me happy. Although still more timid than any of my other Labs in terms of being cowed by harsh tones and reprimands, she never sulks. Of all my dogs, she is the only one who has ever been intimidated by my sneezing! In fact, she often vacates the room the first time I sneeze! I have no idea where or why that aversion arose. In any case, she has been an excellent home dweller and field partner. All my children and friends have been impressed by her friendly, outgoing personality.

As of 2017, Toula's hunting compared favorably to her predecessors. As she hunts, she works the fields and sloughs with unbridled enthusiasm. She retrieves with passion from water or land. On the basis of her three years with me, I look forward to our future together. In short, she represents yet another worthy contributor to that 40-year tradition of blessings my Labrador Retrievers have bequeathed to me.

Although my new puppy Segen has just begun her life with me, I am very optimistic about her and our future together. She appears to have the Lab virtues I so strongly admire—enthusiasm, sense of fun, desire for companionship, interest in life, and ability to show affection. Her hunting skills, I assume, will develop as they did in all the Labs I secured from Scott Snyder's Black Hawk Kennels.

LEGACY FOR MY OFFSPRING

Daughter Johanna's yellow lab Gus

In concluding my Lab reflections, I was faced with the larger question of "so what?" Did my seven Labrador Retrievers have any meaning beyond me and my life? When pondering this, I naturally thought about the other members of the family (but not my ex-wives). I thought of my four now-adult children and my grand-children and asked them the question of the dogs' impact on them.

All responded to me with sincerity and interest. Here are some of their thoughts. There was a surprisingly favorable consistency among their comments. I'll begin with my younger son Rob's response.

After his mother and I divorced, Rob lived with his mother Ann throughout his grade school, middle school and senior high days. During that time, she, who has never been a fan of canines, made dog concessions to him in the form of two non-shedding breeds, first with a French Poodle, and then later with a Chiwawa. Neither dog could eclipse Rob's memories from his time with our Labs. He wrote this about why he favored Labs:

"What I like about Labs is that they have a ton of personality. They are smart and they are people pleasers. You will always have a good friend in a Lab. They give you stories, memories and laughs unlike other pets that I have experience with. They fulfill expectations as family members that far exceed anything you could expect from a pet."

Sister Sarah wrote that she liked Labs because, "I love their warmth and their boundless affection. To come home to Luna (Sarah's present Lab) is to open the door to joy—joy at seeing me after a long day away and joy at the prospect of heading out...to chase tennis balls and greeting every possible dog and human who might cross our path in between. If that love of life doesn't make you smile, I don't know what will.

Of course, I also love how big and cuddly they are. There's something about wrapping your arms around them and giving them a big hug that warms your heart. Dogs are beautiful creatures and Labs are the kings and queens among them."

Nat explained, "I love that our Labs always wear smiles when they are in my company and the joy they take in comradeship. They bond with their humans like many 'working breeds' but with a love and trust in their people that goes beyond any traditional symbiosis. Like many breeds, they adore their parents and enjoy adoration in return, but Labbies smile about it; they smile with their eyes, their tongue and their tails... I love that they are always bringing me things: my birds, my hats, my shoes, my socks... Our Labs always have something in their mouths they want to give us... A constant metaphor for the unfailing love they offer."

Johanna claimed, "I like almost everything about Labs: their thick, soft fur, their beautiful brown eyes, their big webbed feet and especially their soft ears. I love giving a Lab a big hug and squeeze; they are such strong, substantial dogs. You can slap them on the butts affectionately, play with their ears, rub their bellies and grab them in head locks. They don't mind. They especially like to sleep next to you on the bed while you use their backs to prop up a book. As rough as they are, as many tables, chairs, wine glasses, even wine racks they may knock over, either with their cement block heads or tails of iron, they are incredibly gentle with children. They may drag you around when you put them on a leash, but not a small child. They will follow a small child with the leash hanging loosely in front of them as if they were the most obedient dog in the world."

My child with the longest, most varied Lab experiences dating not only from his childhood with me but also from his adulthood with his own family is son Nathaniel. As noted, his experiences with me as a child and adult included not only Lab exposure at home, but also in the field with me as hunting companion. During his married and family life, Nat has owned three Labs (Eddie the black, Grady the chocolate and Luke the yellow). When I asked him to reflect on the meaning of his dogs and which of his Labs were his favorites, he responded with enthusiasm.

"I don't have favorites, but I would celebrate each of our Labs for the important gifts they brought me at different periods of my life. That said, our chocolate Lab Grady is special.

Grady is the most cheerful, happy dog I have ever encountered. His love for his family overflows the vessel of his body. He can barely contain his joy in being. Upon waking, he exudes adoration for his family with his whole body—wagging, panting, smiling, and curling his ears.

He cannot curb the excitement and joy he feels as he shares his life with his clan each and every day.

When, as a puppy, he went to his first vet appointment, the vet saw him wiggling with glee at her attentions and said, 'You're 10-percent Lab and 90-percent happy!' That sentiment captured the trajectory of this chubby chocolate's life. Whether receiving a rectal thermometer or a dog treat, he feels and expresses abundant joy in living. His mission in life: to share with all he encounters his *joie de vivre*. Grady is happy—happy to be alive, happy to be in the same room with you, happy to be part of the constant dance party that is his life.

Grady is also a lover. Where some dogs are most sensitive to pack hierarchies, Grady snuggles up with everyone, giving and taking affection with youngest and oldest, biggest and smallest. My dad says, 'You can measure your life in Labs.' I think that is true. One can also recast that sentiment into a more objective attitude and say, 'You can measure the life of others in their Labs.' I will never be able to think of my youngest daughter Clare's childhood without thinking of Grady. He is her dog the way Boomer was mine.

Grady will always be 'her baby boy.' When she would dress him in skirts, Hawaiian shirts, hats, bows, dresses, any costume of the moment, he would trip down the stairs from her bedroom to show off his outfit just happy to be attended to, happy to share in her games and to give her laughter.

When she trimmed his tail, spritzed him with perfume, and added a dash of glitter to his coat, he was happy to be her playmate, happy to be a part of the show. And when she would collapse on top of him, falling asleep on his wide brown girth, their chests rising and falling in rhythm, he was happy to be her pillow and her support. Grady is a formidable hunting partner, a great family dog, but most of all Grady is Clare's. He is the reason we will always have labs in our household."

Johanna's Lab, a big yellow male which she had to put down recently, was named Gus. In her note to me after his death she wrote, "I miss Gus. He used to wait for me on the bath mat while I took showers, would follow me from room to room, learned how to fetch his bed so that he could be comfortable following me from room to room, would always get up in the middle of the night and come over to the side of the bed when I wanted to pat him, would look at me sadly while I watched TV if his bed was too far away from my chair for my foot to rest on him. (I would have to drag his bed closer—with him on it—to remedy the situation.) When we went hiking, he would run around like crazy, leaping over logs, tugging branches off trees, just generally acting like an insane person. Yet all the while, he would be listening for my steps. If I stopped for any reason, he would come tearing back along the trail to see what was going on.

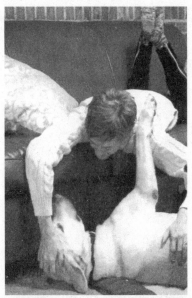

Johanna and Gus upside down and
down side up together

Gus was so loyal, so pure of heart, and so easily made happy. I deeply regret all the times I would go out for runs without him because he would look so sad watching the door close after me. People would tell me that they would see him looking out the window for me when

I was over at the dining hall (at Culver Academy where Johanna was employed). When he would see me coming back from lunch or dinner, his head would sway back and forth gently in the window from the motion of his wagging tail. I feel like I took him for granted. He was an angel sent from God to keep me company!"

Johanna's younger sister Sarah, the anthropologist, responded to my Lab queries: "Your questions, Dad, are seemingly straight forward but in fact they stir up lots of memories, mostly good but also some painful, tied to our family and our beloved Labs. As I write you, my own Luna lies curled up on her bed, just a few feet away.

She turned five-years-old this winter and I find myself comparing her to Roy (her black male from Scott's kennel) and how he aged. Roy was my first black Lab, whom we should all now refer to as St. Roy, because, really, he was the sweetest, most loving and gentle dog I've ever known. What is it your friend Jim Miller says? If you don't think your dog is the best in the world, then something's wrong with you?

*Sarah Luna's launches herself
for an island fetch*

"Roy died very suddenly. In a matter of twelve short hours, he slipped from my life, and I'll never forget the utter despair I felt those days afterwards. I hadn't been prepared; I had told myself that when Roy finally was ready to go, he would die in my arms and in the comfort of his home.

Nothing could have been further from the truth of what happened. He died in some emergency animal hospital in Manhattan, presumably all alone. The tears spring fresh from my eyes when I think about this betrayal of love. I wish I had known the signs, understood their import, and cared for him the way he deserved to be cared for in the last few hours of his life.

Sarah's Saint Roy as an elderly blessing

"Sometimes I think this was Roy's gift to me. He taught me how to love another creature, and the responsibility of that love. His well-being was inextricably bound to mine. I don't have children and maybe this lesson is something akin to what it means to be a parent. I'm not sure.

In his death, he also taught me how to grieve—the depths and course of mourning the loss of another life so dear to you. Finally, he has laid a beautiful path for Luna to follow. I got her when she was just eight weeks old, in fact a gift from you and picked out from the litter by both you and Rob. Luna's a very different dog from Roy (she's bold, not timid; she's high-energy, not mellow; she's got a mischievous streak all of her own), but she's wormed her way in to my heart almost as deeply as Roy. Right now as I type this, she's snoring on her bed, content after her cold nose poking in under the covers managed to rouse me from the bed and fill her bowl with dog food."

Sarah's niece and my ten-year-old granddaughter, Clare, also responded to my request about her favorite Labs. She did so with pleasure. Her special dog turned out to be, not surprisingly, none other than her Dad's favorite, Grady. According to Clare, Grady was "a big dog with a big personality." He has, she wrote "big brown eyes that become golden in the sun and an almost endless mount of neck flab that sways when he walks." His big body is covered by "his thick, chocolatey grown fur." His "stubby, springy legs, generous tail and big-boned frame" are "perfect for dancing." His body is large enough "to block the TV and he loves to stand on our coffee table when we're watching television and stick his face in ours."

Clare claimed she could "write a book on Grady's interests and passions." For example, "he loves to consume liquids and if you spill ice from the ice machine, he will happily eat it because he loves ice cubes. He loves liquids almost as much as he loves peeing. When we take him to the dog park, he pees a lot...Besides liking to pee on Every Single Plant he sees, he slobbers a good deal managing to get his own slobber all over himself, his face, his back, Mom's pants and other dogs that want to play with him." Another favorite Grady activity Clare claimed was tennis ball fetching. "You throw one (a tennis ball) in the living room, he goes for it. You throw one in your brother's lap, he goes for it. You throw one off a bridge, he goes for it."

Although Grady was not a "true athlete or a field champion," he was nevertheless "a champion companion" for her. In Clare's words, "Grady's true calling is companionship. He loves me no matter what. He would endure anything just to be with me. He would happily let me paint his nails, dress him up and of course jam with me in the dance parties in my room. His favorite dance tune is Lady Gaga's Paparazzi which he thinks is Pupperrazzi. He is the fat man on the dance floor who wags his tail with abandon because he knows he is loved."

In summing up her pal, Clare claimed her "favorite part of Grady is his happy rotundity...his chubby layer of flab that makes a perfect pillow. Some dogs might let you sleep near or beside them. Grady let me sleep on him! My Dad would often find us both snoring away on the couch—little girl weightlessly slumbering on her beloved Lab. Those who have met Grady know he is like no other dog. His joy, his smile and his constant and enduring love make him my best friend."

Grady as Clare's champion companion

I would like to end the Lab legacy for my children by quoting the last lines of Sarah's email to me about her Labs: "This little essay of mine," she wrote, "could go on endlessly because there's so much to remember about the dogs that have brought warmth and love into our lives. In this sense, Dad, you have given us an extraordinary gift in raising us with such beautiful creatures, our Sweet Spirits: for all of us that love has extended, almost like new generations through our own

Labs—Penny, Gus, Grady, Eddie, Luke, Roy, and Luna. May there be many more to come. Love Sarah."

P.S. Just recently, Reverend Dr. Johanna Wagner's church bulletin included this bit of information. "The young of heart of every age were thrilled last Saturday to get to meet Rev. Wagner's new fur-kid, a yellow Labrador Retriever puppy named Ozzie! Named after Saint Oswald who gained sanctity in serving the poor and was King of Northumbria from 634 until his dead nine years later, this little prince was certainly king for a day."

FOR ME

In writing this memoir, I have come to understand more profoundly what my Labs mean and have meant to me and my life. From the beginning, I viewed my Labrador Retrievers as physically beautiful, whether black, yellow, chocolate, or red. I enjoyed watching them work in the field, play with one another outside or conform to my regulations at home.

Although my several dogs were unique in the ways I have described, they all shared the same general breed characteristics of non-belligerence, affection, energy, and eagerness to please. Their tolerance and love of fun were entirely predictable.

During the stress of my divorces, their affection for me never wavered. In that time of self-doubt and depredation, they affirmed me with their support. They acted as mentors teaching me with their affirmation that I was not rejected but loved. In so doing, they made it possible for me to be grateful; I could experience joy again.

The loyalty I received from my Three Musketeers, for example, kept me safe from depression during the worst of my Ann and Julie complications. In that low period, my dogs' fun-loving trust, their non-judgmental attitudes, their unwavering interest in me, and their fondness in being close to me I found soothing. It made me capable of transcending the many daily difficulties of those trying times.

The positive characteristics of my dogs just described influenced me both internally and externally. The abiding love of my several Labs inspired me, I believe, to extend my concern and love beyond myself. It evoked a tenderness that allowed me to be more sympathetic to other people. It also inspired in me a sense of wonder—how beautiful was this canine love, how touching, how elevating. In so doing it made me more aware of the beauty of creation itself.

My gentle giant Sherman with his sweet acceptance of his pack mates, my children and me, plus his ongoing willingness to wait his turn inspired me to think beyond myself. My noisy, devoted, loving Diana worked to restore my sense of wonder, to allow me to experience the apparent joy of innocence. I saw Diana as an innocent creature living her life to love and receive love. All my Labs in one form or another exhibited such traits. How beautiful, how uplifting, how like the condition of angels!

Finally, the pain caused by the deaths of my dogs taught me compassion for others. It softened my heart and it made me, I believe, a better person. Jason's sudden death, Clio's prolonged suffering before her demise, and Diana's recent painful end forced me to think of just what their lives had meant to me and how much I would lack without them. Those deaths made me capable of relating to others who suffered similar spiritual and physical losses, whether human or not. I now understand sorrow as never before.

My dogs' energy, humility, enthusiasm, gratitude, loyalty, and joy nearly always involved sharing. What they exhibited is and was model companionship. They loved to be with their best friend, me. That is the sense I have for nearly all my Labs. With the exception of Boomer, none of my dogs were Lone Rangers.

Preferring my company, they were more often than not my shadows. They found pleasure in hunting pheasants and ducks with me, but also in riding next to me in my car, sitting at my feet as I watched television or lying under my desk as I worked on my computer. They were ideal companions for me because they shared so well. That sharing-dog legacy for me began with Satchel and it continued through to Toula. Sharing, I believe, is not only a fundamental element in love but a necessary one as well.

There are many definitions of love, but for me it must involve an intense devotion to or acute appreciation of something. More often than not, that means a commitment to the object loved, a desire to be with that object, and a concern for its well-being. It also has to do with sharing, participating together in an activity, or enjoying some common interest.

As noted in my discussions of the musician Shannon, the physician Ann, and my wood-working wife Julie, I lacked such sharing with my three spouses. On the other hand, my Labs loved me for what I offered them whether it was food at meal time, a run to chase tennis balls or a stint in a pheasant slough.

As this memoir attempts to express, I took great pleasure in recording in my hunting diaries my dogs and their successes in the field. I did so because I wanted to have a record of our efforts together that I could remember after they passed.

In the diary snippets, I described not only their skills and passions as hunters but also their pleasure in serving me, in being with me and in hearing my praise for their efforts.

To friends or acquaintances who have inquired why I hunt pheasants, I always describe my pheasant outings as 80 percent canine and 20 percent human. I have never tried to hunt pheasants, or ducks for that matter, without a dog and never will. The pleasure of a pheasant hunt involves several advantages—the opportunity to be out in nature during the splendid fall season, to harvest not only beautiful birds but culinary delicacies and most importantly, to witness the performance of my dogs as hunting cohorts.

The love for my dogs I had and continue to have in the field and at home has been and still is reciprocated by my marvelous companions. I sense an appreciation of me in them because I have shared these parts of my life with them, that is, because I have loved them.

I can attest that I learned more about love from my dogs than I did from any other source in my life. In my relations with other humans, I try to use my dogs as social models—to appreciate, to admire, to respect, and to want to share of myself with my fellow humans.

In teaching me about companionship and about sharing, my dogs have been major blessings in my life. That I named my last dog with the German word Segen (meaning blessing) captures this sentiment. I fully expect my little Segen child as she grows and matures to bless me and others with her requited love.

I learned what the term "requited love" cited in the manuscript's title really meant from my dogs. A requited love is one that is willingly returned. That is precisely what my several Labrador Retrievers provided for me, some more intensely than others, but all in one form or another.

Their giving constituted initially and still does, I believe, the basis of my attachment to my dogs. It is as well the reason our relationships were so fulfilling and enjoyable. To share, to participate jointly with, to have a fondness for, and to enjoy being in the presence of another constitutes a form of sweet love.

In brief, requited love for me always manifests such identification and sharing. That was the main lesson I learned from my Labs, my Sweet Spirits, and how I came to recognize and value their requited love.

Moreover, in teaching me about love, my dogs have enlightened me to the role of God and the divine in my life. For love is in essence a spiritual force. A lofty desire to appreciate beyond oneself, to venerate the larger force of creation often translates into joy. To sum up and repeat what I noted in the introduction, my dogs inspired in me that marvelous sentiment joy, celebrated so beautifully in Schiller's "An die Freude." A transcendent condition, indeed!

ABOUT THE AUTHOR

Born and raised in Ohio, Jonathan Wagner enjoys his life to the fullest, spending spring and summer in Florence, Wisconsin, on the Brule River and fall and winter in Mercer, North Dakota. He shares his homes with his two Labrador Retrievers, Fortula and Segen. His family also includes four wonderful children and three grandchildren. In his spare time, he enjoys ice fishing, pheasant hunting, fly fishing, bird watching, and kayaking.

Now retired, Jonathan's career as a beloved teacher for forty years has not gone unrecognized. Spending twelve years at the University of Winnipeg in Manitoba, Canada, and twenty-eight years at Minot State University in North Dakota, he considers himself a lifelong educator. He earned a B.A. from Bowdoin College in Maine, an M.A. from the University of Pennsylvania in Philadelphia, and a Ph.D. as well as a J.D. from the University of Wisconsin-Madison. One of his lifelong missions has been to promote conservation and a recognition of the need to preserve wildlife and the habitats that many animals call home.

An ambitious writer of German and Canadian history, *Dogging It Through Divorce and Beyond* is Jonathan's sixth book and first memoir.